Publications of

THE REGENTS' INQUIRY

Into the Character and Cost of Public Education
in the State of New York

GENERAL REPORT

EDUCATION FOR AMERICAN LIFE, A New Program for the State of
New York

ATLAS

SCHOOL DISTRICT ATLAS OF THE STATE OF NEW YORK. *Prepared by
the District Superintendents of Schools under the Direction of the Inquiry*

STUDIES

High School
and Life

High School and Life

By FRANCIS T. SPAULDING

1 9   3 8

THE REGENTS' INQUIRY

THE McGRAW-HILL BOOK COMPANY, INC.

PUBLISHERS · NEW YORK AND LONDON

Printed in the United States of America by the Maple Press Co., York, Pa.

G 28378

THE REGENTS

of the University of the State of New York

FOREWORD

THE Inquiry into the Character and Cost of Public Education in the State of New York was undertaken in order to find out what the educational system of the State is accomplishing, how well its total program fits present-day needs, and what the costs of that program are and should be, and to assist the Regents in considering the present needs and problems of the school system, and in reformulating the fundamental educational policies of the State. Under the provisions of the state Constitution, this responsibility falls primarily upon the Regents.

The Inquiry was organized late in 1935, under the direction of a Special Committee of the Board of Regents, consisting of John Lord O'Brian, William J. Wallin, and Owen D. Young, Chairman. Thomas J. Mangan, the present Chancellor, and James Byrne, the former Chancellor, have sat with the Committee as ex-officio members from its inception.

The work of the Inquiry has been divided into three major undertakings: first, the examination of the educational enterprise of the State and the analysis of its outcomes, methods, and costs; second, the critical appraisal of the work now under way; and third, the formulation of policies and programs for dealing with the immediate problems and issues, and long-range objectives of the educational system of the State. The purpose of the Inquiry has not been to gather great masses of statistics, to devise numerous questionnaires, or to present meticulous factual descriptions of every phase of education within the State. Rather, the Regents' Committee and the staff of the Inquiry have been interested in isolating major issues and in hammering away at the problems which presented themselves in order to find a reasonable comprehensive solution which would commend itself to the forward-minded people of the State of New York.

In conformity with this resolution, the Inquiry is publishing a limited part of the materials which have been brought together—such studies as bear directly upon central issues and major problems emerging in public education. Among these is the study *High School and Life*, by Dr. Francis T. Spaulding, of Harvard University. Dr. Spaulding was in charge of all Inquiry studies in secondary education. Those who assisted Dr. Spaulding in these studies were: Dr. Ruth E. Eckert, Miss Alice L. Edwards, Professor Herbert G. Espy, Professor William S. Gray, Dr. Walter B. Jones, Dr. Bernice E. Leary, Mr. Thomas O. Marshall, Jr., Professor Thomas L. Norton, Dr. Everett B. Sackett, Dr. Harald G. Shields, Professor Dora V. Smith, Dr. Z. M. Smith, Professor Douglas Waples, Dr. Leon Carnovsky, Professor Howard E. Wilson, Professor Dean A. Worcester, and Dr. J. Wayne Wrightstone. Assisting Dr. Spaulding and various other members of his staff were Mrs. Virginia Z. Ehrlich and Miss Evelyn Cummings.

In connection with the extensive programs of testing and interviewing pupils, the helpful services of more than a hundred persons were engaged directly by the Inquiry. In addition, many hundreds of school officials, superintendents, principals and teachers, both public and private, have given voluntarily time, thought, and assistance to the Inquiry staff in their visitations to schools, in their testing and interviewing programs, and in their requests for information. While it is not possible in these few pages to give acknowledgment to each individual, the Inquiry wishes to express its gratitude to each.

In order that it may offer a broad view of the secondary schools and of the problems which the schools must face, this report has been written as much as possible in terms of significant generalizations and of facts which illustrate those generalizations, rather than in the form of a statistical summary. Detailed facts supporting the conclusions here presented will be found in other special reports of the Inquiry, including *When Youth Leave School*, by Ruth E. Eckert and T. O. Marshall; *Education for Citizenship*, by Howard E. Wilson; *Education for Work*, by T. L. Norton; and *School and Community*, by J. B. Maller. Those who are interested in particular phases of the general study of secondary education, will find a full discussion of them in the supplementary reports.

The views expressed in this volume are those of the author; the Regents do not assume responsibility for them. The Regents wish, however, to express their deep appreciation to Dr. Francis T. Spaulding for the important contribution made to education and to the Inquiry through this study.

LUTHER GULICK

CONTENTS

· xvi ·

CHAPTER I

Secondary Education and
Social Competence

M ORE than eighty thousand boys and girls graduate from the public high schools of New York State every year. Almost twice as many others leave school each year without having graduated.

What these thousands of young people are like when they end their high school work is obviously not the school's doing alone. Home and church, playground and street, theatre, magazine, and radio, all have shared in their educational making. The school is only one of the many social agencies, formal and informal, through which they have been educated.

Yet what these young people are like when they leave school is, above everything else, the school's particular concern. In the eyes of the public no less than of school people, the task of the school is to supplement other educational influences, to offer boys and girls appropriate education which they could not otherwise obtain, to offset the negative or unwholesome habits or attitudes which they may have picked up in the street or the neighborhood. As an inevitable consequence of the part it plays in the lives of its pupils, the school is commonly, and no doubt justly, held more largely responsible than any other social institution except the home, for the traits and the abilities of the young people of a given generation.

To discover what the young people of the present generation are like when they leave school is therefore a logical beginning for any study which undertakes to determine whether the existing school program is effective. Such a procedure furnishes

· 1 ·

a particularly appropriate beginning for a study of secondary education. The secondary school is no longer merely a preparatory school for college. For the majority of its pupils the high school has come to be the school in which present-day American boys and girls must complete whatever systematic education they will need to give them a sound start in life. The things these boys and girls know and think and feel and are interested in when they leave the secondary school reflect directly and significantly the adequacy of their schooling.

These considerations have had much to do with the way the Regents' Inquiry has approached the study of secondary education in New York State, and in particular, they have determined a number of important assumptions on which this study has been based.

HOW SHOULD A PROGRAM OF SECONDARY EDUCATION BE JUDGED?

The study of secondary education has attempted to provide answers to two fundamental questions. It has sought, first, to determine to what degree and in what respects the current high school program in New York State is adequate for present-day needs; and second, to define the specific changes which the State should make in its educational policies in order to insure a better program.

Because of the part which the secondary schools have come to play in the education of a majority of the State's boys and girls, the Inquiry has assumed that the present high school program cannot be fairly judged by merely matching that program against some preconceived pattern. Instead, the program needs to be analyzed as dispassionately as possible in terms of its outcomes, that is to say, in terms of the abilities, the interests, the attitudes and habits which high school boys and girls have gained from their school work by the time they leave school.

Accordingly, the Inquiry has tried to discover what the New York State boys and girls who are just out of high school are like. Though young people who are not going to college compose the majority of the high school group, the needs of these young people have in the past been given little direct attention. The Inquiry has therefore paid especial attention to this particular group of boys and girls. At the same time it has not lost sight of the college-preparatory group. Boys and girls who have left school before graduating, as well as those who have earned high school diplomas; boys and girls from country and city, from farming communities and industrial centers, from large schools and small, have been considered. Through an inventory of the qualities of all these young people the Inquiry has attempted to find out what the high school program in New York State is actually accomplishing.

The Inquiry has assumed also that certain characteristics of boys and girls just out of school deserve particular attention. For want of a better expression, the term *social competence* may serve to suggest the nature of these characteristics.

Presumably the State supports public education not so much to teach the formal subjects of the school curriculum as to enable boys and girls to take an effective part in the life that lies ahead of them beyond the school. Whether the young people who are on the point of leaving the secondary school will be able to take an effective part in life outside of school depends on answers to a number of common-sense questions. To what extent are these young people aware of the problems that are likely to confront them immediately after they leave school? How fully are they equipped to deal with these problems? Have they the interests, the knowledge, and the attitudes which will help them to become acceptable citizens? Also, have they the interests, the knowledge, and the attitudes which will enable them to take advantage of their individual talents and abilities? Are those who are not going on to higher schools ready to make a promising beginning vocationally? Are the leaving pupils as a group ready to keep on learning, and do they know where and how to learn when the need or the opportunity arises?

Social competence on the part of boys and girls who are through with high school work implies affirmative answers to such questions. The term is not meant to suggest a conflict between the interests of the individual and the interests of society, nor does it imply that all boys and girls ought to be cast in a uniform mold, without regard for their individual abilities and ambitions. Social competence can be fully achieved only as a person is prepared to make his own best contribution of individual talent or skill. But recognition of social competence as a proper outcome of public education implies that the schools ought to be judged not so much by whether they succeed in "covering" certain predetermined subjects as by their success in developing socially significant abilities and in leading boys and girls to want to put those abilities to use.

Because the qualities which presumably make up social competence are of especial significance to the leaving pupils, as well as to the State as a whole, the Inquiry has sought to keep these qualities in the foreground of its appraisal of the educational program. Through tests, questionnaires, reports from schools, interviews with individual boys and girls, conferences with adults who have been in a position to judge the qualities of particular young people, observation of boys' and girls' in-school and out-of-school activities, the Inquiry has gathered whatever reasonable evidence it could find concerning young people's readiness for normal out-of-school living. Undoubtedly, the desirable attitudes and abilities which leaving pupils possess have not always come from their school work. Undoubtedly also, the school alone cannot be held to blame for a lack of social competence. Nevertheless, a comprehensive assessment of socially important abilities and disabilities among the boys and girls who are leaving school has seemed to offer the soundest basis for appraising the relative influence of the school, and hence for estimating the effectiveness of its program.

IMPROVEMENT OF THE EDUCATIONAL PROGRAM

In arriving at recommendations for the improvement of the State's policy one further assumption has been made. This assumption is that systematic analysis, on the one hand of the social competence of leaving pupils in particular communities, and on the other hand of the influences to which the pupils have been exposed, may make it possible to determine what influences have been chiefly responsible for important characteristics of the pupils.

Significant cause-and-effect relationships have, in truth, seemed clearly apparent. The relationships obviously cannot be proved with the definiteness with which one can prove in the field of physical science that a particular effect follows a particular cause. To disentangle educational cause and educational effect in the varying situations in which schools must operate calls for much reliance on subjective judgment. Thus, different educational methods and materials in different schools have been found to produce essentially the same results; and the judgment of educational specialists has had to be relied on to determine whether the school programs were of equal value, or whether out-of-school influences made up for differences in school work. Again, very different outcomes have been found to accompany the use of what seemed to be the same methods and materials; and it has been necessary to judge whether differences in the abilities of pupils, or in community influences, or in other nonschool factors were responsible for these inequalities in achievement. In spite of the constant need for subjective estimates, certain types of educational outcome have proved to be so frequently associated with the same types of educational practice as to make the existence of a cause-and-effect relationship practically certain. It is on these definite relationships that this study has based its chief recommendations.

The fact should perhaps be noted that many of the cause-and-effect relationships thus discovered have been negative. For reasons which will be discussed in later chapters, New York State secondary schools present a remarkably uniform and, in some respects, a remarkably restricted program of secondary education. Confined within well-recognized limits, that program fails to develop certain types of attitudes and abilities simply because it makes no systematic effort to develop them. The development of other attitudes and abilities is left almost completely to nonschool influences. In numerous instances, therefore, the effort to trace cause-and-effect relationships has led to the conclusion not that the schools positively produce certain outcomes, but that these outcomes appear because the schools do little or nothing about them.

Despite this fact, the recommendations growing out of the study are essentially pragmatic. The basis for the major recommendations has been an analysis of educational practice in large numbers of New York State schools whose pupils' competence has been systematically appraised. The recommendations look toward the extension of practices which have been found to "work"—practices so often accompanied by good outcomes that to extend them more widely will almost certainly lead to improvement in the educational program of the State as a whole.

MAJOR STEPS IN THE PRESENT STUDY

In the light of its basic assumptions, this study has been organized in terms of a number of successive steps.[1]

[1] The study as a whole has included a considerable number of subordinate investigations, each of which was carried out under the supervision of a staff member and led to significant conclusions of its own. A more detailed account of these investigations and of their contributions to the general plan will be found in the Appendix to this report.

First, a group of representative secondary schools was chosen for study. These schools were widely distributed over New York State. They included sixty-two general high schools (among which were four junior high schools) and twelve additional schools emphasizing specialized vocational education. The schools were so chosen as to provide examples of every important variation which the school systems of New York State present, both in their educational programs and in their social, industrial, and economic backgrounds.[2] The schools were not assembled to represent an average for the State. There is ample reason to believe that state policies can be more soundly based on due recognition of variations in problems, needs, and accomplishments than on a consideration merely of averages. An effort was therefore made to have all significant variations fully represented.

Second, a systematic appraisal of the qualities and attainments of its leaving pupils was conducted in each of the selected schools. The appraisal involved a number of separate undertakings. In June, 1936, an extensive testing program was administered in the sixty-two general high schools, to all the school classes from which many pupils were expected to leave school at the end of the year. Tests were given at the same time to pupils in the elementary schools from which

[2] A full account of the method by which appropriate social, industrial, and economic factors were taken into consideration has been prepared for the Inquiry in a special report by Dr. J. B. Maller, *School and Community*, Regents' Inquiry, 1938. To Dr. Maller's account should be added the explanation that a preliminary list of representative school systems which he prepared was examined by the staff of the study of secondary education in the light of information secured from the State Education Department, to make sure that the eventual list would furnish examples of important variations in educational programs. The educational variations especially sought were those of school enrollment, forms of school organization, types of curricula and of teaching method, and school accomplishment as measured by the standards sponsored by the Department. With Dr. Maller's cooperation certain substitutions were made in the preliminary list, so that the school systems finally chosen for study represented important educational variants as well as the major sociological variants.

Italicized

High School and Life

these high school pupils had originally come, so that a general measure of the abilities of the pupils entering each high school was also available. Late in May, 1937, pupils in the specialized vocational schools were similarly tested. During the school year 1936–37 the secondary schools directly involved in the study, together with several hundred others which volunteered to cooperate, submitted special reports on individual pupils withdrawing from school. Within the same period approximately two thousand of the pupils who did not go on to college and who were reported by their schools as having been out of school for six months or more were interviewed by members of the Inquiry staff, and information about them was obtained from their employers or from other adults who were acquainted with them. The data from tests, school reports, and interviews were eventually assembled as a composite, so as to afford a picture of the social competence of a representative leaving group.

Third, two groups of schools were selected for an intensive study of methods and materials of instruction. The selection was made largely on the basis of test results, supplemented by conferences with the school officers involved, to make sure of the dependability of the test scores. Certain schools which stood out because of the relatively high attainments of their pupils in one or more important aspects of social competence comprised the first group. These schools were studied by specialists in various phases of the curriculum—English, the social studies, health education, vocational education. It was the task of the specialists to analyze the work of the schools, to discover the factors either within the schools or in their local environments, which were productive of favorable results, and to make note of especially promising methods or materials of teaching. The second group of schools comprised those which were noteworthy because of the relative lack of social competence among their leaving pupils. Specialists went to these schools also, for the purpose of discovering the

· 8 ·

major obstacles which stood in the way of desirable achievement and of determining whether those obstacles were inherent in the community setting or grew out of weaknesses in
the school program.

Finally, the results of these investigations were examined for
the light which they might throw on strengths and weaknesses
in present state policy and on changes in policy which would
enable high schools throughout the State to contribute more
effectively to their pupils' general and individual competence.
The information gained from the studies suggested certain
desirable changes in the secondary school practices of the
State. A series of proposals was therefore drawn up, outlining a
more effective program of secondary education than that now
in general operation. The final recommendations of this study
are directly related to these proposals, and consist of suggestions
for specific changes in the Education Law, in the policies and
regulations of the State Education Department, and in the
organization of the Department, through which the Board of
Regents may promote widespread adoption of the proposed
program.

These four major steps have constituted the general plan of
the study of secondary education. It should be noted that this
study has not included an independent analysis of the cost of
secondary education in New York State. Such an analysis has
been made by a coordinate division of the Regents' Inquiry.[3]
The recommendations growing out of the present study have
nevertheless been so framed as to take into account the possible
economies in secondary school administration suggested by the
finance study.[4] Furthermore, such recommendations as have
been advanced for extensive new undertakings in secondary
education have been made only after due consideration of the

[3] A brief statement of the relation of the study of secondary education to the
other major studies of the Inquiry will be found in the Appendix to this report.

[4] Alonzo G. Grace and G. A. Moe, *State Aid and School Costs*, Regents' Inquiry,
1938.

cost of these undertakings as estimated on the basis of data provided by the staff of the finance investigation. The policies proposed for adoption by the Board of Regents are therefore not merely defensible from the standpoint of educational need, but consistent with the findings of the separate studies of school costs.

CONCLUSIONS OF THIS STUDY AS A BASIS FOR A LONG-TIME PROGRAM

Because of the unsettled times in which this study has been carried on, there may be a question in the minds of many readers as to the permanence of the conclusions to which the study has led. This question deserves an explicit answer.

The facts underlying the conclusions and recommendations —facts regarding the kind of teaching provided by the secondary schools, what boys and girls are like when they leave school, how these boys and girls fare outside of school—were gathered, with a few exceptions, during the last seven months of 1936 and the first five months of 1937. Economically and industrially, this period was midway between the end of one depression and the beginning of another.

There can be little doubt that both schools and pupils were to some extent affected in 1936 and 1937 by a depression psychology which persisted in spite of the return of comparatively normal economic conditions. School officers occasionally reflected this psychology in a defeatist attitude toward the work of the schools in preparing pupils for employment. In their aimlessness and their doubts about the future, boys and girls about to leave school sometimes showed a similar attitude. Moreover, some of these boys and girls, once they had left school, unquestionably failed to take advantage of jobs that were actually open, because of their apparent assumption that there was no longer any such thing as work for young people.

The facts to which the Inquiry has paid chief attention, however, are largely independent of depressions or of a depression psychology. Whether boys and girls on the point of leaving the high school have learned to read well enough to get along in the world, whether their schools have given them a loyalty to American democracy which will make them active supporters of that democracy, whether they have learned to like decent sports and amusements, whether they know enough about conditions outside of school to take advantage of the jobs that are there—these are matters which will be important whatever the current economic situation may be. It is on facts with respect to matters of this type that the Inquiry's recommendations are chiefly based; and such facts can be as dependably gathered in bad times or in moderately good times as in times of prosperity.

The conclusions of this study have, therefore, more than a temporary bearing on the work of the New York State schools. They look forward, it is true, to a continuance of certain fundamental conditions which now exist: faith on the part of Americans in a democratic government, freedom for each individual to manage his own affairs with proper regard for the rights of other individuals to do likewise, an economic system in which individual ability, integrity, and ambition will have an important place. Granted that such conditions as these will continue, the educational program toward which the facts summarized in this report seem to point is likely to be a sound program long after the economic situation of 1936 and 1937 has been left behind.

PLAN OF THIS REPORT

The principal conclusions of this study are summarized in the three major sections into which this report is divided.

Part I of the report describes the chief outcomes of the current program of secondary education in New York State. Drawing chiefly on data gathered in the second step of the study, it seeks to appraise the social competence of boys and girls who are through with the secondary school—their readiness for citizenship, for leisure-time activities outside the school, for further learning, and for vocation.

Part II endeavors to explain present educational outcomes through an examination of the kinds of education which New York State now provides for its high school pupils. The curriculum and methods of teaching, current provisions for pupils' individual differences, arrangements for the guidance of pupils in their choice of school work and of their vocations, the existing system of school and school district organization, the plan of Regents' Examinations, and the supervisory program of the State Education Department, all exert unmistakable influences on pupils' achievement. To these factors Part II of the report devotes particular attention.

Part III seeks to answer the question as to what can be done to bring about an improved educational program. This part of the report contains proposals for certain modifications in the content, methods, and organization of secondary education throughout the State, recommendations as to the means by which these proposals may be put into effect, and an analysis of the probable cost of an improved educational program.

CHAPTER II

Preparation for Citizenship

NO APPRAISAL of the outcomes of a state-wide program of secondary education can be entirely just if it measures those outcomes merely in terms of the average characteristics of the boys and girls who leave the secondary schools. Young people differ widely in their interests, their abilities, and their personal traits. They may be expected to differ no less widely in many of the qualities which enable them to face the out-of-school world. In any complete estimate of what the schools have done for these young people, their fundamental differences in ability and achievement should eventually be taken into account.

Boys and girls leaving school are nevertheless alike as well as different—alike in certain abilities and characteristics which they all, or nearly all, possess, and alike in that they frequently lack certain traits. Their likenesses in matters with which the schools are or should be concerned may furnish important clues to the general value of the secondary school program. At the risk of passing lightly for the moment over some of their differences, it therefore seems appropriate to look at the characteristics of boys and girls who are leaving the high school from the standpoint, first of all, of qualities which these boys and girls have in common. Among such qualities, those which are of perhaps major importance to a State concerned with boys and girls as its on-coming adult members are the qualities which make these boys and girls ready or unready for citizenship.

MEANING OF CITIZENSHIP

The citizenship which the welfare of a democratic state requires is only partly expressed in the activities of voting, paying taxes, and observing the law. Whether citizens do vote and pay their taxes and obey the law is, to be sure, of no little importance. Present laxity in these matters among adult citizens has occasioned comment by numerous students of government. Hence one basis for judging the readiness for citizenship of boys and girls who are about to become citizens ought to be the degree of conscience which these boys and girls show toward the formal duties of the citizen.

But beyond these formal duties lie any number of informal activities hardly less significant to the social health of the State—activities involved in getting along with family, neighbors, and associates, the day-by-day relationships in which ethics and morals play a part, the normal give-and-take through which the individual participates in the numerous social groups to which he belongs. In a society in which freedom rather than regimentation is to be the rule, it is important that the citizen govern himself in these relationships according to decent standards of honesty and fairness. Any criterion of good citizenship on the part of the individual ought therefore to take account of such relationships as well as of the citizen's formal responsibilities to government.

In these formal and informal activities alike, moreover, the mere fact that an individual "does his duty" offers only a partial measure of his qualities as a citizen. With the growing complexities of government, with the increasing dependence of people on one another for jobs and security and comfort, with the new knowledge that has to be taken into account in dealing with social problems, the citizen who acts ignorantly or blindly, even with the best intentions, may be almost as poor a citizen as the one who makes no attempt to live up to his obligations. How realistically and sensibly a citizen does his duty is as important in a democratic state as whether he does it at all. The social knowledge of the individual and his intelligent awareness of social problems are factors which cannot be overlooked in appraising his citizenship.

This general concept of good citizenship represents the point of view from which the Inquiry has sought to determine how well qualified for citizenship the boys and girls are who are leaving high school in New York State. In many instances the clues to readiness for citizenship have had to be indirect; and the evidence which the Inquiry has been able to obtain has covered no more than a sampling of the activities for which a good citizen ought to be prepared. Tests, reports from schools, and interviews with pupils who have left school nevertheless support a number of highly pertinent conclusions.

DEFICIENCIES IN CITIZENSHIP RECOGNIZED BY THE SCHOOLS

Reports from the schools make it apparent that *among the boys and girls leaving school every year are a considerable number whom the schools themselves are unwilling to recommend for responsible citizenship.* So far as their pupils' readiness for citizenship is concerned, the high schools decline to stand back of one-fourth of all the pupils who are ending their schooling. The schools are surest of the pupils who have been in school long enough to graduate, and especially of those who are graduating from the college-preparatory curriculum. Individual schools ordinarily fail to recommend fewer than one in ten of the boys and girls in their graduating classes. Among the young people who leave without graduating, however, the schools consider every third pupil not adequately prepared for the duties he must assume as a citizen.

The unwillingness of the schools to recommend certain pupils for citizenship does not necessarily mean that these pupils have given evidence that they are likely to be positively bad citizens. There are recognizably bad citizens among the

· 17 ·

leaving group—pupils who have already come into open conflict with the criminal law, or who, for other reasons, are judged by their schools to be not of good character. The far greater number, however, are boys and girls whom the schools fail to recommend because of their lack of understanding of current social problems or their lack of information about the duties of citizenship. The defects which the schools most commonly note are intellectual defects rather than defects in habits or ethical standards.

Probably there will always be some young people leaving the high school who are not ready for citizenship. Schools must often compete with out-of-school influences tending to undo much that the schools themselves may be trying to accomplish. Even when out-of-school influences are not hostile, differences in pupils' capacity to acquire the knowledge and insight and abilities properly demanded of the good citizen will result in quite different degrees of preparation for citizenship. But it is difficult to believe that one out of every four normal boys and girls is incapable of being educated for good citizenship. The fact that so large a number are now recognized by the schools themselves as not ready for citizenship would in itself seem to hold clear implications for the current school program.

SOCIAL INFORMATION OF LEAVING PUPILS

The kinds of intellectual defects of which the schools are no doubt conscious among their pupils are in part revealed by the results of tests given by the Inquiry.[1] Among these tests were various measures of the social information which the pupils possessed at the time they withdrew from school. The results of the latter tests suggest that *irrespective of the schools' judgment of their readiness for citizenship, the leaving pupils as a group*

[1] For a separate analysis of the test results summarized in this and the following chapters, see Ruth E. Eckert and T. O. Marshall, *When Youth Leave School*, Regent's Inquiry, 1938. The significance of the tests bearing on pupils' preparation for citizenship is discussed in detail in Howard E. Wilson, *Education for Citizenship*, Regents' Inquiry, 1938.

are seriously deficient in their knowledge of the problems, the issues, and the present-day facts with which American citizens should be concerned.

The test results show that boys and girls in New York State learn many of the facts of American history. The majority know, for example, that it was Herbert Hoover who gained national prominence as United States food administrator during the World War; they can indicate at least one of the significant results of the Louisiana Purchase; they are familiar with the provisions of the Ordinance of 1787. By the time they leave school they are acquainted also with various aspects of the formal working of government. They know the number of senators in Congress; they know that impeachment is the only legal way of removing federal judges from office; they are acquainted with the pocket veto; they have learned that prohibition came to an end with the ratification of the Twenty-First Amendment. In their information about matters of this sort the young people who are finishing their high school work in New York State are probably at least the equals of similar groups of young people the country over, and they undoubtedly know far more about such matters than the average adult.

Pupils who are on the point of leaving school know a good deal also about the "headline" facts in the current news. A recent National Current Events Survey, conducted in high schools all over the United States, placed the median of New York State pupils definitely above the national median. Particularly in such matters as are currently featured in the newspapers—industrial disputes and broad government activities, for instance—New York State high school pupils are acquainted with "figures in the news" and know in outline about many events of national importance.

The deficiency in their knowledge comes in connection with certain kinds of facts and with their appreciation of underlying issues. Comparatively well-informed though they are about such matters as labor troubles and current government activities, they are not acquainted with recent changes in the structure of government, and they are seriously uninformed or misinformed about foreign affairs. For example, a majority of the pupils tested in 1937 failed to connect the date of President Roosevelt's second inauguration with the "lame-duck" amendment to the Constitution; about a third of those who pretended to any knowledge of it (practically half left the question unanswered) thought that the Fourth Internationale was the Printers' International Society; and only a small minority knew that the important international treaty which expired in 1936 was the Washington Naval Treaty. Obviously it is not to be expected that every boy and girl who left high school in 1937 should have known about these particular matters. The facts cited represent no more than samples of current information which thoughtful followers of the news might well have been informed about; different facts would have provided pertinent samples of information for 1936 or 1938. The important consideration is that few of these and other significant matters were in the minds of pupils leaving school at the very time these matters were significant.

The deficiency in the knowledge of these young people appears again in their lack of familiarity with certain fundamental social concepts. The majority understand what is meant by such terms as "habeas corpus," "ratify," "indictment," "piece-rate wage," "bonds," "immigration," and "acquired characteristics." The kinds of terms which confuse them are exemplified by "constituents," "retail price," "liabilities," "gold certificates," "eugenics," "philanthropy," and "stratified society." They are more frequently acquainted with the relatively restricted, tangible, and limited terms than with the larger, more intangible and nebulous, but often more basic and commonly used terms. Generally speaking, they possess less understanding of sociological terms than of political terms, and less of political terms than of economic terms. It is probable that their misconceptions are no greater or more widespread than those of high school boys and girls in general, or of adult citizens. Nevertheless, in an age which demands so much of the individual citizen in clear understanding and critical judgment, the misunderstandings prevailing among these young people about to become citizens are of serious import.

Deficiencies in knowledge are even more strikingly evident in the results of tests designed to explore pupils' knowledge of social conditions in their own communities. Boys and girls from very large or from very small communities seem to know more about the towns and cities in which they live than do young people from communities of average size, but among young people throughout the State there exists an appalling blindness to local problems. Many boys and girls in a community in which a declining population gives evidence of social pathology may not even realize that the population is declining. The average high school senior knows the ordinary political affiliation of his community, but only a minority know the political outlook of the leading local newspaper. Less than half the young people know how the cost of electricity in their communities compares with the cost in other communities, or how the local death rate compares with the average for the State. Substantial numbers have not found out whether their town has a public library "with magazines and newspapers," or whether their community contains many unemployed, or what the local vocational opportunities are for young people. As with the current events of a given year, information with respect to these matters is obviously less important in itself than as an indication of the alertness of boys and girls to the problems which, with wisdom or ignorance, the citizens of a democracy must inevitably face. Alertness to local problems is clearly not part of the equipment for citizenship of the boys and girls now leaving school in New York State.

It may of course be countered that the ignorance which boys and girls show with respect to current social problems is no greater than the ignorance which adults, similarly tested, would show. The fact that adults do not know all they need to know is hardly a sound reason, however, for being content with an equal lack of knowledge on the part of a new generation. If boys and girls can master historical facts and facts about the machinery of government—and the test results clearly demonstrate their command of many such facts—they can as readily master facts which will give them direct insight into current issues and problems. Coming fresh from school, they might thus have what they do not now have, an appreciation of the major tasks which cities and states and the nation face at the present time.

ATTITUDES TOWARD CONTROVERSIAL ISSUES

Beyond their information and understanding, the question of young people's social attitudes and ideals is obviously of importance. The tests used in the Inquiry provide evidence as to leaving pupils' attitudes with respect to a number of significant matters.

The results of a test on which pupils were asked to indicate their opinions concerning various controversial issues suggest that *the boys and girls who are leaving school are fundamentally conservative in their outlook on social problems.* The test in question was composed of a number of controversial statements which the pupils were asked to mark correct or incorrect, even though the correctness or incorrectness of the statements could not be proved. If a pupil believed a statement to be neither wholly right nor wholly wrong, he was asked to mark it in the way which came closest to his own opinion. The statements were concerned with various aspects of nationalism, international relations, relationships between races, and political affairs. Scores on the test were so computed as to give a measure of pupils' openmindedness and freedom from prejudice.

Pupils from urban areas showed distinctly greater openmindedness than pupils from country districts and small towns. Nevertheless, the responses in general indicated a marked tendency to think in terms of catchwords or slogans rather than in terms of facts. A majority of the leaving pupils approved such statements as that the Constitution should never be changed, that laws should be regarded as sacred enactments, and that American democracy is considered by most of the civilized world the ideal form of government. In spite of the fact that these same boys and girls refused to grant that the Chinese are a backward people who have no culture, or that the United States has always been right in sending marines to South America, or that a patriot should never criticize the faults of his country, they were clearly not willing to confess to any marked tolerance for new institutions or new ways of dealing with social problems.

ATTITUDES TOWARD THE RIGHTS OF CITIZENS

Further light on pupils' social attitudes came from the results of tests which sought a direct measure of pupils' allegiance to certain basic tenets of American democracy. These tests attempted to assay pupils' attitudes toward free speech, freedom of the press, and the right of free assembly. The tests consisted of brief descriptions of a series of situations (in half, school situations, in the other half, situations arising outside of school) in which action affecting one or more of these basic principles of democratic living was involved. In each instance the pupils were to indicate their approval or rejection of the proposed action. Thus, one test question described a situation in which a sheriff had been elected for a year, but seemed to be inefficient in managing his division. A small group of citizens wished to hold a meeting and try to have him removed. The pupils were asked to indicate whether they thought any such meeting should be allowed, and whether the citizens concerned had a right to consider plans for getting another sheriff.

The results of the tests indicate that *most boys and girls on the point of leaving school are ready to give at least verbal allegiance to the principles of democratic living and democratic government.* High school graduates, in particular, confronted with situations in which the rights to free speech and freedom of the press and free assembly apply, can pick out the course of suggested action which most fully respects these rights.

At the same time it should be said that large numbers of pupils were not able to recognize the application of these democratic principles. Boys and girls who were about to leave school before they had completed the secondary school showed much less discernment in these matters than did the graduates. Even among high school seniors, as many as a fourth gave no clear indication on the tests that they knew what freedom in a democracy means. Though the majority of the leaving pupils indicated at least verbal acceptance of the basic principles involved, there is obviously room for far more effective education of boys and girls in the rights and privileges which should go with democratic living.

SOCIAL CONSCIENCE

It must be recognized, however, that mere verbal allegiance to democratic principles may not translate itself into positive action. Young people, and their elders, may know where and how a given principle applies, but may be quite unwilling to do anything in defense of that principle. As a means of testing willingness to act rather than readiness to pay lip-service alone, there were included among the situations presented in the test of allegiance a number which involved personal participation in group action. Pupils' responses to the latter situations suggest an almost wholly unfavorable conclusion. The test results offer unmistakable evidence that *the boys and girls who are on the point of leaving school, whatever they may think about the desirability of certain kinds of action, are reluctant to assume responsibility for civic cooperation, or to commit themselves to action which will involve personal effort or sacrifice.*

The evidence in this matter is so striking and so significant in its implications as to deserve particular attention. Pupils in representative schools were confronted when taking the test with a variety of questions which they were asked to consider as though the questions affected them personally: Should a student volunteer to help clear up the school yard, if doing so would demand his giving up part of his lunch hour? If students experience difficulty in managing their school affairs, should they be encouraged to continue handling such problems or should a teacher settle the problems, assuming that she can do so more efficiently? Should a student accept nomination as president of the student council if he is the best qualified student, provided such acceptance would mean a serious curtailment in his other activities?

To none of these questions did a majority of the pupils at any grade level give answers which indicated willingness to make any personal sacrifices. Moreover, the longer they had been in school the less willing were they, in general, to commit themselves to any sort of responsibility. Of the seventh grade pupils who took the test, one in three indicated that he might exert himself to clean up the school yard, and one in three again would take the presidency of the student council even though it meant a personal loss to him. Of the seniors who were tested, only one in six would assume any responsibility for the yard, and only one in seven would allow himself to be nominated, at personal cost to himself, as president of the council.

That pupils' dispositions in these matters are not limited merely to school affairs is shown by their response to parallel situations involving out-of-school activities. Four-fifths of the seniors reported that they would not, if they were adult citizens, spend any of their own time in trying to beautify a public square near their homes. More than four-fifths believed that if workers who have been given a chance to help manage company affairs are not successful in their efforts, the owner should be encouraged to assume sole control again. Five-sixths were of the opinion that a well-known businessman who is eminently qualified for public office would be justified in refusing the nomination for mayor if it involved his giving up some of his business and social interests.

The questions cited are merely illustrative of a number to which pupils were asked to respond. Their answers to the whole group of questions amply support the conclusion that, in contrast to whatever recognition they may possess of the rights of citizens in a democracy, they have little or no appreciation of the individual duties and obligations through which alone a democracy can survive at its best. In the matter of social conscience, that is to say, they are seriously lacking. For whatever cause, they have been steadily imbibing during their years in school the type of philosophy that "lets George do it," that urges one to forget what happens so that one won't be bothered to testify, that shrugs at proposals for making the world any better.

LEAVING PUPILS' READINESS FOR CITIZENSHIP

Out of these various items of evidence may be constructed a summary picture of the readiness for citizenship of the boys and girls who each year find themselves on the point of leaving high school in New York State. The leaving pupils as a group are at least passably versed in the traditional facts of American history and civics. They have kept up with the headlines in the current news. In most instances they recognize some of the more important of their rights and privileges as American citizens. They know very little, however, about civic and social problems in their own communities. Their acquaintance with the news seldom penetrates beneath the surface of personalities and superficial happenings; they appreciate few of the political, economic, and sociological problems which America faces, particularly the problems reflected in international affairs.

They have developed a generally conservative attitude toward social issues. Most disturbing of all, they are lacking in social conscience—concern for the social good which will lead them to put forth the individual effort necessary to preserve that good.

OUT-OF-SCHOOL CITIZENSHIP ACTIVITIES

There remains to be considered whether the activities of these boys and girls after they have left the secondary school do anything either to confirm or to increase such readiness for citizenship as they have already gained. A minority—less than a fifth of the pupils who enter the secondary schools, except in the larger cities—go on to higher schools. For some of those who do go on, college work may bring wider understandings and a keener appreciation of the parts young people may play as citizens of a democracy. The great majority, once they are through with the secondary school, work or loaf or look for jobs. Interviews with representative boys and girls from this majority suggest that *once he is out of school, the ordinary boy or girl does practically nothing to add to his readiness for citizenship, nor does he even keep alive the knowledge of civic affairs or the interest in social problems which he may have had when he finished his schooling.*

This conclusion does not mean that a large number of the boys and girls who have left school show themselves definitely antisocial. The results of the interviews agree with the reports from the schools in pointing to only a small number who are definitely bad citizens. With reference to young people in general, employers, adults who are acquainted with these young people, and the boys and girls themselves report that they get along well with their associates. Fewer than one in a hundred of the former pupils who are employed full-time seem to have had difficulty in making necessary social adjustments on the job. Possibly one in twenty of the total group who have left school fails to adjust to his family, and most cases of maladjustment in the home are apparently due quite as often to bad conditions within the home as to lack of adaptability on the part of the boy or girl concerned. Young people's relationships with neighbors and with friends and other associates are similarly acceptable. For every boy or girl who is described as "a bad lot," or as "going with a fast crowd," or as being "a tough one," there are scores or hundreds who at worst have attracted no unfavorable attention and at best are highly regarded by those who know them.

Cause for concern is to be found not so much in what these young people do as in what they do not do. If their preparation for citizenship has been effective, it ought to show itself in a continuance of at least some of the activities contributing to good citizenship in which they were engaged while they were in school. The abrupt stopping of these activities, once the pupils are out of school, is all too clearly apparent.

While they are still in school, high school boys and girls do a considerable amount of reading in history and current events, chiefly in response to formal school assignments. As soon as they have left school they cease this type of reading almost entirely. More than half the pupils interviewed had done no reading in books within the two weeks preceding the interview. Of those who had read at least part of one book, fully 90 per cent had read only fiction, and the nonfiction contained few titles bearing even indirectly on problems of citizenship. A larger number of the former pupils had read magazines, but the extent of their interest in the news or in social problems may be inferred from the fact that fewer than one in ten named news magazines—for example, *Time*—and fewer than one in three hundred mentioned magazines of liberal opinion—for example, *The New Republic* or *The Nation*.

High school boys and girls are confirmed radio listeners. Out of school they continue to listen to the radio, but their favorite programs consist overwhelmingly of commercial variety shows. Boake Carter ranked twenty-seventh in the list of preferences of pupils interviewed in 1937; the March of Time came thirty-second; Lowell Thomas was thirty-third; Edwin C. Hill was seventy-first. No other single program of news or comment was mentioned so frequently as were these four; straight "radio news" in general ranked in popularity with Lowell Thomas— thirty-third in the total list. Forums and general educational programs were even less popular: the Town Meeting of the Air, the Farm and Home hour, and the School of the Air, which tied with one another in number of mentions, ranked eighty-fourth.

While they are in school the boys and girls in many high schools have a chance to take part in various social enterprises —student government, homeroom organizations, current events clubs, formal or informal groups engaged in a variety of cooperative undertakings. Out of school fewer than half these young people belong to clubs, organizations, or groups of any sort. Of the total number of leaving pupils, possibly a sixth were found to belong to church groups: the Epworth League, the Young People's Association, the Sacred Heart, the Altar Boys' Club, various choir groups. Fewer than one in sixteen were members of general character-building organizations, such as the Boy and Girl Scouts and the Y.M.C.A. and the Y.W.C.A. Fewer than one in twenty-five were enrolled in 4-H clubs or Future Farmers organizations, and not more than one in forty were members of groups whose aim is general community service. The groups named are the ones which may be expected to have a measure of direct or indirect value in citizenship training; the others to which out-of-school pupils belong are almost exclusively devoted to recreation. There can be little question of the social value of certain of the experiences afforded by the religious, character-building, and service organizations. But the relatively small numbers of young people enrolled in these organizations mean that they have slight influence on the citizenship of the total group of pupils just out of school.

CONTACTS WITH ADULTS

The whole story of the boys and girls who have left school is not told in the general statement that most of them do little or nothing to add to their readiness for citizenship. The interviews make it apparent also that *on leaving school a large proportion of these young people lose touch completely with anyone who can give them intelligent advice or assistance.*

Each boy or girl was asked to name the adult outside his immediate family who knew him best. In the cases of more than a fourth of the young people interviewed, the interviewers were unable to find any adult, other than a former teacher or a member of the young person's family, who was well enough acquainted with the boy or girl in question to give any information about him. Frequently the young people themselves could think of no grown person who knew them well. In other instances they overrated the importance of their contacts with adults; persons whom they mentioned as being well acquainted with them had difficulty in recalling them, or regarded their acquaintance as casual.

The help which these boys and girls can get from members of their own families is often extremely meager. Where family conditions are bad, the young people stay away from home as much as possible. Even when home conditions are good, parents in the cities, particularly, often know little about the activities or whereabouts of their children. "He's home to eat and to sleep; I don't know what he does the rest of the time." And asked about the help they can get from their fathers or mothers on problems of jobs or leisure or social relationships, boys and girls reply again and again that their parents "can't help much. They haven't been up against this kind of thing, and they've got enough on their own minds, anyway."

Nor is the school a source of advice for any large proportion of former pupils. The schools themselves report that fewer than 10 per cent of the pupils who withdraw from school before graduation return for advice or for assistance within three months after leaving school. Approximately twice as many graduates as nongraduates return, but they come back chiefly, it appears, for transcripts of credits for admission to higher institutions, or for credentials or recommendations with which to obtain jobs. From the reports of former pupils, it is evident that boys and girls who have left school do not often consider the school a place to seek help. Many remark flatly that they would not think of going back to school for advice: "The people there don't know anything about the things outside of books." Others say that they would like to go back but hesitate to do so: "Mr. Blank would be a good guy to talk to, but he's so busy I hate to bother him." Still others remark with surprise, "I never thought of that," or "I didn't know you could go back after you'd got your diploma."

Accentuating their lack of contact with adults is an attitude which interviewers reported among boys and girls throughout the State. Young people just out of school reply, in answer to questions about whom they go to for help with their problems: "I'm not asking anybody for advice. I take care of my own troubles." Whether from their school experiences or from outside contacts, large numbers of young people have apparently come to the conclusion that it is wrong or weak to seek advice, and that no matter how serious or difficult the problem, the boy or girl who amounts to anything must "look after it on his own." There is much that is praiseworthy in such an attitude, but in the face of problems about which the only sensible thing to do is to ask for well-informed advice, the boy or girl who thinks it beneath him to accept help is obviously at a serious disadvantage.

SUMMARY

Thus the total impression of these boys and girls newly out of school is one of a group largely adrift, cut off from adult assistance, out of contact with any kind of helpful supervision. Few of them engage in any organized activity which allows them to apply the training in cooperative action that their schools may have given them. The majority become inert, so far as interest in civic affairs is concerned; they neither read about social problems nor listen to discussions of such problems.

Collectively, the leaving pupils constitute a group schooled in academic facts, recognizing their rights as free citizens in a free country, but unconcerned about civic responsibility, and not awake even to the immediate and local problems and issues which will shortly confront them as citizens, taxpayers, and voters.

CHAPTER III

Preparation for Further Learning
and for Wholesome Recreation

IN A society which gives boys and girls, and men and women, a considerable amount of time to spend as they will, what people do with their leisure cannot safely be ignored. One of the purposes of schooling is presumably to see that young people make use of part of their leisure time in learning, even outside of school. Schools are also ordinarily supposed to give young people habits and standards of enjoyment which will make them like to spend part of their free time in worthwhile recreation. The readiness of boys and girls who are leaving school to go on learning, and their interest in wholesome recreation, thus offer further tests of the effectiveness of the secondary school program.

LIMITATIONS OF THE COLLEGE-ENTRANCE
CRITERION

The success of the high school in preparing young people for continued learning is ordinarily measured in terms of pupils' records in college. From this standpoint the New York State high schools enjoy as favorable a reputation as do public secondary schools anywhere. Studies of the success of students in higher institutions have shown that graduates of the New York State schools are distinctly "good risks." In consequence, the evidence of academic ability provided by the Regents' diplomas is accepted by colleges not only in New York but also in most other states, as equivalent to College Board Examinations for admission to the freshman year.

Unfortunately, the criterion of preparation for further education employed by the usual college is very narrow. What liberal arts colleges in general examine in candidates for admission—and this is true of other types of higher institutions also—is the ability to "pass" systematic courses. Few colleges test the capacity or the inclination of entering students to learn of their own accord. Still fewer measure their students' ability to learn outside the areas of French and Latin, formal mathematics, chemistry, biology, and physics, European and American history, and "standard" English literature, which represent the core of the liberal arts program.

The preparation for further education which secondary schools give their pupils should be much broader than this. Whether boys and girls go on to college or end their schooling with the high school, they will have to learn in other ways than through formally organized courses. The radio, the movies, the newspaper, and the magazine are bound to be their teachers. They will have to learn, too, in areas outside the standard academic program, about such matters as getting jobs and holding them, managing their personal finances, conducting their households, living on good terms with their neighbors. Academic tests alone provide little evidence of capacity to learn from impersonal teachers, or about problems of this sort.

Moreover, the tests of readiness for further learning which the colleges administer affect only a minority of high school boys and girls. Of every hundred pupils who enter the ninth grade of New York State high schools, fewer than forty remain to graduate. Only about half the graduates continue their full-time schooling in any type of higher institution. A considerable number of the pupils who do not go on to higher schools will perhaps sometime enroll in apprentice courses, part-time vocational schools, or adult education classes. Except for necessarily piecemeal education of this type, eighty in every hundred young people who enter the ninth grade cannot look forward to having anyone provide systematic teaching for them after their high school work is over. Whatever further learning they do they must do largely for themselves. Their capacity to learn and, perhaps even more, their inclination to learn are matters which deserve serious attention.

The Inquiry has attempted to gauge the readiness of pupils for further education only partly in terms of their preparation for continued school work. It has been concerned even more particularly to discover how much likelihood there is that these pupils will keep on growing educationally, through independent and more or less informal learning, after they have left school. For this purpose it has taken account, among other evidences, of the way that boys and girls, in school and out, spend their time when they are left to their own devices. Much of the free time of young people goes, as it should, into relaxation or fun. Since their leisure affords opportunity for both continued learning and recreation, the two matters are here dealt with together.

PUPILS' ATTITUDES TOWARD SCHOOLING

Interviews with pupils who have left school make it clear that *the boys and girls who are on the point of leaving high school are thoroughly convinced of the value of schooling.*

The young people interviewed were asked whether they thought themselves better off than boys and girls who had had no high school training. More of the pupils who had left before graduating than of the graduates expressed some doubt, but the overwhelming majority of both groups answered yes— often with the express or implied comment that the question was somewhat absurd: "Anybody ought to know that the longer he stays in school the better off he will be." As many as a third of these boys and girls, whether they had graduated from the high school or not, were hoping to be able to continue their school work some day. Though their notions as to when and how they would go back were usually nebulous in the extreme, their faith in the value of schooling was obvious.

The urge to continue with school work was strong enough among large numbers of these young people to have led them to spend a considerable part of their out-of-school time in study. Of the graduates who had not enrolled for full-time work in higher institutions, about a third were studying. About a sixth of the boys and girls who had left school without graduating were also taking a part-time course of one kind or another. It is perhaps worthy of remark that in neither group were there any considerable numbers who were studying "for fun"; they were practically always looking for some advantage which they thought further education might bring them— general improvement or a better job—rather than for relaxation or enjoyment. Moreover, studying seemed to be synonymous in their minds with taking courses, so that the availability of formally organized courses was apparently an important factor in determining not merely what they studied but whether they studied at all. Their desire for better training was nevertheless leading many of them to go to considerable trouble and expense in order to get some sort of further schooling.

THE VOCATIONAL MOTIVE

Despite their faith in school work, it is apparent that *most of these boys and girls have very hazy or limited conceptions of what schooling may be good for.* Asked why they were better off than boys and girls who had had less schooling, many of the young people who had answered promptly that they were better off hesitated and fumbled, not only for convincing replies but often for any replies at all. Some admitted that they didn't know why they were better off: "Maybe I'm not, come to think of it." Others responded with broad generalities: "You know more." " A high school graduate can talk to anybody." "You can feel the difference between the ones who've been to high school and the ones who haven't." A considerable number replied that their high school education had given them "a better social position." The largest group which agreed on any one answer said, in effect, that "if you've had a high school education you're more likely to get a job"— though no greater proportion of this group than of the others actually had jobs.

The conception which these young people hold that school-work is chiefly valuable as training for jobs appears in other connections even more strikingly than in the answers to direct questions. Among those who had taken up part-time study after leaving school almost twice as many had enrolled in vocational courses as in general subjects. Of a large number of pupils still in the high school and planning to stay in school (including seniors expecting to go to college) 60 per cent indicated that they would drop out if they thought that their school work would not improve their vocational chances. Three-fourths of those who were planning to leave (again including the seniors) reported that they would return for at least another year if they could be reasonably sure that doing so would enable them to get better jobs. In most cases only matters of family finance weighed more heavily than the question of vocational preparation in determining whether boys and girls would plan to continue in school or to withdraw.

The seriousness of purpose of most of these boys and girls can hardly be doubted, whatever their attitudes toward the details of their school work. It is therefore a circumstance to be reckoned with that the vocational motive is not merely the chief motive for school attendance in the minds of large numbers of these young people; it is for many of them the only motive which seems to them adequately to justify their continued schooling.

PLANS FOR FURTHER SCHOOLING

The prominence which they give to vocational preparation in their thinking means that the educational plans of most of these young people can be judged best in the light of their vocational goals. Considered from this standpoint, it is evident that *the educational plans of many boys and girls just out of high school are strikingly unrealistic, even if not wholly incapable of fulfillment.*

As long as they continue to be enrolled in the high school, the school itself takes care, after a fashion, of its pupils' educational choices. Once out of school, with no one to advise them, the pupils' very natural ambitions for the future often lead them far astray. Thus pupils who have withdrawn from school with mediocre or failing academic records frequently look forward to vocations which demand extended college training. One in seven of the boys and girls who were interviewed after having left high school without graduating were planning for such careers. Other young people—among them numerous high school graduates—believe that high school training alone will gain them admission to highly specialized occupations. To this group belonged the very intelligent invalid girl who was certain that the 90 in journalism which she had earned during the last semester of her senior year in high school would qualify her for employment as a newspaper feature writer as soon as she was well. Still others, having left the high school, look for specialized training in the short-unit courses offered by proprietary schools of various types, without any clear notion of whether they can master the courses for which they enroll or whether, once mastered, the courses will lead them in appropriate directions.

The lack of realism in the plans of these young people makes them easy prey for the agents of certain unscrupulous proprietary schools. The interviews conducted by the Inquiry brought to light instance after instance of boys and girls enrolling, or planning to enroll, in proprietary school courses in Civil Service, Diesel Mechanics, Radio Engineering, Electrical Engineering, Refrigeration, Air Conditioning, Television, Aeronautics, Art, Dancing, Undertaking, Fashion

Preparation for Learning and Recreation

Designing, Modeling, Laboratory Technique, Dramatics, Beauty Culture, Photography, as well as in a varied assortment of clerical and business courses. Some of these courses undoubtedly represented legitimate and well-planned educational offerings. Others—for example, courses in Diesel Mechanics and Air Conditioning—were obviously designed less to meet an educational need than to appeal to young people who would be attracted by the prospect of being "in on the ground floor" of a new or coming industry. A large number were outright dishonest ventures, employing solicitors who obtained enrollments in complete disregard of pupils' needs or qualifications, by misrepresentation, high-pressure methods, and promises which could not possibly be fulfilled. Few of the young people who were spending time and money on any of these courses had had a chance to pick them out with intelligent understanding of where they would lead or how appropriate they might be.

The zeal with which proprietary schools take advantage of the ignorance of boys and girls just out of school is suggested by the ratio between public and private school enrollments among these young people. One-third of the girls and about one-tenth of the boys planned to enroll, or had already enrolled, in proprietary schools. Not more than one-twentieth of the group as a whole thought of getting similar training through public evening schools or part-time courses. Public schools seldom advertise; proprietary schools do more than advertise. It is not uncommon to find that every member of the graduating class of a small high school has been approached by proprietary school canvassers—with how much success was illustrated in one down-at-heel village of a few hundred inhabitants, in which interviewers discovered that half a dozen boys just out of school were enrolled in the same course in air conditioning.

The educational plans of boys and girls who expect to go directly from high school into college are harder to evaluate.

The fact is noteworthy, however, that a good many high school seniors, in June of their last year, report that they expect to continue their schooling, but are quite unable to indicate what type of school, much less what particular school, they plan to attend. No doubt their uncertainty sometimes results from a lack of assurance that they will have money enough to let them choose the schools they will enter, or it may be due to the pupils' doubts about their ability to meet the admission requirements of the schools of their choice. But often it seems to arise from the absence of any definite planning. Educational planning was obviously lacking among the boys and girls interviewed after they had left school, who volunteered the information that the interviewers' questions about their educational futures were the first questions of this sort that they had ever been called on to consider seriously.

COMMAND OF THE TOOLS OF LEARNING

The vagueness and lack of realism in the pupils' plans for continued schooling become the more significant when it is recognized that *large numbers even of the high school graduates are seriously deficient in the basic tools of learning*.

The tests given to leaving pupils by the Inquiry included a test of ability to read and understand straightforward English. "Literary" English was avoided; the passages presented to the pupils consisted of paragraphs taken from simple scientific articles, historical accounts, discussions of economic problems, and the like. The test was originally constructed for eighth grade pupils. Average eighth grade achievement on such a test represents a level of reading ability which is scholastically desirable, in that high school texts are usually planned for this level or higher, and which is socially desirable as well, in that it enables the reader to comprehend readily the content of a wide range of books and magazines for adults, including some that are above average in difficulty. The high school pupils who took the test were marked "pass" or "fail" according to whether they scored as well in it as average eighth grade pupils. In terms of this standard, one in ten of the seniors in the average high school (and far larger proportions of the pupils in the lower grades) failed the test.

Pupils were also given a test in the ability to solve commonsense problems in arithmetic. The problems were not abstruse, but dealt with computations which any young person or any adult might have to perform:

A book dealer allowed 10 per cent off on a book because it was slightly soiled. What did the book sell for if the regular price was $2?

On an auto trip Harold traveled 29.6 miles the first hour, 32.7 miles the second, 34.1 miles the third, and 30.2 miles the fourth. What was the average number of miles traveled an hour?

A carpenter cut three pieces, each 2 feet 3 inches long, from a board 12 feet 8 inches long. How long was the piece that was left?

This test, like the test in reading, was designed for eighth grade pupils, and was scored by eighth grade standards. More than one-fifth of the seniors in the average high school failed to pass it.

A final measure of ability to use the ordinary tools of learning consisted of a test of pupils' use of written English. Without being told that they were to be marked on the results, pupils were asked to write a letter to the director of the Regents' Inquiry, giving their opinions of the value of the tests which they had been required to take. The results were in certain respects extraordinarily erratic. Originality of content and effectiveness of general expression varied, as might have been expected, from letters which were devoid of thought or almost completely meaningless to others which would have done credit to the ablest adult. Spelling and grammatical usage were more uniformly acceptable. In legibility and in letter form and punctuation, however, there was as great variation as in quality of content. Achievement in letter form may serve as a somewhat extreme illustration of the frequency of outright errors in the letters: among letters representing all four upper grades only one in a hundred was entirely correct as judged by very liberal standards of proper form. The letters in general provided overwhelming evidence that, irrespective of what high school boys and girls may be able to do on demand, large numbers of pupils are leaving school without having attained ingrained habits of good English usage.

In addition to these basic tests the Inquiry administered a number of analytical tests of study skills. Tests of ability to use maps and to interpret charts showed results which were about normal for the various grade levels in which the tests were given. In tests of ability to use the dictionary and to locate library references, however, New York State pupils ranked definitely below the normal level—a matter of some significance if these young people are to undertake any considerable amount of learning outside of formal courses.

The fact that many of the leaving pupils are deficient in the fundamental skills of reading, writing, and arithmetic does not mean that the average pupil's achievement in these subjects is abnormally low. Detailed tests of reading ability given to pupils in selected schools show that the average scores of New York State pupils—the scores of the better pupils balancing those of the poorer—are approximately those found among high school pupils in general. The quality of the English compositions which the pupils write on demand is probably on the average somewhat superior to that achieved by pupils in schools elsewhere. Though no detailed tests of mathematical ability were given by the Inquiry, there is reason to believe that in this field also New York State pupils in general would not suffer by comparison with pupils from other states. But averages alone do not represent the important facts. In skills which everyone must use, everyone should have, if he can possibly achieve it, at least a minimum of competence. The test results suggest that a disturbingly large proportion of New York State boys and girls leave the secondary school—even go on to higher schools—without having attained a desirable minimum.

OUT-OF-SCHOOL READING INTERESTS

The general readiness of the leaving pupils for continued school work may be summarized in the statement that the majority of these boys and girls have adopted an unquestioning faith in schooling, without having gained any clear notion of the probable values of further school work for them individually, and often without having mastered the fundamental learning skills on which real success in school normally depends. Against this background should be considered their readiness to learn independently and informally outside of school.

It has already been noted that young people seldom do continued studying after they have left school unless they find systematic courses for which they can "sign up." The kind of further learning which most of them do in the absence of such courses is typified in part by their out-of-school reading. The results of the interviews show that *once out of school, most boys and girls read almost solely for recreation, chiefly in magazines of mediocre or inferior fiction and in daily newspapers.*

Judged in terms of test results at the time they left school, most of these boys and girls were reasonably well acquainted with the standard school selections: they knew that "The Raven" was written by Edgar Allan Poe, that *Quentin Durward* describes life in feudal times, that Young Lochinvar was a highland hero, that James Fenimore Cooper wrote stories about Indians. They were much less well acquainted with good literature published while they were still in school. In general, they could identify only best-sellers—*Gone With the Wind*, *Drums Along the Mohawk*, *North to the Orient*.

Once out of school, they tend very largely to let books alone. Fewer than 40 per cent of the boys and girls interviewed had read any book or any part of a book in the two weeks preceding the interviews. Only one in ten had read nonfiction books; the titles included a few books on vocations, a number of biographies, occasional books of poetry, drama, and essays, and a scattering of books from other fields. Of the books of fiction which they had read, the largest number were historical novels (which ranked first in the list because of the popularity of *Gone With the Wind* and *Drums Along the Mohawk*), stories of adventure, and novels of romance and glamor. The fiction was in general of either medium or inferior quality. Fewer than a tenth of the pupils who reported having read any books had read fiction that could properly be classed as superior.

Magazine and newspaper reading proved much more common than the reading of books. Nearly four-fifths of the boys and girls interviewed had read parts of at least one magazine in the week preceding the interviews, and practically all reported that they read the daily newspaper. The nature and quality of their magazine reading differed little from that of their reading in books. Most popular among the group as a whole were weekly miscellanies (such as *Liberty* and *The Saturday Evening Post*) and monthly miscellanies, fiction magazines, and women's magazines (*American Magazine, Red Book, Ladies Home Journal, The American Home*). Practically equal to these in popularity with the boys and girls who had not graduated from high school were magazines of out-of-door sports, detective and mystery magazines, and motion picture magazines. Large numbers of the graduates also read these magazines, but the graduates much more than the pupils who had not graduated were interested in digests (particularly *The Reader's Digest*), weekly newsmagazines, and elite and smart magazines (*Esquire, Vogue, Vanity Fair*). Fewer than two young people in a hundred from either group read magazines of the type of *Harper's, Scribner's,* or *The Atlantic Monthly.*

What the pupils had read in magazines is indicated fairly definitely by the general nature of the magazines in which they chose to read. Inquiries as to whether they had read articles, or fiction alone, elicited the information that nearly a third of the graduates, who were clearly the more serious readers, had read only fiction. The most encouraging characteristic of the reading done by the group as a whole was the notable popularity of the digests.

The reading habits of these boys and girls are no doubt directly affected by the fact that many of them have never learned how to read understandingly. Their habits would also seem to be a product of their general attitude toward the reading done in school. Interviewers were frequently told by individual boys and girls that reading was a bore. Certain young people asserted explicitly that the assigned reading they had had to do in school was so dull that they did not want to do any more reading if they could help it. A few—among them the girl who remarked that she had passed civics and consequently did not have to read any more—apparently felt that they were completely educated, and that reading was therefore quite unnecessary. Whether it results from general dislike of reading or from lack of skill in the mere mechanics of reading, the inferior quality of the reading done by large numbers of these boys and girls offers no great hope that their independent reading will add very much to their educational stature.

FAVORITE RADIO PROGRAMS

The claim is frequently made that for people in general radio is fast taking the place of reading as a means of informal education. Among boys and girls just out of school there are, in fact, many more listeners to the radio than readers of books or magazines. Only 4 per cent of the young people interviewed in the Inquiry did not use the radio at least for recreation. The amount of time which they reported spending as listeners was considerable—eleven hours a week for the average boy and fifteen hours a week for the average girl. But the interviews made it apparent that *the radio programs to which these young people prefer to listen are the variety, comedy, and dramatic features, and not the educational features or the "quality" musical programs.*

The four programs most popular with the young people just out of school were those of Jack Benny, the Lux Radio Theatre, Fred Allen, and Eddie Cantor. The programs of Major Bowes, Bing Crosby, and Rudy Vallee also ranked high. Favorites among strictly musical programs were, in order, those of Guy Lombardo (seventh in the total list of preferences), Benny Goodman, and Wayne King. Nelson Eddy, the Ford Sunday Evening Hour, and the Metropolitan Opera Saturday Matinee ranked highest among the "quality" musical programs; they came seventeenth, nineteenth, and twentieth in the list. The low ranking given to news and educational programs has already been commented on. Symphony orchestra and operatic programs together were about as popular as news commentators and educational hours: no programs of either type were listed among their favorites by more than a sixth of the high school graduates, or more than a tenth of the nongraduates.

Whatever may be the future of radio, it does not seem at present to be making up for any deficiencies that there may be in the recreational reading of these boys and girls. The programs to which these young people listen, like the books and magazines they read, provide entertainment. The programs which offer more get at best only an occasional hearing.

ATTENDANCE AT THE MOVIES

Boys and girls who have left school are apparently as confirmed movie-goers as they are listeners to the radio. Only 3 or 4 per cent of the young people who were interviewed reported that they rarely or never attended the movies; three-fourths said that they attended regularly, once a week or oftener. Except for young people in certain villages where there are no movie houses, boys and girls in the country and the small towns apparently go to the movies almost exactly as often, on the average, as boys and girls in the cities. It seems fair to conclude from the interviews, however, that, *despite the fact that movie-going is a habit with them—or possibly even because of that fact—few of these boys and girls use much discrimination in choosing the moving pictures which they see.* Not more than one in five replied to questions about their movie-going in a way which suggested that they had any well-developed standards of appreciation with respect to the movies.

The tendency for boys and girls to go to the movies no matter what the show may be inevitably puts them at the mercy of local exhibitors. Some of the effects of this tendency were discernible in the results of tests given to pupils on the point of leaving school. Pupils in various types of communities —rural and urban, large and small—were tested on their acquaintance with a number of recent films of high quality. The pupils from the large cities stood notably higher on the tests than the boys and girls from the smaller cities and towns, with the New York City group surpassing all the others. Least well acquainted with good movies, even though they went to shows just about as frequently as the city pupils, were the pupils from the rural districts.

A survey of the movies actually attended by high school pupils suggests that the total list of pictures which boys and girls see, while it is likely to contain many harmful films, ordinarily contains a much larger proportion of harmless pictures, and at least some that are distinctly good. One hundred fifteen pictures which pupils in a number of representative communities had attended were evaluated on the basis of ratings published in *The Educational Screen* and *The Parents' Magazine.* Sixteen per cent of these pictures were rated as superior films; 51 per cent were good or fair; 33 per cent were unsuitable for young people. The better films were seen by many more pupils than were the poorer ones. For example, of the seventeen films each seen by forty-four or more pupils, five were rated superior, six good, three fair, and three harmful; whereas of forty-five films attended by one or two pupils each, thirty-one were rated not better than fair and only four were rated superior.

Musical spectacles, for example, "The Great Ziegfeld" and "Swing Time"; comedy and farce, for example, "Kelly the Second," "The Princess Comes Across"; romance as typified by "His Brother's Wife," and "Cain and Mabel"; melodrama, "Navy Born" and "The General Died at Dawn"; and juveniles, for example, "Dimples," constituted the movie fare of about half these pupils. Historical and biographical films, for example, "Mary of Scotland" and "The Gorgeous Hussy," were frequently attended, however, as were plays with a social purpose or emphasis, for example, "Road to Glory" and "Girls' Dormitory." Murder and mystery plays, "westerns," adventure thrillers, and gangster and crime pictures accounted altogether for about one in seven or eight of the pictures seen. Because the films which boys and girls see are so largely determined by what they have a chance to see, no hard-and-fast generalizations about their tastes in pictures can be drawn from this list. It is probably safe to conclude, however, that their interest in movies, as in the radio and in reading, centers chiefly round recreation pure and simple, with little active concern either for standards of enjoyment or for the essential meaning of what they see and hear.

OUT-OF-SCHOOL CLUB ACTIVITIES

In addition to reading, listening to the radio, and going to the movies, *about half the boys and girls who have left school are active in some sort of club or organized group, chiefly recreational in purpose.* The most popular organizations among boys and girls both are church groups, some of which are strictly religious, while others are primarily social in character. Next most popular among the boys are athletic groups, which enroll one in every seven or eight of the boys. The athletic groups consist in many instances of informally organized teams in various sports, rather than of large athletic associations. Common-interest or hobby clubs, including everything from knitting circles to light-opera societies, rank next to the church groups in popularity with the girls, and attract numerous boys as well. The relatively scattered membership in character-building and service groups has already been mentioned in connection with citizenship activities. No other type of organization—fraternal orders, farm groups, small social clubs, military organizations, or factory and office groups—attracts as many as one in ten of either boys or girls; all of them together enroll fewer than one in five or six of the leaving pupils in general.

UNORGANIZED OUT-OF-SCHOOL ACTIVITIES

Organized activities fail to account, however, for a considerable number of interests displayed by these young people. Athletics, music and dramatics, dancing, and numerous individual hobbies claim an important share of their leisure, quite apart from their club activities.

Though only a small proportion belong to regular athletic groups, *nearly nine-tenths of the boys and about three-fourths of the girls engage at least occasionally in athletic games or sports of some sort.* Large-group activities, such as football, baseball, hockey, and basketball, attract most of the boys and about a fourth of the girls. More than half the young people of both sexes report that they engage in some form of individual sport—hiking, hunting, fishing, skating, skiing, archery, swimming, and the like. Small-group games—tennis, golf, ping-pong, badminton, fencing, horseshoe pitching, and similar sports

· 49 ·

in which from two to four persons compete with one another—attract fewer than a third of either group. Lacking the stimulus of organized groups, it is probable that most of these boys and girls engage only irregularly in the games which they say they like. Moreover, the fact that the boys in particular favor large-group as contrasted with small-group games suggests that a marked readjustment in their activities may soon be necessary; the large-group sports are likely to become increasingly difficult for them to arrange and carry on as they grow older. The general interest of both boys and girls in athletic activities is nevertheless a striking characteristic of the group as a whole.

Almost as striking is the extent of their interest in amateur music and dramatics. *Approximately one-eighth of these young people either play musical instruments or sing with some group, and one-seventh participate in amateur dramatics.* Boys take part in both types of activity somewhat less frequently than girls, and nongraduates are less often represented than graduates, but there is an appreciable amount of such participation among all groups. The kinds of radio programs to which the leaving pupils habitually listen suggest no high development among them of consumer interest in good music; their interest in listening to good plays is perhaps somewhat stronger. In view of their lack of highly developed standards of consumer appreciation, it is noteworthy that so many are interested in the production of music and dramatics.

Their interest in dancing is significant because of the types of social contacts which result from it. *From a third to a half of the young people dance at private and club parties; about a fourth of the boys and a third of the girls dance in public dance halls, roadhouses, and night clubs.* The two groups apparently do not mingle; those who dance at private parties usually do not frequent public dance halls and night clubs, and vice versa. In a few communities, however, the local schools invite out-of-school boys and girls to attend school dances. The school parties, where they are given, are generally popular, but their comparative rarity is responsible for the fact that only a sixth of the out-of-school group ordinarily attend them.

Nearly 60 per cent of these young people claim to have a hobby of one kind or another. The most popular of these seem to be handwork, in which the interest of girls somewhat exceeds that of boys, and the making of collections, which is about equally favored by girls and boys. The handwork reported by the girls who were interviewed included chiefly knitting, dressmaking, and embroidery. The handwork of the boys was represented by woodwork, repairing old automobiles, and building models of various sorts. The collections were almost infinitely varied with respect to the types of articles which they included— stamps, foreign coins, recipes, Indian-head pennies, pictures, guns, matchboxes, World War relics, and so on. They were likewise varied in the amount of thought and care which was given to them. Many represented mere random accumulations; a few were the products of hours on end of intelligent study and careful arrangement.

In addition to handwork and collections there were reported various other hobbies, each enrolling a relatively small number of young people, but the group as a whole accounting for an impressive total number of participants. The only major hobbies peculiar to one sex were radio experimentation and building, and home laboratory work, which were reported only by boys. Boys engaged in photography, outdoor activities (target-shooting, diving, figure-skating, hiking), and certain miscellaneous activities more frequently than girls. Girls more often than boys were interested in the arts (drawing, painting, and sculpture, as well as music and dramatics), reading and writing, and the making of scrapbooks.

Not all these hobbies can be regarded as constructive, or as educational in any fundamental sense; many of them seem to represent no more than casual and harmless diversions, likely to be quickly outgrown or forgotten. With due regard for this fact, however, it is significant that a large group of boys and girls leave school with avocational interests strong enough so that the young people themselves recognize these interests as important and want to do something about them.

SUMMARY

The picture presented by these varied glimpses of the attitudes and leisure-time activities of leaving pupils might have been slightly different if the 20 per cent of high school pupils who go on to college had been represented among the young people who were interviewed. No doubt the college group would have shown greater interest and higher standards of taste in their reading. Possibly this group would have displayed more discrimination in the radio programs they listened to and the movies they attended; and they might have added to the number and variety of the interests and hobbies which the noncollege pupils reported.

Even without the college group, the picture is in many respects encouraging. High school pupils value their school work. A considerable number of them continue to take various types of school courses after they have given up full-time school attendance; even more plan eventually to do so. Their recreations display a wide variety of interests, most of them reasonably wholesome. Their individual hobbies are numerous and often valuable.

Much less encouraging is the complete abandonment by the boys and girls who do not go on to higher schools of many of the activities on which secondary schools commonly lay great emphasis. Left to their own devices, most of these young people cease to read serious books and articles or good fiction; they seldom listen to the best music; they study as a means of preparing for a vocation, rather than for fun or to add to their general education.

Less encouraging also is the lack of realism with which large numbers of these boys and girls face the future. A considerable proportion are not competent enough in the three R's to take courses beyond the level at which they have dropped out of school, much less to go on learning by themselves. Even those who are competent as learners frequently have no clear notion of what sort of education is appropriate to their individual needs. Educational swindlers and confidence men take advantage of their uncertainty. As a result, their out-of-school educational experiences, instead of being stimulating and constructive, are often abortive, haphazard, and thoroughly disheartening.

CHAPTER IV

Preparation for Vocations

A T LEAST three-fourths of the boys and girls who leave high school every year need to begin as soon as possible to earn their own livings. From the point of view of these boys and girls, quite as important as anything else the schools may do for them is the preparation the schools may give them for employment.

Boys and girls in a few of the large-city school systems in New York State can be sure of getting direct vocational preparation by enrolling in specialized vocational schools. The chance for a high school pupil to enter such a school is at present limited, however, both because only a few specialized schools have been established and because the number of pupils seeking admission to these schools is far greater than the number that can be accommodated. In most towns and cities all high school pupils attend comprehensive schools (in New York State traditionally called "academic high schools") which occasionally include vocational departments, but which provide core programs of general academic subjects. Inasmuch as these comprehensive schools are responsible for whatever vocational education is now supplied for the great majority of young people of high school age, the pupils from these schools, rather than the pupils from the specialized vocational schools, demand immediate consideration in any broad assessment of the vocational competence of New York State boys and girls.

VOCATIONAL PLANS OF PUPILS

The concern of the pupils in the academic high schools that their education should lead them somewhere vocationally has already been referred to. Widespread though it is, this concern does not seem to be accompanied by any realistic planning for jobs. Pupils' replies to questions about their vocational futures reveal that *large numbers of boys and girls on the point of leaving school either have no vocational plans or have plans which are quite out of line with their own demonstrated abilities and with opportunities for employment.*

From 17 to 40 per cent of the various groups of pupils questioned had no long-range vocational objectives—no idea, that is to say, of the kinds of jobs they wanted to hold when they were finally through with school or college. The least uncertainty was found among the girls who were completing a year of postgraduate work in the high school; the greatest, among boys withdrawing before graduation. In general, the less successful a boy or girl had been in school, the vaguer he was about what he wanted to do vocationally.

Even more marked than their lack of long-range objectives was the uncertainty of the leaving pupils about their immediate jobs. Pupils who definitely intended to get jobs for the following year were questioned about their vocational chances as they saw them. The questions were asked in June of the pupils' last year in school—less than a month before they would actually be hunting for work. Pupils who had been "promised a job" or "knew of a job" were in the minority. Far more would commit themselves only to the statement that they thought they could get "some sort of job," or that they were uncertain whether they could get any job at all. Girls were in general less sure of their chances than boys. The graduates and postgraduates, despite the fact that they were the ones who most often had long-range objectives, tended to be less certain that they could get full-time jobs of the kinds they had specified than were the pupils who were leaving school without having graduated.

A clue to the wisdom with which pupils were making their plans was provided by their answers to a question about their long-range objectives. Specifically, the pupils were asked whether there was anything that might make them change their minds about the kinds of jobs they wanted. About half the boys and girls who had decided on what they wanted to do considered their long-range plans quite unalterable. Girls were more "set" in their minds than boys. Also, the young people withdrawing before graduation were more inflexible than the graduates. Among the pupils who foresaw that they might have to change their plans, the largest number thought that they might need to shift to other vocational fields because of a lack of money necessary to obtain further training. A smaller number conceived that other fields might eventually prove more attractive to them than those they had chosen. In spite of the lesson that an economic depression might be supposed to have taught them, relatively few pupils recognized that the lack of opportunities for actual jobs might have to be reckoned with.

The wisdom or lack of wisdom with which pupils were making their long-range plans was reflected also in the relation between their choices and the abilities they had shown in school. Pupils' vocational choices in general appeared to be geared roughly to their intelligence, the financial levels of their homes, and their school achievement. The pupils who ranked lowest in these measures more often hoped to be mechanics, commercial artists, beauticians, and bookkeepers; the pupils who ranked highest tended to choose such occupations as engineering, teaching, medicine, and the law. The inclination of all groups of pupils, however, was to choose much more frequently occupations at or approaching the professional levels than at lower levels, with the result that the number of choices at the upper levels was entirely out of proportion to present job opportunities. Furthermore, there was almost the widest possible range of choice among the pupils at any one level of ability, home background, or achievement. Large numbers of boys and girls of exceptional intellectual ability were looking forward to occupations which would never offer them a real challenge. Young people from homes ranking very low economically were often planning on careers which, if not quite out of the question from the financial standpoint, could be achieved in their cases only with extraordinary difficulty. Many pupils with mediocre or poor school records or with training in curricula offering no substantial basis for continued academic work, had in mind vocations which could be prepared for only by graduate study in a higher institution. Whatever degree of realistic wisdom was shown in the average choice of any large group of these pupils, individual unwisdom on the part of its members proved a more significant characteristic.

Nor were these boys and girls much more realistic in planning for their immediate futures. Some, as has been noted, reported that they knew of jobs they could get, or were sure they could get some sort of job; others were uncertain. Of the whole group who left school planning to go to work, only a third were known by their schools to be employed at the end of three months. Among this third, those who had been sure of their chances were represented in almost exactly the same proportion as those who had claimed to have no "leads." Whatever the information on which these pupils had based their plans, most of their expectations as to the jobs they could actually get proved to have been quite unjustified.

It is not to be assumed that definiteness of vocational plans on the part of boys and girls about to leave school is either possible or desirable. The boy or girl who has not extraordinary ability, energy, and persistence is likely to be seriously handicapped by absolute definiteness of plan at a time when occupations are constantly shifting and vocational adaptability is more and more necessary. Young people's initial plans must necessarily be flexible if those plans are to be sensible, and every boy and girl must be ready to take advantage of opportunities which he may not have foreseen when he made his plans.

It is not to be assumed, either, that there should be complete agreement between pupils' aspirations and their eventual achievement. Vocational opportunities change, and individual futures may contain unexpected chances for success. Sometimes the change works disadvantageously: the boy or girl must be satisfied with a second best, or a tenth best, or any chance, if he is to get his feet on the ground economically. Partly because youth seems bound to be optimistic, partly because optimism is in itself a spur to success, there is no serious ground for disquiet in the fact that boys and girls aim somewhat above the mark which sober experience shows they are likely to attain.

But there is ground for disquiet in complete planlessness on the part of boys and girls who are face to face with the necessity of earning a living. There is ground for disquiet also in vocational ambitions which are not so much optimistic as thoroughly fantastic. There is ground for disquiet in young people's confident reliance on information about jobs which turns out to have been no information at all. Each of these weaknesses in their readiness to make a living is characteristic of large numbers of the boys and girls who are now leaving school in New York State.

SCHOOLS' JUDGMENTS OF VOCATIONAL COMPETENCE

How well-prepared these young people are to hold successfully whatever jobs they may get is difficult to determine for the group as a whole. Reliable tests of vocational ability which could be given to all the pupils before they left school were lacking in most fields, or were too cumbersome to be useful for survey purposes. Hence there can be presented no objective measurement of readiness for vocations corresponding to the measures used in nonvocational fields.

In the cases of leaving pupils for whom individual reports were furnished by the schools, however, school officials were asked to indicate their willingness or unwillingness to recommend the boy or girl concerned, at the time he left school, for any type of full-time employment which would allow him to be self-supporting. The replies from the schools were analyzed in relation to the actual success of these young people in getting jobs. The results make it evident that while schools are willing to recommend the majority of their leaving pupils for employment, *the high school's opinion of its pupils' vocational competence bears little relation to the actual success of these boys and girls in getting jobs.*

The schools were readier to recommend graduates than boys and girls who withdrew before graduating. Between 85 and 90 per cent of the graduates were reported as capable of holding a job with reasonable success, whereas somewhat fewer than 50 per cent of the withdrawing pupils were recommended.

The schools' recommendations appeared to be based in a measure on the curricula which the pupils had followed. Pupils taking college-preparatory and business courses were recommended with about equal frequency—the former, according to reports on individual pupils, because of superior intelligence and a well-rounded general education, the latter because of specialized vocational skills. Students of the general curriculum were considered poorer risks.

In general, the schools based their recommendations less often on specialized vocational training than on high intelligence, unusual aggressiveness, physical development, or favorable personality traits. Specialized training was prominently mentioned, in connection with the group as a whole, only with reference to pupils who were not recommended. The lack of special training among these pupils, together with the lack of a well-rounded general education, constituted the most common defects as the schools noted them.

But nearly all such distinctions lost their significance in the light of what actually became of the pupils concerned. As between nongraduates and graduates, almost exactly as large a proportion of one group as of the other was found by interviewers to be holding jobs within six to eleven months after they had left school. As among pupils who had taken various types of curricula, no widespread differences in employment or unemployment could be traced to curricular differences as such[1]—though pupils who had been enrolled in different types of curricula did show some tendency to gravitate toward different kinds of jobs. As between graduates whom the schools were willing to recommend for jobs and graduates whom they were unwilling to recommend, approximately the same proportions were known actually to have got jobs within three months after leaving school. Only in the cases of non-recommended pupils who had withdrawn from school before graduating did the schools' judgments seem to have a modicum of predictive value—partly, no doubt, because the schools were chariest of their recommendations with this particular group.

The high school pupils in New York State who now receive schooling that is definitely vocational in purpose represent a minority of the total high school enrollment. The vocational pupils tend to be recruited from the academically less able or less interested. It is understandable, therefore, that school officials should estimate the vocational competence of leaving pupils generally in terms of such factors as intellectual intelligence, personality, and academic success. Quite conceivably the schools' appraisal of these factors provides a fair measure of potential vocational competence. The schools may be much more nearly right, indeed, than the employers who eventually hire, or refuse to hire, these same boys and girls. But the fact that schools and employers do not agree suggests that the kinds of abilities to which the schools pay chief attention may be of

[1] This statement holds true for curricula within academic high schools. Attention is given in Chapter V to differences between the job placements of pupils from academic high schools and pupils from specialized vocational schools.

little direct use to young people once they begin to work for their living.

SUCCESS IN GETTING WORK

Leaving school under these conditions, most young people proceed more or less actively to look for work. Interviews both with the boys and girls and with their employers indicate that *whether boys and girls just out of school succeed in getting jobs depends chiefly on luck, accidental contacts, and "personality."*

The boys and girls who get jobs locate them in most cases either through a blind round of door-to-door applications, or by "knowing the right people." Many of the pupils who were interviewed had found their jobs by such devices as looking for "help-wanted" signs; many others had been given jobs by relatives or by employers with whom they were acquainted, or had taken advantage of "tips" from friends who knew where there were vacancies. Fewer than 7 per cent of the graduates, and fewer than 3 per cent of the young people who left school without graduating, were directed to their jobs by their schools. A much smaller number—no more than one in a hundred of the total group—found their jobs through government placement agencies.

Interviews with employers showed clearly that the personal impressions made by the boys and girls who apply for jobs weigh far more heavily than school records or direct recommendations from school people. When they were questioned as to the traits which had led them to employ particular applicants, the employers as a group mentioned personality first, then intelligence, then general education.[2] Personality is judged chiefly by the applicant's "approach." The approach made by many boys and girls is apparently so unfortunate—

[2] It may be noted in passing that industry, rather than personality, ranks first among the traits which employers value on the job—a circumstance which suggests that the boys and girls to whom employers are most inclined to give jobs may not be the boys and girls who will hold those jobs most successfully.

as in the case of several boys whose notion of a favorable beginning was to ask, "Do you pay good wages here?"—that applicants are sometimes turned down even when there are vacancies which the employer knows they might be able to fill.

As to letters of recommendation from school people, or transcripts of school records, only a minority of employers make any use of them: "The schools never try to find out what kind of people we need." "I've tried going on what teachers say about these kids, and it doesn't mean a thing." Even where particular boys and girls are employed because they are high school graduates rather than nongraduates, or because they have graduated from a given high school curriculum, an employer is more likely to have chosen them because he thinks their school records are probable signs of intelligence than because he values the specific training they have received.

JOBS AND PREVIOUS SCHOOLING

Hunting for jobs chiefly by a hit-or-miss method, hired more largely on the basis of their looks and the way they talk than on the basis of their educational background, the majority of these boys and girls eventually get jobs of one sort or another. Among the former pupils interviewed between six and eleven months after they had left school in 1936, about three-fourths of the boys and a little more than half the girls were working for pay. The proportions cannot be taken as any lasting index of probable employment; chances for jobs obviously fluctuate with economic conditions. Nor does the distribution of these young people among various types of jobs have much permanent meaning. More significant is the fact that *the kinds of jobs that these boys and girls get bear only a crude relation to the amount or nature of their previous school work.*

The lack of correspondence between the schools' judgments of pupils' readiness for employment and the pupils' success in getting any jobs at all has already been pointed out. There is some connection by contrast between what boys and girls have studied, or how far they have gone in school, and the kind of employment they find, but the connection is striking chiefly because it is so slight.

The connection is least obscure in the case of high school graduates as contrasted with nongraduates. "White-collar" jobs—clerical work and selling—accounted for more than a third of the employment among boy graduates and for slightly less than a fourth among the nongraduates. Similar jobs were held by three-fifths of the employed girl graduates, as compared with only one-fifth of the nongraduates. Nearly half the boys who had not graduated were employed in physical labor, repetitive manual work, or as learners in trades; they outranked the graduates in these occupations by about four to three. The same kinds of work were extensively represented among the girls, except that various forms of domestic and personal or nonpersonal service took the place of physical labor. Occupations of this type claimed three-fourths of the nongraduate girls who were employed, as contrasted with only a third of the graduates. So far as there exists a caste system in present-day industry, that system tends to distinguish roughly between young people who have finished high school and young people who have not.[3] The distinction would seem to be most effective in the case of the girls.

There is much less connection between the kinds of jobs boys and girls hold and the curricula they have followed in school. Pupils who have been enrolled in the business curriculum tend to go into clerical work more frequently than do

[3] The system tends to distinguish also, of course, between high school graduates and college graduates. Interviews with employers of sales people and clerical workers indicated that many such employers are looking increasingly for college graduates to fill positions for which high school graduates were once eligible after a few years of experience. The range of jobs open to high school graduates, and the opportunities which these young people have open to them for promotion, are thus becoming increasingly limited. For a further discussion of these matters see T. L. Norton, *Education for Work*, Regents' Inquiry, 1938.

pupils from other curricula. Except for this single tendency, young people just out of high school seem not to pick and choose, but to take whatever jobs they come across. Whether because of employers' lack of interest in their high school work or because of their own indifference to the kinds of immediate jobs they get, relatively few step out of school into occupations which place any special premium on what they have studied.

ATTITUDES TOWARD JOBS

The pupils' own attitudes no doubt have much to do with the random nature of their immediate job placements. The interviews with pupils who were working suggested that *the boys and girls who succeed in getting jobs are more concerned with the superficial conditions of their work, or the satisfaction of having any kind of job, than with particular opportunities which their jobs offer.* No doubt the attitudes of these young people will change as they increase in maturity and in vocational experience. No doubt also, their satisfaction at merely having jobs was explained often by the fact that they had fresh in their minds the recollection of a severe economic depression. Their statements about their jobs would seem to be of some significance, nevertheless, as indications of the extent of their readiness to go on from their present jobs to better ones.

All the boys and girls who were working were asked what, if anything, they liked about their jobs. A considerable number said, "Nothing," or gave no answer at all. Others answered simply that they liked the work, but were unable to say what features of it they liked; some of them replied, in effect, "It's a job, and that's a lot." Among those who were more articulate, a number commented that the work was challenging—they liked having to "use their heads" on it. Girls in particular spoke of enjoying the chance to meet people. Boys spoke of appreciating the opportunity to be out-of-doors. Both groups frequently referred to pay, or satisfactory hours, or pleasant working conditions, or a routine which let them work without too much effort. Among all these young people hardly one in six mentioned either the training that they were getting from their jobs, or the chance to advance from their present jobs to better jobs, as being among the attractive features of their work.

Lack of concern for the future was also apparent in the responses to questions about what these young people disliked in their jobs. From 3 to 5 per cent said that they disliked the routine—by which some of them may possibly have meant the lack of opportunity to acquire new skills. About half as many spoke of the lack of a chance for advancement. The remainder, if they saw anything to dislike, complained most frequently of hard work or long hours, low pay, or unpleasant working conditions—the references to unpleasant working conditions resulting more often, it seemed, from unfulfilled "white-collar" ambitions than from actually unhealthy or dangerous employment.

The answers to questions about dislikes did not necessarily indicate complete lack of interest in the jobs. On the contrary, the majority of the boys and girls who were employed seemed definitely to like their work. Judging from the reports of employers, however, only about a third of the group as a whole had put forth enough extra effort to demonstrate their interest to their employers. Relatively few were reported by their employers to be studying or doing outside work which would help them with their jobs; a few made it a practice to watch what was going on about them and to learn about the work of others as well as their own work; a smaller number had done voluntary overtime work; and a handful had made constructive suggestions about their jobs.

But their failure to pay attention to chances for advancement seemed to mean that a majority of these young people were largely unmindful of the future. When they were asked what positions they expected to hold next, about half seemed to have no idea. Among the others, the largest number looked forward to jobs similar to their present ones, but with a higher rank or higher pay. A few expected to be promoted to a different type of work under the same employer. About one in twenty counted on changing from industrial work, agriculture, or domestic service to a "white-collar" occupation; an almost negligible number expected to change in the opposite direction. The expectations of those who had any clear ideas of what might happen to them accorded fairly closely with what their employers reported about their probable chances. The group as a whole, however, were apparently thinking ahead— so far as they thought ahead at all—with little reference to long-range plans or to the ambitious futures which many of them had laid out for themselves just before they left high school.

CHANCES FOR ADVANCEMENT

Their lack of concern for the future is significant in the light of their actual long-range prospects. Statements by employers, and an analysis of the wage-scales under which representative boys and girls are working, indicate that *more than half the young people who have jobs will have to leave their present employers if they are to earn enough to marry, live decently, and stay out of debt.*

Employers in general were optimistic about the chances for advancement of the young people they had hired. They reported themselves at least reasonably satisfied with the work of nearly all these young people; boys and girls whom they regarded as unsatisfactory they had either refused to employ in the first place or discharged after brief trial. Among the boys who were working, employers estimated that three out of five had a good chance to advance to better jobs. Among the girls the estimates differed between high school graduates and nongraduates; about half the graduates were reported to be in line for advancement, whereas chances were said to be good for fewer than two-fifths of the nongraduates. Boys and girls who were not regarded as likely to advance were described in a few instances as having reached the limits of their ability. Ordinarily, however, any lack of opportunity for promotion was apparently due to the fact that employers were engaged in a type of work offering a restricted range of jobs, rather than to doubts about the ability of individual boys and girls to improve in vocational competence.

The employers' optimism was based chiefly on boys' and girls' immediate chances for advancement. For a considerable number of young people it was possible to obtain some estimate of their long-range chances under their present employers, in terms of the wages they might look forward to. Their outlook from the long-range standpoint was less promising. More than 40 per cent of the boys and girls who were working were employed by individuals or business concerns— farmers, small store-owners, filling-station or garage owners, small businessmen or contractors—hiring fewer than five persons each. These small-scale employers were seldom in a position to offer more than minimum wages. Of the young people working for employers of larger groups, well over a third held jobs with concerns paying 75 per cent of their employees less than twenty dollars a week, and more than two-thirds with concerns ordinarily paying less than thirty dollars a week. Obviously, not all these boys and girls can look forward to being advanced by their present employers to positions paying the top wages. If they are to receive much higher pay than they now earn, most of them must leave their present jobs. Their immediate chances for advancement may be good, but their ultimate chances will almost inevitably depend on their getting new jobs elsewhere, even though they may not change the kinds of jobs at which they work.

All facts considered, it is apparent that the first year out of school is likely to be no more than a year of adjustment for most boys and girls fortunate enough to obtain employment. They get jobs, but only by chance do they get the kinds of jobs at which they will be most successful. They are chiefly engrossed with the superficial aspects of their work. Though they like their duties and though their employers are reasonably satisfied with their performance, they see only the next step ahead vocationally, and often not even that. Few of them have any long-range plans, despite the fact that the majority will be obliged to find themselves new jobs before they can look forward to more than a bare subsistence-wage.

Thus it is for the boys and girls who get jobs. Of those who leave school and get no jobs (or none that last), only a brief and somewhat general accounting can be given.

UNEMPLOYED LEAVING PUPILS

One-fourth of the boys and nearly half the girls, it will be recalled, fell among the group who were unemployed at the time the check was made. A small proportion of these young people were temporarily unemployable because of immaturity or ill-health, and a further small proportion were permanently unemployable because of mental or physical defects. About one in ten of the unemployed boys and one in five of the girls were not looking for employment; they were occupied with part-time school work, or were "helping out" at home, or were waiting to get married. The others wanted work, and for the most part were willing to take any kind of work they could get.

The interviews reveal that *in the absence of a chance to work for pay, the boys and girls who get no jobs spend their time chiefly in part-time schooling which is likely to have little direct relation to their needs, in random looking for work, and in aimless loafing.*

What makes these young people different from the working group is chiefly the accident of their not having found jobs. So far as can be determined through tests, reports from school officials, and questionnaires addressed to the boys and girls themselves, the two groups were essentially alike at the time they left school. Those who got no jobs knew as much about some matters and as little about others as those who were vocationally more fortunate. They had the same indefiniteness about their plans, the same aspirations, the same kinds of school records. They came from the same communities and from the same types of homes.

Out of school, the unemployed boys and girls tend to retain certain types of optimism which the working boys and girls speedily lose. The great majority of unemployed young people, if they know what kinds of jobs they want, believe that they are adequately trained for them. The working young people, in contrast, much more often report that they were not adequately trained when they took their present jobs. Again, the jobs which the unemployed boys and girls say that they want are very different from most of the jobs which the working boys and girls have actually obtained. The jobless group seem not to have realized that the kinds of jobs they are looking for may be particularly scarce. Probably neither kind of optimism differentiated the jobless from the working group when the two groups left school. The more practical realism of the young people who are working points to something that they have learned which the jobless have not.

Having tried to get jobs and failed, the unemployed boys and girls attribute their joblessness to various factors. Most often they blame general economic conditions: a large majority of the boys and from a fourth to a third of the girls believe—probably with some justice—that they are unemployed chiefly because there are not enough jobs available. One out of six or seven thinks that his own lack of specialized training may be at fault, particularly if he has had only an academic education. A smaller number conclude that they have failed to qualify because of lack of experience. Only a few seem to have set their standards so high that they have refused to take proffered jobs which did not measure up to their hopes or ambitions. None attributes his failure to find work to his lack of "personality," or to a lack of skill in finding or applying for a job.

So few credit their lack of employment to their own lack of education that the frequency with which they enroll for continued part-time schooling must be explained on other grounds. Certain explanations are obvious: they have time on their hands, and they listen readily to arguments about "insuring their futures." Whether for these or other reasons, the jobless boys and girls enroll more frequently for part-time courses than do the young people who are employed. Among the unemployed boys and girls the salesmen for proprietary schools find their best prospects. Not counting those who were continuing part-time schooling in preference to going to work, at least one-fourth of the unemployed graduates and about half as many of the nongraduates were enrolled for some sort of part-time training at the time they were interviewed. Others reported that they would have taken part-time courses if they could have afforded the tuition. A considerable number, preferring vocational experience to further study, had been looking for apprenticeship openings or jobs as learners in trades.

Commendable though their effort to get further training is, it must be recalled that much of the out-of-school studying done by the leaving pupils is inappropriate or ineffective. The part-time courses in which they enroll keep the unemployed pupils temporarily busy. For many of them their studying may give point to an otherwise aimless round of activities. It is seldom guided, however, by anyone competent to judge the educational needs of the boys and girls concerned, or interested in planning constructively for their vocational futures.

In their recreational activities and their general social relationships the unemployed boys and girls differ from the employed chiefly in the amount of time they have at their disposal. There are perhaps more in the unemployed group who are reported to be loafing or keeping bad company than there are in the group who have jobs, but neither group contains any large number of openly "bad actors" a year after they are out of school. In what they read and do not read, in their favorite radio programs, in the kinds of clubs they belong to, and in their interests and hobbies, the two groups are much alike. Lack of employment merely accentuates, to a degree, the place which these activities occupy in the lives of the young people who have no jobs.

But the fact cannot be overlooked that the jobless are adrift to a far greater extent than are the young people who are at work. The latter have the steadying influence of their working associates and their superiors. Though that influence may be limited in its effect and narrow in its scope, it is at least recurrent and on the whole positive. The boys and girls who are without jobs largely lack any such purposeful contacts with others. Like the group who are employed, they know few adults, they do not go back to the school for advice and help, they can often find little wisdom at home. Having no one to look to for guidance, they especially are in danger not just of turning their out-of-school experience to small account, but of losing much that their previous education has given them.

SUMMARY

Opportunities for employment during the period in which this study was made obviously had much to do with the number of boys and girls just out of high school who were able to find work. To a large extent this same factor determined the kinds of jobs which were open to these young people, and the wages which the jobs offered. The persistence of a depression psychology among the boys and girls themselves no doubt also affected their vocational adjustment. The attitudes of some of these young people toward the jobs which they eventually got, and their views of their own predicaments if they were unsuccessful in finding work, were probably colored in considerable measure by their memory of the several years of hard times which preceded their leaving school.

Such factors as these, however, account only in part for the hit-or-miss adjustments which these boys and girls had made. The economic conditions which young people must face outside of school will necessarily vary from year to year. Whatever these out-of-school conditions may be, boys and girls who are to be adequately prepared for employment need some realistic conception of their actual chances to get work, and some conception also of how to make the most of conditions as they find them. The fact that large numbers of the boys and girls now leaving school seem to have no such conception reflects seriously on their competence.

The readiness of these boys and girls to take any sort of work that may offer itself, and the fact that most of them are not unsuccessful in the work they get, may be thought, perhaps, to give evidence of a desirable versatility. But such versatility as the majority of them possess would seem to be the versatility of ignorance. They do not know what jobs are available; they do not know what kinds of work are likely to be most appropriate for them individually; they do not know how to use their jobs, once they have stumbled on them, to advance themselves to better jobs.

Ignorance about these matters is the more serious in view of the fact that of the young people who go to work as soon as they leave school, large numbers will probably always have to take jobs which offer only meager chances for advancement. The boys and girls who hold such jobs must eventually find other employers if they are to earn enough to support themselves independently. Looking for new jobs, most of these boys and girls have at present no recourse but to start over again the process of random search through which they gained their first positions.

Their ignorance about jobs is a matter for particular concern in the cases of the boys and girls who are unemployed. Though current figures give no sure index of future unemployment, it is noteworthy that even in the spring of 1937—a period of relative prosperity—large numbers of young people were unable to find work. Economic conditions are unlikely to change radically enough to provide employment for all the boys and girls who may desire it, however effective their vocational preparation may have been. The group of unemployed will in all probability, therefore, be a permanent one. Even more cut off from guidance and help than the boys and girls who are working, this group under present conditions seems destined to largely random and profitless activity.

CHAPTER V

School Achievement and
Social Competence

THE competence of the young people who leave the high schools each year has been considered thus far in terms of these young people in general. Though a number of striking differences between graduates and nongraduates, and between boys and girls, have been briefly commented on, chief attention has been given to the likenesses, rather than the differences, among the leaving pupils.

The schools themselves explicitly recognize differences in certain types of competence among the pupils who are ending their full-time schooling, by the fact that they give diplomas to some of these pupils and not to others. Moreover, the schools award different types of diplomas to pupils who have been enrolled in different curricula. The respect with which these school distinctions are generally regarded, not merely by the boys and girls who graduate or fail to graduate but by the public at large, raises certain obvious questions. How much does it actually mean, in terms of social competence in general, that some boys and girls fail to finish their high school work? How much difference in social competence is there between the pupils who graduate from one curriculum and those who graduate from another? The answers to these questions may afford not merely a further check on the adequacy of the present high school program, but also some measure of the realism with which the schools now appraise their own work.

EARLY ELIMINATION OF PUPILS
FROM HIGH SCHOOL

It has already been pointed out that in New York State the boys and girls who leave high school without graduating outnumber the graduates nearly two to one. Pupils' persistence in high school in New York is relatively low—lower, according to United States Office of Education figures, than that in three-fourths of the States of the Union.

Comparatively rapid elimination of pupils from school does not in itself mean that the high schools are failing in their responsibility. In the National Survey of Secondary Education, completed in 1932 under the Office of Education, the retention of pupils in two major types of secondary schools was systematically analyzed. Junior and senior high schools, offering programs designed in part for the very purpose of encouraging pupils to stay in school, were found to be holding their pupils no longer than four-year high schools offering more or less conventional programs. The kind of education the pupils received might be much better under the one type of program than under the other. How long the pupils stayed in school, however, seemed to depend less on the nature of the school program than on certain out-of-school factors—the availability of jobs, or local confidence in the value of formal education, or the ability of parents to provide for their children during a prolonged period of schooling.

It is probable, therefore, that *the tendency of pupils to leave the high school relatively early in New York State is due to social and economic conditions in the State more directly than to the nature of the secondary school program*. The tendency is nevertheless of the utmost significance from the standpoint of educational planning. It obviously means a yearly release into business and industry and general social life of large numbers of young people for whom the high schools have not been able to do all hey set out to do. Since these young people are to become citizens of the State as truly as are those who earn high school diplomas, their social competence is a matter of no less serious concern.

CHARACTERISTICS OF NONGRADUATES AS REPORTED BY THE SCHOOLS

The schools' judgments of the characteristics of boys and girls who leave school early are in general unfavorable. *According to reports from the schools on individual leaving pupils, the pupils who do not graduate come from homes which offer few educational advantages; they are usually failing in their school work; they have few exceptionally desirable personal traits and many undesirable traits.*

Pronounced economic and social selection operates among high school pupils in New York State as it does in most other states. More than half the boys and girls who drop out of school without graduating, as contrasted with fewer than a fifth of the graduates, are reported to belong to poor or indigent families. Boys and girls whose fathers are engaged in unskilled labor graduate much less often than do those who come from professional families. More frequently than the graduates, the nongraduates have been brought up in homes in which some other language than English is spoken. Handicaps arising from all these sources—poverty, parental occupations which provide small opportunity for parents to assist in their children's education, home backgrounds colored by foreign outlooks— are clearly reflected in reports from the schools on unusual features in their pupils' home environments. When unusual features are mentioned, those noted for graduates are predominantly advantages. Those mentioned with reference to nongraduates tend to be disadvantages, the limited cultural opportunities provided by the homes being especially emphasized.

A conspicuous characteristic of the young people who leave school early is their lack of success in school work. More than half of a representative group of tenth and eleventh grade pupils who were planning to leave school said that they would stay in school if they could be sure of getting a Regents' diploma; almost as many said they would stay if they could even count on being promoted to the next grade. The implication that the withdrawing pupils' chances to "pass" in their school work are not good is borne out by their school records. Failures in school subjects were the rule among the pupils reported by the schools as leaving before graduation, though no one subject or group of subjects stood out as special stumbling blocks for these pupils in general. Their school records suggested not so much low achievement in particular parts of the present high school program as a general lack of scholastic success.

In view of their backgrounds and of their school accomplishment, it is hardly surprising that schools are relatively hesitant to recommend nongraduates for citizenship, and especially for jobs. More nongraduates than graduates, it will be recalled, are judged by their schools to be unprepared for the responsibilities of citizenship at the time they leave school, and from half to two-thirds of the nongraduates are reported not ready to get and hold jobs. The schools' lack of confidence in the pupils who leave school early is reflected not merely in their unwillingness to recommend these pupils for out-of-school activities, but in their replies to questions about exceptional personal qualities possessed by individual leaving pupils. Whereas among graduates the schools frequently mention unusual intellectual ability, special talents of various sorts, or exceptional drive and persistence, for the nongraduates the best they can say in any considerable number of cases is that these pupils are well developed physically, or have pleasing personalities, or display good moral qualities. On the negative side, the schools report exceptionally unfavorable characteristics much more often among the nongraduates than among the graduates. The only unfavorable trait listed frequently enough to appear characteristic of any appreciable number of the graduating group—and this trait is mentioned in the case of not more than one graduate in a hundred—is laziness or indifference; whereas among the nongraduates low intelligence is repeatedly mentioned (particularly in the cases of pupils leaving from the earlier grades), and laziness, indifference, and untrustworthiness are also commonly reported.

OBJECTIVE EVIDENCE AS TO SOCIAL COMPETENCE OF NONGRADUATES

The reports from the schools as to the lack of competence of the pupils who leave school early are in many respects corroborated by more objective evidence. Test results, among other data, definitely support the schools' judgments. Interpreted in terms of the length of time individual boys and girls stay in school, the tests given by the Inquiry indicate that *the poorer a pupil's school accomplishment, the earlier he is likely to leave school.*

Pupils who do not graduate from the high school may drop out of school at any grade level from the seventh to the twelfth. Those who end their schooling with the seventh or the eighth grade are relatively few in number, and in most cases are reported by the schools as having unusual mental or physical disabilities; the great majority of pupils tend to persist at least into grade nine. Balancing early leavers against pupils who stay until they reach the upper grades, the average leaving point for nongraduates occurs at some time within the tenth grade. Nongraduates in general are thus at an educational disadvantage, as compared with graduates, amounting to the equivalent of two full years or more of schooling.

This disadvantage is clearly reflected in the results of objective tests of achievement. In the tests used by the Inquiry, the pupils leaving school early ranked so far below those staying till graduation that the best of the nongraduates tended to be the equals of only the poorer graduates. Tests of general scholastic aptitude illustrate these differences especially forcefully. Only one group of nongraduates—the boys (but not the girls) leaving the twelfth grade—were not markedly inferior in scholastic aptitude to the graduates. The scholastic aptitude of the nongraduates in general proved to be so far below that of the graduates as to give ample confirmation to an inference already suggested by the reports from the schools: fundamental scholastic inability, rather than lack of success in particular school subjects, furnishes a primary reason for early withdrawal.

As might be anticipated, the contrast between nongraduates and graduates tends to be more pronounced the earlier the nongraduates leave school. The handicap in scholastic aptitude grows steadily greater for pupils leaving school at lower and lower grade levels. Handicaps in special types of achievement show a similar trend, though with two or three noteworthy exceptions. One exception occurs in spelling: boys who leave school early (but not girls) make fewer mistakes in spelling words in their letters the lower the school grade from which they withdraw. A second exception is found in pupils' acquaintance with public affairs: boys and girls withdrawing at the end of the ninth grade display more familiarity with matters recently in the news than pupils leaving the tenth or eleventh grade. Again, scores on tests of attitudes toward controversial issues show no appreciable differences among pupils withdrawing at different grade levels. Notwithstanding these exceptions, the general trend is exemplified in so many of the measures used that it stands out clearly: the pupils who leave school early are not merely less able academically than the great majority of those who stay, but the earlier they leave the more certain one can be that they have had serious difficulty with their school work.

Further light is thrown on the competence of the nongraduates as a group by their replies to questions about their plans for the future, and by their activities after they have left school. The evidence from these sources tends to suggest that *boys and girls who leave school before graduating are likely to have especial difficulty in coping with out-of-school problems of vocation, citizenship, and further education.*

The major differences between nongraduates and graduates which were revealed by the questionnaires on pupils' plans for the future and by the interviews with boys and girls who were out of school have been commented on in earlier chapters. It will therefore be sufficient to review very briefly those differences which have particular bearing on the general social competence of the nongraduates.

Only a fourth of the pupils who left school before graduating (as contrasted with nearly two-thirds of the graduates) were able to come reasonably close to carrying out the plans they had outlined for the following year. Almost half the non-graduates were found to have submitted to complete reversals of their plans. Thus, many boys and girls who expected to be in school were not there, and many who looked forward to going to work had been unable to find jobs. More than a fourth who had had definite plans for being in school or at work were actually in school or working, but were taking quite different school programs or were working at very different jobs from those they had anticipated. Even when they were on the brink of leaving school, the great majority of the nongraduates thus had no accurate notion of what lay ahead of them.

A larger proportion of the pupils withdrawing before graduation than of the graduates reported that they had no long-range vocational plans. Among the boys and girls who were leaving school early, however, those who had made long-range plans tended more often both to consider their plans absolutely unchangeable and to have hit upon plans which were out of keeping with their own demonstrated abilities.

School Achievement and Social Competence

Out of school the pupils who left before graduating got jobs about as often as the graduates, but they got jobs which paid less, which ranked lower in the industrial scale, and which offered fewer chances for advancement. Six months to a year after they had left school, the median earnings of the boy non-graduates—$13.63 a week—averaged about a dollar a week less than those of the boy graduates; the wage of $9.63 which the median girl nongraduate received was approximately $1.25 less than that of the girl graduate. Not merely with respect to wages but in practically all other vocational matters, failure to have completed the high school program represented an especially serious disadvantage among the girls.

Though few of either the graduates or the nongraduates were found to have become actual offenders against society within their first year out of school, an appreciably larger proportion of the nongraduates were reported by adults who knew them to have undesirable personal traits—over-confidence, immaturity, lack of ambition, sometimes outright immorality. Two-thirds of the nongraduates (as compared with fewer than half the graduates) belonged to no clubs, organizations, or groups of any sort. A much smaller proportion of nongraduates than of graduates read news-magazines or listened to radio news programs or programs of comment.

Boys and girls who had left school early went to the movies somewhat more often than did the graduates; they took part about as frequently in out-of-school athletics, and they spent about the same amount of time in listening to the radio. The nongraduates read less than the graduates, however, and what they read was for the most part less substantial. Their radio fare was even more narrowly limited to variety shows, popular music, short plays, sketches, and stories than was that of the graduates. They had fewer hobbies than the graduates and those which they did have consisted chiefly of collections and handwork. As compared with the graduates, less than two-thirds as large a proportion were doing any sort of systematic study, either for vocational purposes, to add to their general education, or for fun.

These various types of evidence clearly suggest that wherever the nongraduates and the graduates differ in their out-of-school plans and activities—and they differ in many respects—the nongraduates are at a marked disadvantage. In the light of this evidence, it is significant that both the interviews and the reports from the schools show that *boys and girls who leave school without graduating can count even less often than the graduates on dependable help or advice from adults.* Schools and government employment agencies place almost none of the nongraduates in jobs. Once they have left, fewer than one in ten go back to their schools for any sort of assistance. In most cases these boys and girls either have no one on whom they can rely for counsel (this proved to be the situation among nearly a fifth of the nongraduates interviewed), or they are obliged to get such help as they can from their parents. In view of the poverty and lack of resources which characterize most of the homes from which these young people come, the help on which they can rely at home is likely to be all too meager.

CONTRAST BETWEEN NONGRADUATES AND GRADUATES

Thus the picture of the boys and girls who leave the high school before they have completed the standard program is that of a group seriously handicapped by a lack of information and skills which they will need out of school, less ready than the high school graduates to meet the demands of adult society, making less purposeful and less profitable beginnings than the graduates in almost every phase of their out-of-school life, and even more cut off from adult guidance and help. The graduates themselves are poorly prepared for many of the problems which they must inevitably face; the plight of the nongraduates, by comparison, is much more serious.

For emphasis it should be repeated that the boys and girls who leave school without graduating outnumber the high school graduates every year by nearly two to one. The problem of adequate schooling for the nongraduates, therefore, cannot be waved aside as one of small dimensions. Nor can it be regarded as a problem which will disappear of its own accord as soon as out-of-school factors cause young people to stay longer in school. The length of a pupil's schooling has an important bearing, obviously, on his eventual competence. Even more important, however, is the pupil's ability to succeed in the kind of education the schools provide for him. That thousands of pupils now in school in New York State are not succeeding under the existing school program is attested both by the reports of the schools themselves and by objective measures of the pupils' achievement. Clearly there can be no effective preparation of these pupils for out-of-school citizenship or vocation or leisure, as long as the present school offerings are their only recourse.

GRADUATES OF DIFFERENT CURRICULA

The pupils who receive high school diplomas are in general set off from the pupils who do not by differences which have much to do with social competence. Are the various groups of young people who receive different types of diplomas similarly distinguishable from one another?

Academic high schools in New York State, like comprehensive high schools everywhere, ordinarily offer a number of more or less specialized curricula. Each pupil is expected to elect an appropriate curriculum in the ninth grade, and barring failure in his work or some radical change in his plans, to follow it through until he leaves the high school. The number of curricula offered by any one school varies with the size of the school and the educational philosophy of its administrative officers. At the core of practically every academic high school program is to be found a college-preparatory curriculum, built up of courses required for college admission and designed to meet the requirements of the most prized of the Regents' diplomas. Most schools also provide a general curriculum, which includes chiefly academic courses but allows freer choice of nonacademic work than is possible in the college-preparatory curriculum. Less usual, but still a part of the offering of a majority of the schools, is a business curriculum, preparing for clerical work or selling. Various types of vocational curricula, emphasizing vocational technical, industrial, agricultural, and homemaking courses, are becoming increasingy common in the form of special departments in the academic high schools. Least frequently found, but prominent enough to be included in a list of the major types of curricula, are specialized programs for pupils majoring in music or art. Each of these curricula is commonly planned to lead to a high school diploma for the pupil who successfully completes four years of work above the eighth grade.

Analysis of the results of tests used by the Regents' Inquiry shows that *at the time they leave school the graduates of the major curricula form a distinct academic hierarchy, with the college-preparatory graduates at the top and the vocational industrial, agriculture, and homemaking graduates at the bottom.*

The best pupils—that is, best in terms of general scholastic aptitude, liberality of outlook, and knowledge of affairs outside the school, as well as in terms of academic achievement—tend to graduate from the college-preparatory curriculum. The boy or girl who ranks at the bottom of the next-to-lowest quarter of this group is likely to be superior on measures of school achievement to the average pupil in any other curriculum except the general curriculum. Graduates of the vocational technical curriculum, which is a preparatory curriculum for technical and scientific colleges as well as a vocational curriculum, rank in scholastic aptitude and in most measures of achievement with the liberal arts preparatory group.

Young people graduating from the general curriculum constitute a mixed group. Many of them attain test scores well above the average for the college-preparatory curriculum. Others, in spite of high scholastic aptitude, show notably low achievement in school subjects. Though the average standing of the general curriculum group is relatively high, the discrepancies among its members between ability and school records suggest that it includes many pupils who have been drifting through school without definite purpose, and without having learned to put forth serious effort.

Most of the graduates of the music and art curricula rank below graduates of the general curriculum on measures of school achievement. They appear to be handicapped in mathematics, and surprisingly enough, they show less acquaintance with current personalities in music and art than graduates of other academic curricula.

Graduates of the business curriculum rank on the average above the other vocational groups, but below the average graduate of the strictly academic curriculum. Most of the pupils whom the business curriculum attracts hope to obtain secretarial positions. It is noteworthy, therefore, that the group as a whole obtain relatively low scores on letter form and on content in letters written not as required exercises but in the form in which the pupils themselves choose to write them.

The scholastically least able pupils tend to be those graduating from the vocational homemaking, agriculture, and industrial curricula. Were they to be tested in manipulative skills or in knowledge of vocational processes, these pupils might show themselves superior to the rest of the high school group, but in such abilities as could actually be measured in the general testing program they are consistently at a disadvantage. The disparity between the homemaking, agriculture, and industrial graduates and the graduates of the academic and business curricula is especially evident in tests which emphasize reading, or which place a premium on general cultural background. The most seriously handicapped among the vocational graduates are the girls from the homemaking curriculum. Despite their possession of high school diplomas, more than half the girls graduating from this curriculum rank below the average girl leaving school at the end of the eleventh grade in types of achievement which are appropriately the concern of all secondary school curricula.

This academic hierarchy repeats itself in other matters than measurable school accomplishment. Ranked in terms of the socio-economic status of their homes, the college-preparatory pupils come highest in the scale and the vocational pupils lowest. Pupils enrolled in the academically "better" curricula are more likely to stay in school until they graduate than are pupils enrolled in curricula which are less select academically. Pupils' plans for continuing their full-time school work vary in similar fashion: more than three-fourths of the college-preparatory group look forward to continued schooling after they have graduated from the high school, while fewer than a sixth of some of the vocational groups have any further schooling in mind, notwithstanding the fact that numerous schools of noncollegiate rank are open to them.

THE OUT-OF-SCHOOL COMPETENCE OF GRADUATES OF DIFFERENT CURRICULA

Clean-cut as these groupings are from the academic standpoint, they lose much of their significance as soon as pupils get out of school. The first evidence of their lack of meaning in relation to nonschool matters appears in the schools' judgments of the general competence of their leaving pupils. *Schools tend to recommend leaving pupils for citizenship or for jobs with no very definite relationship to the nature of the curricula in which the pupils have been enrolled.* For example, only a small proportion of secondary school graduates—and this is true of the graduates of specialized vocational schools as well as of the academic high schools—fail to be recommended by their schools as ready to assume the responsibilities of citizenship. Whether a pupil has graduated or has not graduated makes an important difference in this connection; the particular curriculum from which he has graduated has little apparent bearing on the school's judgment. Again, college-preparatory pupils are recommended for jobs (the nature of the jobs not being definitely specified) almost exactly as often as business curriculum graduates; and business graduates, though their training has presumably been definitely vocational, are recommended somewhat less often than are the graduates of the vocational industrial curriculum. Here, also, whether a pupil has or has not graduated seems to weigh more heavily in the school's judgment than the curriculum he has followed.

Efforts to distinguish important differences among the out-of-school activities of boys and girls from different curricula lead, with two possible exceptions, to even less confidence in the significance of the curricular groupings. *The general citizenship and leisure-time activities of pupils who have left school—their relations with friends and associates, their interests and hobbies, the part which they take in civic affairs—bear no apparent relation to the curricula they have followed.* The academically abler boys and girls, it is true, have more intellectual interests and show more discrimination in what they do than the less able. Thus they read more and better books, they listen more often to serious programs on the radio, they have more substantial hobbies. The attempt to trace the origin of these tendencies, however, leads much less often to what the pupils have studied in school than to various nonschool influences. The accident of whether a young person is employed or unemployed apparently has more to do with the way he spends his free time than does the nature of his high school diploma. The fact that he belongs or does not belong to a church club outside of school seems to be more largely responsible for the part he takes in civic affairs than does the knowledge of current events which his school

· 87 ·

may have given him. The interests and general attitudes of his parents and friends, and not the subject matter of his high school course, largely determine what he reads, or listens to on the radio, or thinks about most seriously.

Boys and girls who have succeeded in the academically "better" curricula do, however, tend to continue their schooling after they have left the high school more often than do the young people who have graduated from curricula lower in the academic scale. This tendency represents perhaps the most prominent exception to the disappearance of curricular distinctions among the boys and girls who have finished with the high school. From one point of view it follows so obviously from the nature of the educational program that it is hardly worth pointing out. The high school has set some of its pupils on the academic track which leads on to higher institutions; other pupils it has not tried to put on that track. The pupils who have a clear academic road ahead of them naturally follow that road more often than do the pupils whose high school path has led nowhere in terms of strictly academic goals. But this is not all the story. Boys and girls who do not go on to higher institutions—and nearly half even of the college-preparatory graduates do not—must ordinarily find jobs for themselves. Business and vocational curriculum graduates have at least a modicum of salable vocational skills; graduates of the college-preparatory and general curricula have no corresponding skills, and after they have looked in vain for jobs they begin to realize that fact. The unemployed graduates of the latter curricula are therefore often enrolled in part-time vocational courses. Their tendency to undertake such study, motivated as it is by vocational need, furnishes evidence not so much of the effectiveness of their high school training as of its serious shortcomings.

The second exception has direct bearing on the vocational programs of the secondary schools. Interviews with pupils, as well as reports from schools, show that *the graduates of certain specialized vocational curricula make far more successful vocational adjustments outside of school than the graduates of the academic curricula.* This tendency does not hold to any appreciable degree among the graduates of the general high schools—even (so far the Inquiry data would indicate) in schools maintaining separate vocational departments. The tendency is clearly apparent, however, as it affects graduates of the industrial and homemaking curricula in specialized vocational schools.

Tests given to pupils on the point of leaving school reveal no substantial differences either in scholastic aptitude or in school achievement between pupils enrolled in the industrial and homemaking curricula in specialized vocational schools and pupils in the corresponding curricula in academic high schools. Whichever type of school these pupils attended, they were at the bottom of the academic heap—overage chronologically, low in scholastic aptitude, handicapped particularly in their ability to read and to deal with the usual academic subject matter. Furthermore, interest inventories showed that the vocational-school pupils were interested in about the same kinds of activities as academic high school pupils from lower grades and smaller communities. Their educational and vocational plans were similar in character to those of the pupils of low ability in the academic schools. All factors considered, the specialized vocational schools appeared to be under no advantage in the abilities or backgrounds of the pupils whom they enrolled, with the possible exception that many of these pupils had believed in the need for direct vocational training strongly enough to have chosen to enter a vocational school rather than an academic high school.

Nevertheless, of the boys and girls who did not continue their full-time schooling, at least a third more of the vocational school graduates than of the academic high school graduates secured employment within a year after they left school. At the time both groups were interviewed, 82 per cent of the boys who had graduated from vocational schools were working at full-time jobs, while only 60 per cent of the boy graduates of the academic high schools were employed full time. The corresponding percentages for girls were 53 per cent and 40 per cent respectively.

The vocational school graduates went into other than white-collar occupations more often than did the academic graduates. Few were engaged in clerical work; the largest numbers were working as learners in trades, or were employed in various forms of repetitive manual work, personal service, or machine work. These were the types of jobs considered least desirable by the graduates of the academic high schools. The vocational school pupils not merely did not seem to dislike them, but were doing well in them. The average wages of the employed vocational school graduates were notably higher than were those of the academic high school graduates, despite the fact that the two groups had been out of school the same length of time. Thus, the vocational school boys were being paid an average of $18.50 a week, whereas the academic high school boys were receiving an average of only $14.63 a week. Moreover, the vocational school graduates were more often reported by their employers as likely to advance on the job: about 80 per cent of all the vocational school graduates, as compared with only 60 per cent of the boys from the academic high schools, and a much smaller proportion of the academic girls, were found to be in line for promotion.

To compare the two groups in their success in getting the kinds of jobs for which they were trained is impossible, since most of the academic pupils were trained for no jobs in particular. It is perhaps worth noting, however, that the chief source of dissatisfaction among the vocational school graduates was that they had not been able to find work in the occupations for which their school programs had supposedly prepared them. Approximately a third of the boys reported that so far as they themselves could see, their school courses had had no bearing on their present jobs. Once they got jobs, the vocational school graduates were less afflicted than the academic graduates with unsatisfied white-collar ambitions. In this respect, as in the matter of their having any sort of jobs, they were notably better adjusted than were the boys and girls from the academic high schools.

GENERAL SIGNIFICANCE OF PRESENT CURRICULAR DISTINCTIONS

The difference in vocational adjustment noted above would seem to be the most important out-of-school difference actually produced by pupils' choice of one secondary school curriculum rather than another. The fact that pupils fall into an academic hierarchy within the schools is apparently not a result of their having elected particular curricula. The curricula are there, the pupils gravitate toward them or are steered into them, and the pupils whose intellectual ability and social background admit them to the preferred curricula tend to get preferred academic ratings. Thus the curricula act as fairly effective sorting devices in the matter of academic ability. But in most instances the curricula themselves do not produce different kinds or degrees of out-of-school competence. The fact that a pupil has succeeded in a given curriculum tells something about his general ability. That fact provides almost no indication of whether he has developed special interests, or any high degree of competence, which distinguish him from pupils who have followed different curricula.

All of this means that except for the specialized vocational curricula the supposed differentiations among the present curricula have little more than academic significance. The differentiations could be made significant in out-of-school terms: the comparative success of the vocational schools in contributing to pupils' vocational adjustment is evidence of what can be done. Most of the present differentiations, however, seem to contribute principally to the smooth operation of in-school affairs. The varied curricula serve to supply certain pupils with the academic wherewithal for getting into college. They allow other pupils to go through school without being subjected to any very exacting academic demands. They make it possible for a third group to "succeed" chiefly by spending four years in more or less earnest attendance. They fail almost entirely to bring about the differences in actual competence which would justify the relative degrees of respect now accorded them by pupils, parents, and the general public.

SUMMARY

If all that should be expected of schools were that they should pick out and label the academically successful boys and girls, the current program of secondary education in New York State might be judged reasonably satisfactory. In the granting of diplomas to some pupils and not to others, the schools obviously distinguish between pupils who are good and poor from the standpoint of academic accomplishment. They make further distinctions of the same sort in their award of various kinds of diplomas. Moreover, in selecting the pupils who eventually graduate, the schools somewhat automatically differentiate between young people who are good and those who are poor from the standpoint of social competence.

But if schools can fairly be expected to provide every normal boy and girl with the educational equipment that he will need to give him a fair start toward making the most of his particular abilities, the view which this chapter gives of the competence of various groups of leaving pupils is disturbing. The young people whom the schools do not graduate, though they constitute a majority of all the boys and girls who enter the high school, are especially unprepared for the problems they must face as soon as they end their schooling. They leave school without having finished any program designed to make them ready for out-of-school activities, and they flounder with extraordinary aimlessness and lack of understanding in their efforts to adjust themselves to out-of-school conditions.

Among the graduates, the academic criterion by which the schools distinguish one group of pupils from another has little meaning after young people get out into the world. Its significance is denied in part by the failure of the present educational program to stimulate to their best work a considerable number of relatively able boys and girls. Its significance is even more directly denied by the fact that the schools themselves, in judging the probable out-of-school competence of individual graduates, pay slight attention to the nature of the school work which these pupils have had.

CHAPTER VI

Social Competence of Various Types of Pupils

DIFFERENCES in competence among young people leaving school are, of course, to be accounted for partly by the fact that these young people were in many respects widely different when they entered school. Some of the differences that boys and girls bring with them into school—differences caused by unequal out-of-school advantages, for example— it is the task of a democratic educational system to diminish as far as possible, so that young people of equal ability may have reasonably equal chances to make a successful beginning outside of school. Other differences—differences, especially, in the kinds of ability or of interests which individual pupils show—the schools ought to foster, in order that each boy or girl may take advantage of any special talent that he may have. How far the schools succeed in lessening differences of the one sort and in recognizing and building on differences of the other sort is a further measure of the effectiveness of the educational program.

Evidence as to the success of the New York State schools in dealing with differences in background or in ability among their pupils has been sought through comparing the competence of certain groups of leaving pupils. Under an ideally effective program, young people leaving the rural high schools might be expected to be as competent, in general, as young people of equal native ability leaving school in the cities. Girls should be as competent as boys, in the kinds of knowledge and ability which both girls and boys need to possess. Young people of exceptional intelligence should be more competent than leaving pupils in general, in proportion to their ability to learn. The facts as to the actual competence of these various groups of young people may serve to show how well the current program is adjusted to the differing needs of high school pupils.

RURAL AND URBAN YOUTH

The comparison of leaving pupils from the country schools with leaving pupils from the city schools points to a number of significant differences between the two groups of young people. In general, *boys and girls leave school at an earlier grade in the rural communities than in the cities; they are less well educated than the city pupils whenever they leave; they take up fewer out-of-school activities which will add to their education.*

In New York City, boys and girls who do not complete the high school program stay in school, on the average, until about the middle of the eleventh grade. In communities of less than 2,500 population they tend to withdraw from school near the beginning of the tenth grade. Furthermore, the boys and girls who eventually graduate from the rural schools tend to be older than those who graduate from the city schools. When they finish high school the girls from towns of less than 2,500 population are as a group about eight months older than the girls from the larger cities; the rural boys are more than a year older than the city boys.

In spite of the fact that they go through school more slowly than city pupils, the rural boys and girls do not gain as much from their school work. The tests given by the Inquiry in formal school subjects, high school literature, algebra, general science, civics, and American history, showed generally lower attainment in such subjects, grade for grade, by pupils in rural schools than by pupils in city schools. In the ability to solve arithmetic problems and to use the fundamental operations in arithmetic, a type of ability not particularly well developed among high school pupils in general, the rural pupils were on the whole about equal to pupils from the cities. In the use of English, however, the rural pupils were at a disadvantage except when compared with the pupils from New York City, where mixtures of nationalities make the problem of developing correct usage exceptionally complicated. Tests of comprehension in reading placed the pupils from the rural schools notably below the urban pupils both in New York City and in other cities. None of the differences in school achievement consistently favored the rural pupils, and the majority of test-by-test comparisons were to their definite disadvantage.

The pupils from small communities appear at a similar disadvantage in tests not so directly based on formal school subject matter. In the tests measuring attitudes toward controversial social questions, and particularly in the tests dealing with racial and political questions, the rural pupils tended to show greater prejudice than did the pupils from the cities. The rural pupils were at a disadvantage also in their information about matters of health, about current literature, and about music and art. Their lack of information was especially striking in connection with social, economic, and political affairs. The average twelfth grade pupil in New York City proved to be better informed on public affairs than 60 per cent of all the high school seniors tested; the average rural school twelfth grade pupil knew more about such matters than only the lowest 25 per cent of high school seniors in general.

Furthermore, boys and girls from rural communities display, in general, narrower and less active individual interests than the young people from the cities. Pupils leaving school were asked to tell whether they liked, disliked, or were neutral toward each of a large number of specific activities in which young people frequently engage—reading books and articles of various sorts, taking care of household appliances, playing musical instruments, earning money, managing various types of group undertakings. Though city and country pupils reported many interests in common, the country boys and girls tended more often to favor routine work-activities, such as cutting the lawn or clipping shrubs; taking charge of the home when parents were away; operating, adjusting, and repairing machinery; ironing, washing dishes, and making beds. Boys and girls from the cities more often reported an interest in social or intellectual activities, such as arranging for meetings, making speeches, designing dresses, inventing stories or planning articles. As a composite measure of the influence of school and out-of-school experiences, the interest inventories suggested that whereas the city boy or girl has been educated to respond to opportunities for leadership, aesthetic activities of various sorts, and chances to exercise creative imagination, the country boy or girl thinks of his interests largely in terms of physical or manual activities.

In the light both of what they know and of the range and intensity of their interests, the boys and girls from the country schools are thus less well off than the boys and girls from the cities. Their handicap does not reflect itself in their vocational plans at the time they leave school: they look forward to the necessity of getting jobs with no less definiteness or realism, and no more, than the urban young people. Nor is their disadvantage immediately apparent after they leave school. They are not notably different from city young people in their ability to get along acceptably with their families and their friends. Their habits with respect to reading, listening to the radio, going to the movies when movies are available, and taking part in various kinds of organized activities do not especially differentiate them from boys and girls who have left school in the cities. They look for work in the hit-or-miss fashion characteristic of city boys and girls; they get jobs, or fail to get them, just about as often; they like and dislike the same sorts of things about the jobs which eventually fall to their lot.

The rural young people are distinguished from those who have been to school in the cities, however, by the fact that rural school pupils are recommended by their schools less readily than are city school pupils, as being prepared for vocations and for the responsibilities of citizenship. Differences in the schools' judgments with respect to their pupils' readiness for general social and civic duties are greater than the differences in their attitudes toward their pupils' vocational fitness. In the case of boys and girls leaving before graduation, in particular, the rural schools refuse to recommend for citizenship very much larger proportions of their pupils than the city schools. At one extreme in this respect stands New York City, in which the general high schools reporting to the Inquiry refused such recommendations to approximately one-seventh of the boys and one-fourth of the girls who were leaving school without having graduated. At the other extreme, the schools in communities of less than 2,500 population denied recommendations to nearly half the boys and to three-fifths of the girls in this same group. Studies carried out by the Inquiry show that pupils whom the schools recommend tend as a group to display more than average ability according to various objective measures, and that pupils whom the schools fail to recommend are likely to be weak in important respects. Hence the large numbers of leaving pupils not recommended by the rural schools are evidence which directly corroborates the evidence provided by the test results, as to the relative lack of competence among these pupils.

Finally, having left the high school the boys and girls from rural communities are less likely to continue with any sort of school work than are the city boys and girls. This difference is apparent among both the graduates and the nongraduates. Among the graduates, only a little over a third of the boys leaving the rural schools in 1936 were reported to be in school at the beginning of the following year, as compared with more than half the New York City graduates and some 45 per cent of the graduates of large-city schools outside New York; the differences between girls from country and from city schools were of much the same order. Among the nongraduates, only one girl in seven from the rural schools (to choose girls rather than boys as an example) was reported to have enrolled for part-time schooling within three months after having left the high school, whereas one in three or four was reported thus enrolled in the large-city school systems; and again the tendency among boys and girls was essentially the same. Perhaps the growing interest in adult education will eventually attract many of these young people, graduates and nongraduates alike, back to school. At the present time, however deficient their education at the conclusion of their full-time schooling, a far larger proportion of rural pupils than of city pupils seem destined to get no systematic school work beyond the work they have had in high school.

The significance of these various facts lies not so much in the facts themselves as in the evidence which they give that *the present educational system is very far from providing educational opportunities for rural boys and girls equal to those open to young people in the cities.*

Boys and girls in the city have the advantage of an out-of-school environment which offers greater stimulation and a much greater variety of experience than are usually the lot of boys and girls in the country. Ideally, the rural school program ought to be rich enough and varied enough to make up for these out-of-school differences. That it falls far short of the ideal is apparent in the more limited interests with which rural boys and girls leave school, and in their meager acquaintance with many nonacademic matters which should be of as much concern to them as to young people in the city.

Even as judged by less than ideal standards, the educational program of the rural schools would seem to be seriously deficient. Common justice to rural boys and girls would demand that the rural schools do as well as city schools in teaching the formal school subject matter that is the present stock in trade of all high schools. The schools are not successful in this respect at the present time. Their pupils leave them not merely handicapped with respect to the kind of education which the city environment gives to pupils brought up in that environment, but handicapped as well in the academic abilities and information for which rural schools and city schools alike hold themselves directly responsible.

BOYS COMPARED WITH GIRLS

Any widespread differences in competence which appear between boys as a group and girls as a group at the time they leave school ought presumably to be in keeping with differences in the kinds of activities in which boys and girls will be engaged outside of school. Girls will obviously enter other vocations than those which attract most of the boys; their contributions to civic activities will be somewhat different; they may be expected to spend their leisure in different ways. Most girls who are ending their full-time schooling may normally be expected, therefore, to have acquired various interests and abilities distinct from those characteristic of boys.

Boys and girls will nevertheless need many of the same kinds of competence. Girls should be as well prepared as boys to recognize and deal with the social problems which are the concern of every voting citizen; they should be able to go on learning after they have left the high school; they should have acquired standards of enjoyment which will lead them to make wholesome use of their leisure; they should be ready to take proper advantage of their opportunities for employment. So far as their innate ability to learn is concerned, girls are as able as boys to master the knowledge and abilities which such types of competence demand. Investigations have repeatedly shown that the intelligence of a group of girls drawn from any particular social background or community setting corresponds closely with the intelligence of a group of boys similarly selected. Though girls may not be able to acquire certain physical skills which are readily attained by boys, boys and girls are apparently equally capable of the intellectual learning which they need to do in common. It has accordingly seemed fair to apply many of the same intellectual measures of social competence to young people of both sexes.

Judged in terms of these common measures, the girls leaving school in New York State have apparently got much less out of the educational program than the boys. The first of the measures which the Inquiry used—the various survey tests given to pupils on the point of leaving school—indicate that *at the time they leave the high school, girls in general are less well informed, less objective in their attitudes, and less actively interested in using their minds, than are the boys leaving at the same grade levels and from the same curricula.*

In matters of information, the boys' superiority is most apparent on tests of general science knowledge and acquaintance with public affairs. Here the boy who ranks below three-fourths of his own group makes a better score than the average girl. But the boys tend to be definitely superior also in their knowledge of American history, civics, and mathematics, and are at least equal to the girls in their knowledge of literature and in their acquaintance with fundamental rules of health. The only consistent advantage shown by the girls is in their knowledge of aesthetic matters (acquaintance with current personalities in music, art, and the drama), and in their use of spelling, grammar, and correct letter-form.

In the leaving pupils' attitudes toward civic affairs, as judged by their opinions on national, international, racial, and political questions, the differences between boys and girls are somewhat less pronounced than in matters of information. Again, however, the advantage is on the side of the boys; as a group, they show less biased attitudes than the majority of girls.

The boys' and girls' individual interests discriminate between the two groups in somewhat different fashion. The boys in general reported both keener and wider interests than the girls. The activities which the boys favored tended to place considerable emphasis on imagination and ingenuity: "being allowed to go ahead with your own ideas"; "doing something that others have not attempted"; "picking out the best things for your money"; "discovering how tools and machinery work." The girls rated first such activities as "taking long walks, climbing, rowing a boat," "arranging flowers artistically," "observing textures and colors of fine cloth," "watching clouds and other beauties of nature." The boys reported that they vigorously disliked drawing and literary activities; the girls were even more emphatically averse to anything suggesting quantitative analysis. The differences between the two groups may be not unjustly summarized by saying that the boys expressed keen interest in a wide range of activities calling for study, investigation, and active effort, whereas the girls favored fewer activities, preferring on the whole those demanding contemplation and passive enjoyment.

In various respects the results of these tests run counter to the common judgment of teachers and no doubt of most parents. School people in general tend to believe that girls get more from their school work than boys do. That judgment is clearly evident in the reports submitted by the New York State schools on their leaving pupils. Among boys and girls of the same levels of ability as measured by scholastic-aptitude tests, the girls are consistently given higher school ratings than the boys—so much higher that girls who rank in the lowest fifth of their classes in scholastic aptitude commonly receive school ratings equivalent to those of boys in the middle fifth. The school histories of the girls show that they are promoted more rapidly and graduate earlier than the boys, despite the fact that both groups enter the elementary school at the same average age. Though the schools' recommendations as to vocational competence seem to favor neither group, in recommendations as to citizenship the girls are again more readily approved. The schools' judgments in these matters are in the main unsupported by the objective measures of achievement. Positive strengths peculiar to girls are almost entirely lacking in the range of abilities and interests which the Inquiry canvassed for boys and girls alike. To balance the boys' superior knowledge of science, mathematics, and public affairs, and their greater disposition to think objectively about controversial questions, the girls have only a somewhat better acquaintance with current aesthetic activities, and slightly better habits in the use of English. To offset the boys' interests in active inquiry the girls possess chiefly a liking for pleasant surroundings and pretty things.

In addition to the differences between boys and girls in such matters as these, there are noteworthy differences between the two groups in their attitudes toward jobs. The boys' and girls' replies to questions about their vocational goals suggest that *the majority of girls think even less realistically about jobs and job opportunities than do most of the boys.* Moreover, it is evident from the interviews with working young people and their employers that *though girls can look forward to advancement on their jobs less often than boys, they are less inclined to be dissatisfied with whatever jobs they may happen to get.*

More girls than boys indicated that they had made at least tentative decisions as to their long-range vocational plans at the time they left school; fewer girls than boys reported that they knew of immediate vocational openings. Neither group showed themselves particularly well informed or clear-sighted with respect to vocational opportunities. A notably smaller proportion of the girls, however, were inclined to regard their long-range plans as subject to change; even more frequently than the boys they seemed to consider their objectives fixed and unalterable. In the matter of immediate jobs the girls were still more at a disadvantage. Whereas approximately a third of the boys who had been sure of jobs were later reported to be actually working, fewer than a fourth of the corresponding group of girls were known to be employed.

Of the young people who did not go to college and who had been six or more months out of school, approximately twice as large a proportion of girls as of boys had no jobs. More often than the boys, the girls who actually held jobs were in positions requiring them to use skills developed in their high school work. This situation seemed not to have resulted from any greater intelligence in hunting for jobs on the part of the girls; it came about merely because openings for girls were more numerous in clerical occupations, and many of the girls had followed a clerical curriculum. Accordingly, it gave the girls no advantage over the boys either in earnings or in opportunities for advancement. Their average wages were, in fact, notably lower than were those of the boys with equal training and experience, and employers less often reported that girls whom they had hired could expect to be promoted either in rank or in pay. Notwithstanding these disadvantages, only half as large a proportion of the girls as of the boys seemed to have in mind any reasons for disliking their jobs. Furthermore, what the girls did dislike, if they were at all dissatisfied, was rarely connected with chances to learn on the job or to move to a better job. Unquestionably many girls were looking forward to marriage, and hence considered a paid job as something which needed to concern them only for a time. Their attitudes toward their jobs are nevertheless of interest: their tendency to be satisfied with whatever had come their way would seem to mark a definite continuance of the habit of acceptance rather than of active concern, which was earlier found to characterize these same girls when they were on the point of leaving school.

A similar passiveness is evident in the girls' use of their leisure time. Girls who are through with school, being less frequently employed than boys, enroll more often for part-time study. On the average they read more than boys, and spend more time listening to the radio. They more often have individual hobbies. Of greater significance than the amount of time girls devote to leisure activities, however, are the kinds of interests which chiefly occupy them. Like the boys, they seem to have vocational ambitions primarily in mind in enrolling for continued school work. Apart from their schooling, *girls' leisure activities differ from boys' in that the girls' activities are more often purely recreational and less often concerned with civic interests or with matters involving intellectual problems.*

Thus, more girls than boys are members of organizations sponsoring parties or, purely social "get-togethers"; fewer girls than boys belong to character-building or service organizations. Girls read more fiction than boys, and a larger proportion of mediocre and inferior fiction. In what they read, they tend to give first place to stories of romance and glamor, and only a subordinate place to books and articles dealing with adventure, science, or sports, which are subjects definitely favored by the boys. In choosing their hobbies the girls more frequently incline to aesthetic or literary activities— keeping scrapbooks, reading or writing, taking part in plays. The boys more often pick some phase of science, or elect to make experiments, or try to build something calling for ingenuity or invention.

These differences in out-of-school activities are clearly of the same nature as the differences in the interests expressed by boys and girls still in school. They serve to reinforce a conclusion already suggested by the test results: girls go out of school less competent in civic and vocational matters than boys, and less likely to add to their competence through voluntary out-of-school activities. The passive quality of the girls' interests calls for particular notice; it would seem to stand directly in the way of any very constructive participation by many girls, either in the kinds of civic, vocational, and leisure activities in which boys engage or in other activities more directly appropriate to girls.

In so far as the schools are to be held responsible for the final readiness of young people for adult citizenship, *the present inequalities in achievement between boys and girls point to an unmistakable weakness in the educational program.* Boys and girls seemingly have equal capacity to acquire strong interests and to succeed in tasks calling for intellectual drive. The radical differences in the educational achievements of boys and girls, in matters in which the two groups ought to be equally competent, can hardly be attributed to anything else than a difference in the relative effectiveness of the education that boys and girls receive. Schooling alone cannot be held responsible for the difference; the influences affecting both boys and girls outside of school are unquestionably of at least as much importance as the experiences which the schools provide. But the schools are quite obviously not counteracting the out-of-school factors which press boys into one mold and girls into another, to the present educational disadvantage of the girls.

EDUCATIONAL OUTCOMES AMONG EXCEPTIONALLY CAPABLE PUPILS

Whatever its shortcomings in other respects, the present educational program has been shown to have the merit of discriminating at least roughly among pupils of various degrees of academic ability. In the ablest of its young people New York has much at stake. As an additional test of the effectiveness with which the schools deal with differences among their pupils, the questions which may fairly be raised concerning the education now provided for boys and girls of exceptional capacity are of particular significance. Do these boys and girls come out of high school with the attitudes, interests, and knowledge which will lead them to make the most of their talents? Having completed their high school work, do they continue their education in institutions which will give them a chance to develop still further?

"Exceptional capacity" ought to mean unusual talents in any field. Mechanical or artistic or musical or social talents are all important to a state which depends for its well-being on a great variety of specialized activities. Unfortunately the only kind of special ability that can now be identified at all accurately before it has become so outstanding that it is apparent even to the casual observer is intellectual ability— the sort of ability that expresses itself most fully in the work of the academic scholar. Present tests of intellectual ability are by no means infallible. They do show with reasonable exactness, however, how much academic achievement may fairly be expected of boys and girls who are still in the high school. Because such tests represent the only dependable measures now available of general capacity as distinguished from specific accomplishment, they have been used as the basis for singling out the exceptionally capable high school pupils.

The data gathered by the Inquiry show that *though the boys and girls who are ablest intellectually are fairly certain to complete the high school program, exceptionally promising young people frequently graduate from curricula which have not brought out the most they are capable of in intellectual achievement.* The data also show that *at the time they leave school the ablest pupils possess notably greater information about all sorts of matters than do pupils of lesser intellectual promise; but the ablest pupils are not greatly different from the average in their general social attitudes.*

Notwithstanding the social and economic selection which persists among high school pupils, the great majority of the "best" pupils find means to stay in high school until they have earned diplomas. There are, of course, individual exceptions to this tendency. Every experienced high school principal can doubtless recall instances of young people who showed unusual promise but who, because of family pressure or financial need, were forced to leave school before they had graduated. A number of such instances appeared, in particular, among the twelfth grade boys reported to the Inquiry who withdrew from school in order to go to work. But if by the ablest are meant those boys and girls who rank in scholastic aptitude among the highest fifth of the total secondary school group, the exceptions are relatively few. The school progress of the ablest pupils is comparatively rapid. Such pupils tend to complete the high school program before they are old enough to take advantage of work opportunities outside of school. Hence most of them have neither the chances nor the incentives which surround less capable boys and girls to leave school before they have finished.

The majority of the intellectually ablest young people graduate from the college-preparatory curriculum. Under present conditions it is understandable and quite appropriate that not all should do so. Both their individual interests and their need for jobs may make it desirable for certain pupils of high academic ability to choose curricula pointed toward nonacademic goals. Consequently some of these pupils specialize in music or art rather than in college-preparatory subjects, or elect commercial, industrial, agricultural, or vocational homemaking curricula.

Reports from the schools indicate, however, that a considerable number of very able pupils have gone through school taking courses which are addressed to no definite aims and which impose no high academic standards. Pupils often find it possible to make their whole programs out of such courses by electing the general curriculum—a curriculum serving chiefly to provide academic work for pupils who cannot meet college entrance standards. The presence in this curriculum of exceptionally capable boys and girls who are not working to the full level of their ability has already been commented on in Chapter V; it suggests a serious defect in the training the high schools are now giving to some of their most promising young people.

In tests of information the ablest boys and girls, irrespective of their curricula, rank in general much above the average of the total group of leaving pupils; they show definite superiority not merely in their command of academic subject matter but in their acquaintance with out-of-school activities and events.[1] To some extent they surpass the rest of the leaving pupils also in the liberality of their social attitudes. Their superiority in this respect was evident both in the test of opinions on national, international, racial, and political questions and in the test of attitudes toward basic principles of democracy. But the ablest pupils appear to much less advantage in tests of attitudes than in matters of pure information. Many individual boys and girls who score high in acquaintance with facts stand very low in the scale of tolerance or enlightenment with respect to social issues. For the group as a whole, the advantage in liberality of thinking is hardly large enough to offer assurance that the young people who are intellectually ablest are learning to be correspondingly able in dealing with social problems.

Considered all together, the high school histories of the boys and girls who show outstanding scholastic aptitude, and the relative attainments of these boys and girls by the time they have come to the end of their high school work, suggest that the present educational program "takes care" of such pupils but takes care of them without much attention to their par-

---

[1] It should perhaps be noted that in spite of their relative superiority, the ablest pupils frequently know very little about nonacademic matters. The blind spots which the tests revealed among the pupils of high scholastic aptitude as well as among the boys and girls of average ability have been pointed out in the first three chapters of Part I of this report.

ticular needs. Though the able young people are in general outstanding in academic achievement, a considerable number of them fail to live up to their capacities. The group as a whole is deficient—as are pupils of merely average ability—in types of competence which will be needed eventually by every boy and girl, and which should be possessed in especial measure by boys and girls capable of playing a more constructive part than the average in general out-of-school activities.

Thus far the academically superior pupils have been considered as a separate group. From the time they graduate from the high school the fortunes of these pupils can be better traced in terms of what happens to high school graduates in general.

Reports from the schools show that *liberal arts colleges or junior colleges tend to attract the top group of the high school graduates,* which of course includes the pupils of outstanding intellectual ability. Judged by the pupils who entered higher institutions from representative New York State high schools in 1936, four-year colleges and junior colleges enroll about equally competent groups of entering students. In terms of scholastic aptitude, more than half the boys and girls who were admitted to these institutions stood in the upper third of their graduating classes. The school records of the junior college entrants tended to be slightly inferior to those of pupils entering the standard colleges, a fact which suggests that the former group may have made somewhat less effective use of their abilities than the latter. Both the college and the junior college entrants were nevertheless definitely superior, in terms of their average school standing, to the pupils enrolled in other types of higher institutions.

It should be noted, however, that there is great overlapping in the abilities of pupils admitted to various kinds of higher institutions. The groups of pupils who enter institutions of different kinds can be ranked in fairly definite order so long as only the average abilities of the groups are considered. Among the boys, for example, the college and junior college group stands at the top; then comes the group entering professional and technical schools; next are those who enroll in business schools; and at the bottom are the three boys in a hundred who enter normal schools or teachers colleges. Among the girls, the college and junior college group is followed in order by the group entering normal schools, the girls enrolling in business schools, the few girls entering professional and technical schools, and the group admitted to schools of nursing. But individual pupils in any one of these groups may stand either high or low among the graduates in general. Though higher institutions succeed in attracting the ablest of the graduates, the range in abilities of the pupils whom they enroll and the overlapping among the groups entering different types of institutions are such as to suggest no very systematic discrimination in terms of scholastic achievement.

Reports from the schools also support the conclusion, as might be expected, that *financial rather than educational considerations often dictate the choice of particular higher institutions, or the decision as to whether a given boy or girl will go to any higher institution at all.* Many of the junior colleges entered by the 1936 graduates were tuition-free emergency collegiate centers. It is therefore significant that the junior college pupils included approximately three times as large a proportion of young people from poor or indigent homes as the group entering standard colleges. Financial considerations would seem to have been responsible not merely for the choice of junior colleges by certain pupils, but also for the fact that considerable numbers of able young people from poor families entered short-term professional, business, and technical institutes, rather than four-year colleges. Furthermore, poverty undoubtedly kept an appreciable number of pupils from entering any higher institution. Between 25 and 30 per cent of the graduates whom the schools reported as not attending any school after they had left high school came from poor or indigent homes. Though the average scholastic level of this group was lower than that of any of the groups of pupils who went on with their schooling, the group contained many individual boys and girls who could undoubtedly have profited by further school work.

Important as financial considerations may be, the data from the schools suggest that whether an individual boy or girl goes to college may be less often determined by the cost of a college education than by certain other factors. Poverty alone obviously does not shut tight the door to higher education: there are boys and girls from poor homes in every type of institution to which the high school graduates commonly go. The tendency of pupils in certain communities to return to their high schools for postgraduate work instead of entering college, and the varying proportions of pupils who enter college from different communities, make it seem probable that *the nearness or remoteness of higher institutions, coupled with local traditions as to college-going, may be quite as important as individual finances in leading able young people to go to college or not to go.*

It is frequently assumed that high school postgraduates are predominantly able pupils who continue in the high school instead of going on to college because they cannot afford higher education away from home. The Inquiry sought to test this assumption by comparing the scholastic aptitude scores and the school reports on individual postgraduates who had formerly been enrolled in college-preparatory curricula, with the corresponding data for college-preparatory graduates from the same schools who had gone immediately into college. The two groups proved to be practically identical in character. The scholastic-aptitude scores of the postgraduates, like those of the college students, placed them on the average in the upper third of their classes. Their school records gave them a group ranking almost exactly the same as that of the group entering college. The two groups were of the same average age. Their average indices of socio-economic status approximated each other closely. Even their distributions according to the financial levels of their homes were similar, the sole notable difference being that the postgraduates included fewer young people from very wealthy families. Furthermore, a check on what became of the postgraduates at the end of their extra year in high school showed that more than half of them—at least as large a proportion as of the corresponding group of graduates —eventually went on to college anyway, entering a year later and a year older than the usual high school graduate. The conclusion is inescapable that whatever the factors leading certain high school graduates to go to college and others to return to the high school, poverty is not of major importance among them.

The considerations which probably do apply are suggested by the varying proportions of pupils who enter college from different communities. The fact that a larger proportion of the graduates of city high schools than of country high schools continue their education beyond the high school has already been noted. It would seem to be especially significant that the New York City schools, in particular, send more than half their graduates on to higher institutions, as contrasted with only a third of the graduates of rural schools who enter such institutions. The disproportionately large college enrollment from New York City can hardly be accounted for except by the consideration that colleges are extraordinarily numerous in the metropolitan area, and are often closely related to the public school system. Scholastically able young people from New York City naturally consider going to college the thing to do. Equally able boys and girls from upstate New York end their schooling with the high school, or continue with a more or less aimless postgraduate year, apparently because no colleges are near enough to make college-going a natural sequel to high school graduation. Not lack of money to continue their education, but the absence of a type of guidance which might direct individual boys and girls into the kinds of higher institutions appropriate for them, would seem to be responsible for the fact that many exceptionally able pupils now drop out of school as soon as they have completed their high school education.

In the light of what happens to able young people after they leave the high school, as well as of their attainments when they end their high school work, it seems fair to conclude that *the current program of secondary education is only partially successful in making the most of the abilities of exceptionally capable boys and girls.* That these young people ordinarily finish high school, that they have a greater fund of information than high school graduates in general, that they form a group from whom higher institutions, particularly liberal arts colleges, chiefly draw their students, are matters in which New York State can justly find satisfaction. But in other respects the histories of these boys and girls point to certain serious problems. One such problem is evident in the tendency of many able young people to go through high school without having obliged themselves, or having been stimulated, to make full use of their scholastic ability. A second grows out of the circumstance that large numbers of exceptionally able high school pupils, for all their superiority in terms of sheer knowledge, develop no commensurate insight into social issues and no real concern for social problems. A third, affecting the higher institutions as well as the secondary schools, appears in the withdrawal of promising boys and girls at the end of their high school courses, sometimes because of poverty but perhaps especially because of the lack of active encouragement to continue their schooling. Until some way can be found to meet these problems, the educational program is not likely to give full scope to the abilities of the young people who are most able to profit by continued school work.

Social Competence of Various Types of Pupils

SUMMARY

So far as the data which have been available to the Inquiry allow a sound judgment, the current educational program in New York State would seem to be not very effective in meeting the differing needs of various important groups of boys and girls. The schools come closest to providing for the particular needs of pupils who show unusual academic ability. Though a good many such pupils are lost through the meshes of the educational system, intellectually able boys and girls in general have their abilities recognized and are given opportunity to put those abilities to use in high school and college. The present educational system does not succeed, however, in making up for the differences in out-of-school environment which put country pupils at a disadvantage as compared with city pupils. It does not provide school work which is as profitable for girls as for boys. Its weakness in these latter respects would suggest that young people who differ from the ordinary in other ways than through their possession of unusual intellectual ability are unlikely to have their special needs adequately met through the work which the high schools commonly offer.

CHAPTER VII

Effectiveness of the Current Program

TO ATTEMPT any brief summary of the outcomes of a state-wide educational program is a dangerous undertaking. Those outcomes are infinitely numerous and highly complex. They vary from one community to another, from school to school, from pupil to pupil. No simple statement can comprehend them all, or give due weight to many important exceptions.

To try to summarize educational outcomes in terms of the measures which the Regents' Inquiry has used is particularly dangerous. Large-scale educational programs have seldom been examined in terms of the social competence of the boys and girls who have been subject to those programs. There are almost no standards, therefore, by which to tell whether one state is producing a more competent or less competent group of young people than other states. The standard which must chiefly be referred to is that of whether a state is doing as well as it needs to do and wants to do. Any such standard is bound to be exacting. Examined in the light of it, an educational program is likely to seem far less praiseworthy than that same program would appear to be if it were merely compared in conventional fashion with similar programs.

It seems desirable, nevertheless, to undertake a concise and somewhat general interpretation of the outcomes described in the preceding chapters. Insofar as those outcomes are what New York State needs and wants from its educational program, they point to phases of the program which ought to be retained. The outcomes which are unsatisfactory or inadequate provide a significant clue to essential changes in that program.

POSITIVE OUTCOMES
OF THE EDUCATIONAL PROGRAM

Whether through its schools or its homes or its community environments, New York State is now accomplishing certain positive educational results with its boys and girls of high school age. Most prominently, it is teaching them academic subject matter. By the time they leave the high school the majority of its young people have read enough to have mastered certain facts about the standard English classics; they have gained at least an elementary acquaintance with general science and with the principles of personal hygiene; they probably know more than their elders know about American history and civics. In addition, they have acquired a good many less academic attainments. They have learned various somewhat evanescent facts about the personalities and events of contemporary national and international life. They have acquired fairly clear ideas of their rights as citizens in a democracy, and considerable understanding of where and when those rights apply. They have come to believe that one of the most important things a young person has to do is to prepare himself to earn a living. They have adopted a surprising variety of individual hobbies. They have learned to like dancing and athletic activities, particularly large-group sports. In many instances they have learned to enjoy singing, playing musical instruments, and acting in amateur theatricals. They have become habitual movie-goers and listeners to the radio. They have also become habitual readers, chiefly of newspapers and magazines.

The high school program has set a considerable number of these young people on the road to continued schooling. By the time they leave high school a majority of them believe firmly in the value of schooling. Large numbers act on this belief to the extent of going on with part-time school work, even though they cannot or do not enter higher institutions.

Numerous and varied though its positive effects have been, the educational program has not been equally successful with all types of young people. It has done more, on the whole, for boys than for girls. It has been more effective with the academically able pupils than with those whose talents have lain in other directions. It has provided better for city pupils than for boys and girls in the small towns and the country.

Moreover, the current program has not always swept clean in those areas in which its positive results are most apparent. Though it has equipped most young people with the tools of learning, it has allowed appreciable numbers of boys and girls to leave school without having learned to read and write and use arithmetic well enough to meet normal out-of-school needs. It has been most effective, in the main, with young people whose abilities are of a bookish sort; but even among boys and girls of marked academic ability it has failed to challenge many to their best achievement.

AREAS OF SOCIAL COMPETENCE NOT TOUCHED BY THE PRESENT PROGRAM

The present educational program has notably failed to develop certain types of competence. Though it has supplied much academic information, it has neglected to equip boys and girls with pertinent knowledge about their local communities, their chances to make a living, and the educational opportunities open to them once they leave the high school. As a result, thousands of young people just out of school are equipped to take no well-informed part in civic affairs; they look at random for jobs which may never materialize; they plan for further education which they can never attain, and which would often be of little use to them even if they could get it.

Despite some success in acquainting boys and girls with their rights as citizens, neither the schools nor any other social influences have developed in these boys and girls an active social conscience. High school pupils on the point of leaving school display, on the contrary, a disturbing inclination to evade social responsibility, and young people who have left school undertake few activities which will contribute in any way to the public good.

Nor have any large numbers of these young people attained standards of enjoyment which lead them to make particularly discriminating use of their leisure time. What boys and girls read when they are free to choose what they will read, what they like to listen to on the radio, what they see in the movies, give evidence of little discriminating preference, except the preference for something that is exciting, romantic, or "funny."

In the field of competence which is most on the minds of the boys and girls themselves—vocational ability—the present program seems to have done least of all for the young people who have been subject to it. The great majority have developed no salable vocational skills; they have learned nothing about the kinds of work in which they are most likely to be successful; they do not know how to make the most of the jobs they eventually get.

In all these matters the present educational program fails large numbers of high school pupils in New York State. It falls farthest short of developing competence on the part of the boys and girls who most need help—the young people from homes low in the social scale, whom financial need or lack of encouragement or lack of success with traditional academic work drives out of school before they have earned a high school diploma.

· 119 ·

EDUCATIONAL PROBLEMS DEMANDING ATTENTION

This listing of present educational outcomes will serve to suggest the educational problems which most demand attention in New York State.

Academic education, in the sense of training for scholarship, is not the most pressing of these problems. There is no denying the need for more discriminating selection of the young people who can best profit by academic education, or for more thorough and systematic preparation of these young people for an education beyond the high school. But that need applies at present only to some of the young people of high school age, and is not the whole need even of the boys and girls most directly affected by it.

The more serious problems are to be found in the lack of tangible connection between what boys and girls learn while they are in school and what they will need to know after they leave school. A fund of largely academic information, a set of social attitudes picked up at random, tastes and interests developed as chance may dictate, provide no stable basis for the welfare either of individuals or of the State to which they belong. If it is to deserve public support, the program of secondary education must produce more tangible results than at present in the form of systematic preparation for citizenship and leisure and jobs. If it is to accomplish all that needs accomplishing, that program must concern itself quite as much with the young people who are not academically successful as with those whose easiest learning comes from books.

PART II

The Secondary School Program

CHAPTER VIII

The Secondary School Curriculum

SECONDARY education in New York State has been considered thus far from the standpoint of its outcomes. The question of why those outcomes are reasonably adequate in certain respects but quite inadequate in others must obviously be answered in terms of the educational process—of what is done to and for boys and girls in the course of their educational growing up. The schools, it should be said again, are only one of the agencies which determine the eventual social competence of young people. Yet the influence of the schools is so important that an accounting for young people's present competence may properly give first place to a consideration of what the schools in particular do for boys and girls. Such an accounting ought logically to begin with a description of the schools' programs of studies and their methods of teaching.

SUBJECTS STUDIED

The programs of studies of the New York State high schools are remarkably uniform from school to school. Their fundamental pattern is chiefly determined by the requirements of the State Education Department for Regents' diplomas. Certain subjects must be included in the work of pupils who are to be candidates for the diplomas; these subjects accordingly tend to be provided for first of all in the programs of individual high schools. Though small schools offer fewer subjects than large schools, and the relatively few schools which have been organized as junior and senior high schools present occasional departures from the standard list of subjects, the core of the program is essentially the same irrespective of the size of the school concerned or of the type of organization the school has adopted.

Under this program, *the subjects that high school pupils have a chance to study are usually restricted to the general academic subjects required or accepted for college admission, to subjects intended as preparation for commercial work, and to courses in home economics.* English; Latin and French; algebra and geometry; general science, physics, and chemistry; history, civics, and economics; design and representation; mechanical drawing; harmony and the rudiments of music—these subjects, with one or two periods a week of required physical training,[1] represent the basic offerings of the majority of secondary schools. For boys and girls to whom the standard courses are ill-suited, most schools offer introduction to business, business arithmetic, economic geography, bookkeeping, typewriting and short-hand, and business law. For girls the schools are likely to provide also a limited amount of training in household arts, frequently confined to cooking and sewing.

The omissions from this program are striking. In recent years the high schools in rural areas have more and more often offered vocational work in agriculture as a part of their programs. Despite this trend, courses in agriculture are still entirely lacking in the programs of almost 60 per cent of the schools in predominantly agricultural districts. Courses in industrial arts for boys are even rarer than are courses in agriculture. The ninth grade general shop course, which is more frequently offered than any other course in this field, is given in fewer than 25 per cent of the high schools of the State. Most noteworthy of all is the omission of specialized vocational training in industrial subjects. There are 110 towns and cities in New York State with populations of 5,000 or

[1] Secondary school offerings in health education and physical training are not extensively dealt with in this report. For a discussion of the health program in the New York State schools, see C.-E. A. Winslow, *The School Health Program*, Regents' Inquiry, 1938.

more, nearly all of which are industrial communities. Ninety-seven of these towns and cities make no provision for vocational industrial or technical education.

With the program of studies limited in this way, it is not surprising that *more than three-fourths of all the work which boys and girls were "taking" in New York State high schools in 1937 was academic work or work in music and art, and most of the remainder consisted of training for business.* Courses in English accounted for a fifth of all subject enrollments; courses in history and other social studies for a seventh; foreign language courses for an eighth; courses in science for a tenth; courses in mathematics for a twelfth. All the art courses and all the music courses together attracted about the same enrollments as the courses in foreign languages. Commercial work accounted for approximately a sixth of all subject enrollments. In other vocational and semivocational fields combined, the total enrollments were fewer than in the single subject of French: $2\frac{1}{4}$ per cent in industrial arts, one fifth of 1 per cent in agriculture, $1\frac{7}{8}$ per cent in homemaking and home economics.

CONTENT AND METHODS OF TEACHING

The General Subjects

The predominantly academic flavor of the high school program is only partly indicated by the names of the subjects which pupils study. English, the social studies, science, and the other general subjects might be taught—and in some schools they are taught—in such a way as to have direct bearing on pupils' out-of-school concerns. Analysis of courses of study and visits to hundreds of classrooms make it evident, however, that in the main there is little relation between the general school courses and out-of-school problems. *Most of the teaching of general subjects in the high schools consists of drill on technical skills, and memorization of a kind of factual material which is significant to pupils chiefly because it is useful in passing examinations.*

· 125 ·

The content of the high school subjects and the methods by which they are taught can be described in broad terms because, like the basic program of studies, the subject matter of the separate courses is remarkably standardized. In order to be eligible for state diplomas, pupils must pass Regents' Examinations in specified subjects. These examinations, administered on a state-wide basis, tend to establish the goals of teaching in individual schools. Uniformity in preparing for the examinations is encouraged by the issuance of state syllabi, outlining for teachers the recommended subject matter in the various fields. Occasionally the syllabi are much more liberal than the examinations. This is true in the field of English, for example: the course of study which the state syllabus outlines in that field is a model in its realistic attention to a wide range of pupils' interests, abilities, and needs, whereas the Examinations ordinarily test merely acquaintance with "standard" literature and ability in formal language usage. But the success of teachers and pupils alike is largely gauged by the results of the Examinations; so that whatever the syllabus may suggest, the usual practice is to emphasize in the classroom the particular kind of subject matter most likely to make a good showing in terms of examination marks.

This practice leads, in the teaching of English, to extensive drills on technical grammar, a large amount of work in more or less formal written composition, and the reading by all members of the class of a few standard selections from English literature of the type usually included in the traditional college-preparatory English course. The high schools rarely pay any great amount of attention to oral expression, notwithstanding the fact that the major problem of English teaching in a large proportion of schools in New York State is a speech problem. Nor do they teach pupils who are deficient in reading ability how to read. Instruction in the mechanics of reading finds a place in the high school program only as some individual teacher or supervisor, aware of the seriousness of the problem, seeks to deal with it independently.

The courses in foreign languages offered in the majority of high schools are what their names imply—courses intended to develop ability to read and write Latin, or to read, write, and speak French or Spanish or German or Italian.[2] The language courses emphasize drill on vocabulary and grammar, written and oral translation from the foreign language into English, written and oral translation from English into the foreign language. Enrolling few pupils who follow them for more than two or three years, the courses give to the majority of the boys and the girls who elect them only the most rudimentary acquaintance with a foreign tongue.

In the field of the social studies the teaching chiefly emphasizes historical facts. The study of government that is provided for in the classes in civics usually pays more attention to the structure of government than to a realistic analysis of how government works. The economics taught is largely impersonal and institutional; it deals with broad tendencies rather than with immediate problems, and with abstract economic "laws" rather than with the personal and individual uses of economics. Many schools deal with current events in connection with their history courses, but the teaching is likely to dwell on factual information, with little attention to underlying social tendencies or fundamental social problems. Question-and-answer represents the characteristic teaching method, directed toward the acquisition of a large amount of information about dates, names, and events. Pupils' attitudes are almost entirely neglected: items of knowledge, rather than loyalties, ideals, or ways of thinking, represent the outcomes by which pupils' learning is chiefly judged.

Courses in science and mathematics are for the most part designed as introductions to advanced study in these fields. General science has been added to the traditional courses

[2] Greek has practically disappeared from the high school offering.

in physics and chemistry, and general biology is being offered in increasing numbers of schools, but specialized courses aimed chiefly at preparation for college still outnumber the courses planned to help pupils understand common aspects of their environment or appreciate the significance of science in everyday life. In mathematics the usual subject matter is even more formal than it is in science. Elementary, intermediate, and advanced algebra, plane and solid geometry, and trigonometry constitute the bulk of the courses offered; general mathematics, either as a substitute for elementary algebra or as a course for pupils who lack the ability or the inclination to do specialized work in mathematics, is found in less than one school in eight.

In music and art chief attention is devoted to technical performance. Instruction in music is in many schools curiously akin to coaching in athletic activities: its emphasis is on the development of musical "teams," namely, bands, orchestras, and choruses, which compete with similar organizations from other schools. Where musical expression is not the chief aim, the teaching has to do with the technical matters of harmony and the rudiments of composition more often than with the general appreciation of music. Courses in appreciation are rarely offered for pupils who do not elect specialized work in music, so that most pupils have little or no opportunity in school to develop habits or attitudes which will make them intelligent listeners to the music that comes to them through the sound film or the radio or the phonograph. The work in art is likewise largely concerned with techniques. Courses in the appreciation of art are ordinarily found only in the larger schools; the courses in design and representation and in mechanical drawing which are more commonly offered lay chief emphasis on developing pupils' ability to draw.

It is apparent that in all these fields of study the subject matter chiefly emphasized is that which is commonly regarded as important in academic scholarship. Unfortunately the methods of teaching most often used are not those which can be expected to produce scholarship in any real sense. The daily routine consists principally of drill by memoriter methods on more or less disconnected items of information, practice in formal skills for which high school boys and girls have little immediate use and whose value to scholars they are in no position to appreciate, and examinations and quizzes in preparation for the all-important tests by which high school success is measured. Practically all the class time of pupils who are candidates for academic diplomas is spent in this kind of study. Even the pupils who elect to specialize in business or homemaking are likely to devote not less than half their school hours to work in which the traditional motive of academic scholarship is dominant.

Business and Household Arts

The courses in business and in homemaking and home economics with which the majority of high schools supplement their academic work are primarily intended as terminal courses for pupils who will not go on to college. Planned in part to meet the needs of pupils who cannot attain traditional high school standards, they differ in important respects from the general academic work.

Business courses are in most schools so organized as to lead to a special business diploma. They may be credited, however, as part of the programs of pupils enrolled in the general curriculum, and are frequently chosen by such pupils either for their supposedly general values or as an escape from more exacting academic work. They are often chosen by other pupils who become candidates for the business diploma but who have no definite intention of going into business as a vocation.

Despite their popularity for nonvocational purposes, almost none of the business subjects are so planned as to contribute effectively to general education. The present courses

are not designed to provide pupils with any broad understanding of business relationships as a part of their individual
economic education, nor do these courses offer an opportunity
to develop the knowledge and skills most useful to the consumer of business services. Instead, the work is conceived
strictly as preparation for vocational life. It consists for the
most part of practice on specialized vocational skills and drill
on information supposedly useful in business occupations.
Its outcomes are tested by Regents' Examinations similar to
those in the general academic fields.

The business courses, notwithstanding their vocational
aims, offer useful vocational preparation to only a fraction
of the pupils enrolled in them. The vocational values of the
courses are limited in part by the fact that the training which
they provide is usually training merely for clerical service—
chiefly routine typewriting, stenography, and bookkeeping.
A few large schools offer training for office machine workers
and retail sales people. The majority of high schools, lacking
any equipment except typewriters, provide courses which
fall short even in the clerical field of meeting present-day
needs and standards in business practice.

The vocational values of the courses are limited also by the
general lack of valid standards either for admission to such
courses or for graduation from the business curriculum. In
many schools business subjects offer the only recourse for
pupils who have been unsuccessful in the traditional academic
program. Such pupils are often freely admitted to business
training regardless of deficiencies in general capacity or in
fundamental skills; they find it possible to "pass" because the
standards of the business courses and the examinations
applying to these courses have been gradually adjusted to
pupils of lower and lower ability. In all schools the factors
of age and maturity as requirements for entrance into business occupations are largely ignored. Few business concerns
will employ young people who are not at least eighteen years

of age; yet a majority of representative high schools offering specialized training for business reported in 1937 that the average age of their business graduates was below eighteen. Because of a general disregard for business standards, graduation from the business curriculum bears little relation to readiness for vocational employment. The absence of realistic standards was strikingly emphasized by the statements of fifty-eight high school principals who submitted supplementary reports to the Inquiry on their business curricula. Only six of these principals reported that all their business graduates were fully prepared for employment. Seventeen estimated that of the pupils leaving their schools who had met the requirements for business diplomas, 60 per cent or more were not employable in business occupations at the going rate of pay for beginners—were not competent, that is, to start at the bottom rung of the ladder.[3]

Thus, *the principal value of the present business-education courses in New York State high schools is to provide elementary clerical training for the relatively few boys and girls who are to become stenographers and typists.* The content of these courses bears only remotely on the probable vocational needs of the great majority of the pupils who enroll in them. The courses do not provide general economic education. Neither do they offer any essentially new kind of learning for most pupils, since the methods of teaching ordinarily used in them represent little variation from the drill and memoriter learning characteristic of the academic subjects in the high school program.

The offering in household arts, unlike that in business training, is definitely planned both for vocational pupils and for pupils who elect work in household arts as part of their general education. For the vocational pupils, high schools commonly provide a group of courses in vocational home-

---

[3] These figures are based not on reports with respect to individual leaving pupils, but on principals' replies to a general question as to the competence of graduates of vocational curricula.

making, emphasizing the development of desirable habits and skills in home and family life, and including supervised home projects as a part of the training program. Nonvocational pupils have open to them in many schools a parallel group of courses emphasizing the understanding and appreciation of home problems, rather than the development of particular skills. Both groups of courses treat much the same general topics—the selection and preparation of food and clothing, house planning, house furnishing, and house care. The vocational homemaking curriculum devotes a year's work, in addition, to home management, home nursing, child study, and family life. The vocational courses meet for double class-periods and represent a major part of the school program of pupils who elect them. The nonvocational courses, like elective courses in other fields, are organized in single-period classes.

Despite the fact that they deal with various problems of concern to both men and women, the courses in homemaking and household arts seldom enroll boys. For girls these courses may provide an opportunity to learn about matters of obvious importance, under methods of teaching which give a large place to dealing with real materials, discussing immediate problems, and measuring results in terms of habits and skills useful in normal out-of-school life. In numerous schools the courses are actively sought by girls who recognize the work as a valuable preparation for home activities and home life.

The courses in household arts have frequently suffered, however, and in some schools they still suffer, from over-emphasis on the mere mechanics of housekeeping. Furthermore, the nonvocational courses tend to be offered only to the extent to which the demands for vocational work do not completely preempt available equipment and teachers' time. In schools which provide only the vocational courses, girls who are interested in home economics as a part of their general education are likely to elect little or no work in this field because of the large time allotments which the vocational work requires. For this reason as well as because of the lack of favor in which they are sometimes held, the contribution which the courses actually make to general education is notably limited.

The value of the courses is limited also from the standpoint of vocational training. The program in vocational home-making, as its name implies, is restricted to the development of domestic abilities. Only in the largest schools does this program provide direct training for vocations outside the home, for example, for restaurant and cafeteria service, beauty-shop work, and related occupations. In the majority of high schools the sole type of paid employment toward which the home-making program clearly leads is domestic service. Few high school girls except those who despair of succeeding in other fields are willing to look forward to being servants. As a result, the vocational homemaking courses in most schools attract relatively few pupils, and those from the least able intellectually of the schools' enrollment.

Of the present courses in household arts it may be said, in summary, that *the home economics courses, designed as a part of general secondary education, often deal directly and constructively with problems of real concern in family life, but attract a very meager proportion of the girls who might profit from them, and enroll almost no boys. The vocational homemaking courses tend to lead only to domestic service as a strictly vocational outcome; their possible value as a contribution to general education is for the most part defeated by their large time allotments and their frequent overemphasis on mechanics.*

It should be recalled that business courses and courses in home economics and homemaking represent the only alternatives to conventional academic work for the pupils in most New York State high schools. The narrowness of the resulting program is apparent. Boys may choose between courses chiefly designed to start them on the road toward academic scholarship—a road which few will follow beyond the high school—and courses which train them in certain routine clerical skills. Girls are offered these same choices. In addition, girls in certain schools have an opportunity to elect courses which may enable them to take a more intelligent part in family life. Girls also have open to them the chance to prepare for employment as domestic servants.

Industrial and Technical Courses

Though they appear at present in the programs of few schools and are open to relatively small numbers of pupils, industrial and technical courses deserve special consideration as an expanding part of the secondary school program. Enrollments in vocational industrial curricula, in particular, more than tripled during the depression, rising from 18,370 in 1932 to 63,572 in 1937.

The industrial education program at the secondary school level comprises four major types of courses. Offered as a part of the program of general education in about a fourth of the academic high schools are courses in industrial arts, designed to give boys some acquaintance with industrial processes and industrial occupations. Similar courses are offered in the seventh and eighth grades of certain elementary schools, with the result that pupils in approximately one-third of the school systems of the State have a chance to elect work in industrial arts. Specialized vocational industrial curricula, leading to industrial certificates or diplomas, are provided by two state agricultural schools and by academic high schools or separate vocational schools in thirteen school systems, including New York City and Buffalo. Vocational technical curricula are offered by ten of these school systems. Part-time continuation school courses, required by law in the larger school systems for pupils who leave school to go to work before they have reached the age limit of compulsory attendance, provide instruction in general school subjects for employed young people between sixteen and eighteen years of age.

Of these four types of courses, the continuation school programs may be dismissed with very brief comment. These courses were instituted at a time when boys and girls sixteen years old found it relatively easy to obtain employment in unskilled or semiskilled industrial and commercial occupations. With the growing scarcity of work among adults, it has become increasingly difficult for young people in the cities to get jobs before they are at least eighteen years old, the age at which the continuation school law ceases to apply. Continuation school enrollments have therefore fallen off so rapidly in recent years that many continuation schools have been either abandoned or, as in New York City, converted into full-time industrial schools. General economic trends make it seem practically certain that opportunities for industrial and commercial employment will not again be open to any large number of sixteen- and seventeen-year-old pupils. The few remaining continuation courses thus represent an educational anachronism; their place will eventually be filled almost automatically by full-time school work.

General industrial arts courses, unlike the continuation courses, are a growing part of the secondary school program. These courses represent a constructive development of the manual training courses introduced in the upper elementary and lower high school grades early in the twentieth century. Ideally, their purpose is to give boys, and girls who are interested, first-hand acquaintance with various simple industrial processes, as a means of broadening their understanding of modern occupations and providing them with possible avocational interests. They are not intended to develop vocational skills. Organized in such a way as to allow pupils to try themselves out in a variety of manipulative processes—work with wood and metal, plastics and stone, textiles and electricity— they may nevertheless contribute to effective educational and vocational guidance, and for pupils who eventually go into

· 135 ·

industrial occupations they may lay the foundation for valuable vocational adaptability. Unfortunately only a few of the industrial arts courses in New York State high schools are thus organized. Many of the present courses are limited to woodworking; they emphasize practice on formal skills more often than an understanding of general processes. So far as their direct contribution to general education is concerned, the majority of the industrial arts courses as now given are likely to have, at most, a somewhat limited avocational value for the relatively few pupils to whom they are open.

The vocational industrial courses are intended to provide thorough training for specific trades. Certain of these courses enroll pupils fourteen years of age who have completed the sixth grade but have demonstrated a lack of capacity for the regular school program. The majority are planned for pupils who have completed the eighth grade; they are usually open without other admission requirements to any pupils who choose to elect them, though in various school systems the numbers of pupils applying for admission have increased so rapidly that divers means of selection are being employed. All the vocational industrial courses are so administered as to be eligible for federal subsidies under the Smith-Hughes Act. This means that vocational pupils are required to devote half the school day to shopwork, and to divide the remainder of their time equally between classroom work related to their shopwork and general or academic subjects. In the shop experience which they present, the vocational courses parallel as closely as can be managed under school conditions the shop conditions which pupils must face on the jobs for which they are preparing. Instruction in shopwork is largely individualized; each pupil completes a prearranged series of jobs, working as rapidly as his ability permits. Related classroom work, like the shopwork, draws its subject matter from actual job requirements. The academic subjects studied by vocational pupils (usually English and social studies) differ little in content from the academic courses open to nonvocational pupils, though they may be stepped down in difficulty to accord with the generally lower academic ability of the vocational group.

The restriction of the vocational industrial work to a very few school systems has already been mentioned. Of equal interest is the high degree of specialization characteristic of the industrial courses. In the schools in which these courses are offered, the industrial program has tended to ramify into a large number of specialized curricula. New York City offers 42 kinds of vocational industrial curricula for boys, 18 kinds for girls, and 8 vocational commercial curricula for both boys and girls—a total of 68 specialized vocational programs, not counting technical programs. Buffalo provides 25 separate and distinct vocational curricula. Rochester offers 19 such curricula, and Yonkers and Mount Vernon each offer 10. Academic high schools with vocational departments are less likely than the specialized vocational schools to provide large numbers of separate curricula, but even in the academic schools the usual number of specialized vocational curricula is four or five.

This high degree of specialization is particularly significant in view of the nature of the training which the vocational courses present. Under the provisions of the Smith-Hughes Act the instruction given in these courses is not expected to be general, that is to say, preparatory to a variety of industrial occupations, but relatively specific—directed toward a particular occupation. Accordingly, the work in each curriculum ordinarily tends to be focused on a single kind of job. In the vocational departments of academic high schools the occupations for which training is most frequently offered are electrical work, machine shop work, woodwork, auto mechanics, drafting, and sheet-metal work. The specialized vocational schools present training for these same occupations, and in addition, offer separate curricula in aviation mechanics, barbering, beauty culture, clock and optical mechanics, dress manufacturing, fur manufacturing, ladies' garment design, jewelry making, meat merchandising, shoe manufacturing and repairing, sign and show card making, to list only a few of the sixty-eight curricula offered in New York City.

Insofar as ability in one occupation may fit a boy or girl to engage successfully in a closely related occupation, training in any of these curricula may prepare for a number of different jobs. Indeed, much of the training presented in certain of the separate curricula—auto mechanics and aviation mechanics, for instance—is practically identical. The courses are not ordinarily taught, however, in such a way as to make pupils fully aware of these facts. So far as could be determined by the Inquiry staff, the work in most of the vocational courses emphasizes specialization to such an extent that pupils completing the courses often regard themselves as ready only for a single very limited kind of job.[4]

Moreover, the training offered in certain of the vocational industrial courses is not well adjusted to requirements for beginning workers in industry. Though shop courses parallel job conditions, the courses sometimes graduate large numbers of specialized workers for whom there is no demand. In one small city, for example, the vocational school principal reported that none of the pupils who were being regularly graduated from the woodworking curriculum in his school could expect to obtain jobs in the occupation in which they had been trained, for the simple reason that for some years there had been no local openings in woodworking. In other schools lack of adjustment is due not so much to lack of job opportunities as to the poor calibre of certain of the pupils graduated from vocational courses. Principals of nine out of nineteen industrial and technical schools whose officers pre-

[4] Note, in this connection, the frequent complaint of vocational school graduates that they had been unable to find employment in exactly the kind of occupation for which they had been prepared. (See Chapter V.)

pared detailed reports for the Inquiry estimated that appreciable numbers of their graduates were unemployable at the going rate of pay for beginners in the occupations for which they had been trained. In one city the principal reported that 40 per cent were below par in employability because of lack of skill, lack of ambition, or absence of any honest desire to do a good job. In another city the principal of a girls' vocational school estimated that as many as 45 per cent of the graduates of the curriculum in vocational dressmaking were below the necessary level of attainment for similar reasons.

Lack of adjustment between the industrial courses and job requirements also appears in the fact that certain of the courses train pupils to a degree of specialization which is of no practical advantage to them even in the occupations for which they have been prepared. An outstanding example of overtraining is furnished by some of the courses in printing. Certain of these courses provide training which is sufficiently intensive to prepare large numbers of pupils for journeyman's work; yet organized labor will not accept the graduates of these schools at the journeyman level. Therefore the pupils are obliged to enter the trade as apprentices, going through the same schedule of learning on the job that pupils do who have not had the advanced training. In connection with various other vocational courses principals reported that their schools were providing specialized training definitely beyond that which would give beginning pupils an advantage either in initial employment or in later promotion.

It should be noted that the vocational industrial program in general rarely includes training for semiskilled occupations. Boys and girls who lack the physical dexterity or the general intelligence necessary to let them become skilled workers may sometimes graduate from the vocational courses, but not more than four or five of the present vocational schools have developed a training program systematically adapted to their abilities and needs. It should be noted also that little has been done at the secondary level to provide apprenticeship training in cooperation with industry. The vocational courses are almost without exception in-school courses; they do not ordinarily provide for either part-time or full-time job placements as a substitute for work in the school shops.

Vocational technical curricula, the fourth major type of industrial program, are intended to prepare pupils for employment in industrial occupations in which knowledge of processes or methods is more important than skill of hand. Current industrial conditions have led to an increasing demand for workers who can produce, operate, and maintain machines, and for large numbers of trained draftsmen, technicians, junior engineers, and junior supervisors. The technical curricula represent an effort to meet this demand. They are so planned as to give as broad an education as possible at the secondary level, in mathematics, science, and technology in a given field of industry. At present they prepare for only a limited number of fields—chiefly electrical engineering, mechanical engineering, chemistry, and architecture and building construction.

Unlike the vocational industrial curricula, most of the technical curricula prepare pupils for entrance to higher institutions. This fact lends them a social respectability which the industrial curricula do not have. The emphasis commonly given to college preparation in the technical curricula, and the respect accorded these curricula because they do prepare for college, partially defeat their purpose as terminal curricula for pupils planning to go to work as soon as they leave the high school. Pupils are not ordinarily admitted to technical courses unless they give promise of being unusually successful in academic work. Once admitted, they are held to academic standards of such a nature that large numbers either transfer to other programs or drop out of school without graduating. As a result, the technical curricula now serve relatively few of the pupils who might actually benefit by vocational training on a higher level than that offered in the trade courses, but who are not looking forward to college work.

The educational value of the technical courses is restricted also by the fact that they are limited to four years. Between those occupations which can be adequately prepared for by a four-year high school program and those which demand a college degree lie an increasing number which require a year or two years or three years of training beyond the high school level. Junior engineering occupations, for example, can be prepared for only by exceptionally capable young people if the training program must be compressed within four years of high school work, though these occupations do not necessarily demand four additional years of college education. Laboratory assistants, dental technicians, junior surveyors, supervisors of various industrial processes likewise need more than high school and less than four-year college training. Higher institutions in New York State have been slow to recognize the educational requirements of these intermediate vocations. The high school technical curricula do not adequately meet such requirements, partly because they offer training for a very limited number of technical fields, partly because they have thus far been confined within a rigid four-year pattern.[5]

All the various industrial programs together, in school systems which offer the major types of industrial courses, represent a notable effort to extend the educational opportunities open to high school boys and girls. At the same time these courses are subject to limitations which need to be clearly recognized. With positive contributions and limitations both in mind, the current program of industrial education may be summarized as follows, in terms of the three most important groups of industrial courses:

[5] Though one or two schools are now planning fifth-year programs, postgraduate pupils in technical high schools have not regularly had open to them a fifth year of training offered as part of a unified five-year curriculum. In common with academic postgraduates, they have ordinarily had a chance merely to elect undergraduate subjects which they have not already taken.

The courses in industrial arts, which are intended to form a part of the high school program of general education, provide for the development of certain avocational interests and skills (principally in woodworking), but are rarely comprehensive enough or sufficiently concerned with basic processes to add much to pupils' understanding of industrial occupations in general.

The vocational industrial curricula offer training for a large number of skilled occupations under school conditions paralleling shop conditions in the occupations themselves. These curricula seldom prepare pupils to shift from one vocation to another, nor do they ordinarily offer training for semiskilled work. They graduate many pupils who are well prepared for specific skilled occupations. They also graduate many pupils who are admittedly not ready to succeed in the occupations for which these pupils have been trained; certain other pupils they overtrain; and they sometimes prepare considerable numbers of pupils for occupations in which there are few local openings.

The vocational technical courses, though designed as terminal courses for pupils planning to enter junior technical occupations, are often chiefly college-preparatory courses. They attract an able group of pupils, to whom they furnish preparation in fundamental mathematics, science, and technology, but they are at present neither long enough nor varied enough to offer a comprehensive program of technical education.

Courses in Agriculture

Whereas industrial curricula tend to be found only in school systems in the largest cities, courses in agriculture in the New York State high schools are offered almost exclusively in small rural schools. The two types of courses are seldom offered in the same schools. Though enrollments in agriculture have grown less rapidly than enrollments in industrial courses—from 3,442 in 1932 to 7,154 in 1937—agricultural education, like industrial education, has become an increasingly important part of the secondary school program.

High school work in agriculture is offered entirely for purposes of vocational training. Except for the first year of the four-year program, classes are ordinarily scheduled for double periods, and pupils are required to carry out extensive home projects as a part of their training. The work of the first year includes an agricultural survey of the local community; that of the later years is intended both to give pupils some acquaintance with farm operations in general—animal husbandry, the raising of the commoner farm crops, the care of farm implements—and to develop initial skills in the particular types of operations most appropriate locally. The courses give considerably less attention to the social and economic problems of farm life than to agricultural processes and skills. Though teachers of agriculture are allowed considerable latitude in varying the content of their courses to meet local needs, the present courses in agriculture generally follow a fairly uniform pattern, both as to the subjects with which they deal and as to the time allotted to these subjects.

In the majority of schools any pupil may be admitted to the work in agriculture who is at least fourteen years old, has completed the eighth grade, and is interested in taking up farming as a vocation. Reports from individual schools indicate that a majority of the graduates of the curriculum in agriculture do actually go into farming after they leave high school. The schools which provide the training in agriculture are commonly village schools, however, and enroll numerous pupils who have neither immediate opportunities to carry on effective home projects nor any real expectation of taking up farm work. Considerable numbers of these pupils elect work in agriculture because they have been unsuccessful in academic work or business training or both, and because the local school provides no other outlet for them. The courses in agriculture do not prepare these pupils for the nonagricultural vocations which are to be found in small communities, nor do they offer a substitute for the kind of general education which the academic program is intended to provide.

Concerning the total part played by the work in agriculture in the small schools in which this work is offered, it may therefore be said that *the agricultural curriculum is largely restricted to the provision of direct vocational training for pupils who are to earn their livings on farms.* The courses are not planned either as part of a program of general education or as a substitute for the academic program. They offer little of direct value to the numerous pupils who elect them for non-vocational purposes.

EXTRACURRICULAR ACTIVITIES

Academic work, courses in music and art, business training, general courses in home economics and industrial arts, and specialized industrial, technical, agricultural, and vocational homemaking curricula represent the range of the formal program of studies in New York State high schools. The teaching that the schools do cannot be completely assessed, however, without considering their extracurricular programs.

Reports from the schools show that *in addition to studying formal school subjects, pupils have a chance to take part under school auspices in a variety of recreational activities, in the meetings of informal subject matter clubs, in the publication of some sort of school periodical, and in character-building or school service organizations.*

Almost all the high schools provide dances, organized athletics, and musical organizations, and a large proportion of high school pupils participate actively in these recreations. The dances are ordinarily the only form of purely social activity which the schools sponsor. The organized athletics tend to be restricted to large-group sports. Boys usually have a chance to engage in football, baseball, track, and soccer; girls may take part in volleyball, softball, and soccer.[6] Spectator participation in sports is often actively encouraged among both boys and girls, in connection with interschool athletic competitions. The musical organizations, like the athletics, tend to place chief emphasis on large-group activities. A majority of the schools

[6] Basketball, interestingly enough, is not an outstanding sport in the New York State high schools in general.

have orchestras and glee clubs or choirs, and in all but the smallest schools there are likely, in addition, to be school bands. Except in the case of dancing, the school's supervision of these activities involves a considerable amount of teaching— perhaps more accurately described, in the case of musical activities as well as athletics, as coaching.

Subject matter clubs emphasize teaching of a different sort. The commonest of these clubs are sponsored as adjuncts to their class work by teachers of academic subjects, particularly English, foreign languages, and science. Clubs in social studies, mathematics, art, music, and vocational subjects, though frequently found in schools of all sizes, are less common than are clubs in the other three subjects. Whatever the subject with which the club deals, the membership of each club is usually drawn from the regular classes in that subject. Usually the club activities are not essentially different from classroom activities. The pupils in English clubs chiefly read and discuss books; foreign language club members read books and talk about them; mathematics club members solve mathematics problems; natural science club members perform "experiments"; social-studies club members study and discuss social problems and current events; and so on. The clubs frequently serve, indeed, as elective classes in school subjects: they meet on school time, in special periods of the weekly schedule, and they are sometimes administered in such a way that each pupil is required to "belong" to one or more of them. The chief difference between club activities and the usual classroom activities seems to be that most schools make club work more pleasant than class work. Club work is commonly less rigorous, and the club program frequently includes dancing, games, and refreshments.

School publications serve various and somewhat ill-defined purposes in the various high schools. In the larger schools, school newspapers often represent an outgrowth of elective classes in journalism. Other schools support newspapers, class annuals, and occasional "literary" magazines (these last are less and less common) partly as a means of motivating the work in English composition, partly because of long-established custom. The number of pupils actively engaged in producing the school publications is usually small; participation by the majority is likely to be limited to buying and reading.

Character-building organizations in the schools most commonly take the form of Boy Scout and Girl Scout troops, chapters of the Junior Red Cross, and Hi-Y and 4-H clubs. Adults from outside the school are frequently in charge of these groups. The schools themselves tend to sponsor some form of student council, together with subordinate organizations which provide various types of personal service to the school. The student councils range from a relatively small number which are enthusiastically supported by pupils and teachers alike, and which take an important and responsible part in the direction and oversight of the life of the school, to many which serve chiefly as agents of the faculty in administering routine forms of pupil control. The subordinate personal-service groups are usually entrusted with responsibility not so much for planning and organizing as for performing certain recurrent duties. Their most common type of service consists of the supervision of student traffic at street crossings. Messenger service and management of traffic in school corridors, oversight of pupils being transported in school busses, and ushering and the sale of tickets in connection with school programs to which the public are admitted, are illustrations of other duties frequently undertaken by such groups. Most of these duties enlist relatively small numbers of pupils as active participants. Neither the character-building organizations nor the service groups enroll a majority of the pupils in most high schools, and in numerous schools only a small fraction of the total group of pupils are actively enlisted in any sort of school civic activity.

Reports from the schools show further that *the extracurricular program as a whole almost never engages all the pupils in any single school*. Certain schools exclude from participation in non-athletic extracurricular activities, as well as in interscholastic athletics, all pupils whose scholarship is unsatisfactory. The majority exclude those whose personal conduct is objectionable. These policies probably account for only a small amount of nonparticipation, but the cost of the extracurricular program to individual pupils (from three dollars a year in the smaller schools to five dollars or more in large schools), the limited scope of the program in many schools, and the fact that most of the extracurricular activities are voluntary, tend to keep other pupils from engaging actively in them. In large schools particularly, it is usual to find fewer than a fourth of the pupils participating. Among schools of small or moderate size a substantial proportion report that fewer than half their pupils are actively engaged in any form of extracurricular activity.[7]

Consideration of the total program of extracurricular activities commonly found in the high schools makes it clear that *in most schools these informal activities reinforce, but do not greatly extend, the opportunities for learning provided by the formal program of studies*. For the most part the extracurricular program gives pupils a chance to apply the learning they have been doing in their classes. A few schools, but only a few in terms of relative numbers, have introduced clubs devoted to photography, crafts, aviation, etiquette, movies, conversation, exploring, marionettes, automobile driving, and similar unconventional and unacademic activities. A few others have sought to develop pupils' interests in small-group sports, for example, boxing, golf, tennis, swimming, bowling, ping-pong, horseshoes, fencing. Certain schools provide opportunity, like-

[7] Exact figures on the numbers of pupils engaged in extracurricular activities are difficult to obtain, partly because many schools keep no definite records of pupil participation, partly because various activities regarded as extracurricular in some schools are considered curricular in others.

wise, for small-group musical activities—fife-and-drum corps, harmonica clubs, vocal quartets, sextets, or octets. A very small number have attempted through the extracurricular program to extend their pupils' acquaintance with the local community, bringing boys and girls in touch with vocational activities, with civic affairs, and with social problems through firsthand contacts of a sort which the usual classwork fails to provide. But in most schools the extracurricular activities are as scholastic as the curricular work, in the sense that they are confined to matters which can be readily dealt with in the school building or on the school grounds. Like the program of studies, they tend to be focused on performance rather than on appreciation. Initiated and almost entirely dominated by the faculty in the great majority of schools, they seldom give opportunity for the development of pupil initiative and leadership, and they introduce few methods of teaching not already well established in the curricular program.

THE HIGH SCHOOL PROGRAM IN RELATION TO SOCIAL COMPETENCE

Young people cannot reasonably be expected to learn what they are given no chance to learn. If the boys and girls now leaving high school in New York State have not attained the kinds of competence they will need to make them good citizens and successful workers, it is fair to ask whether the schools have given them a chance to develop that competence.

The schools now emphasize, in their curricular and extra-curricular programs, the mastery of academic information, the development of certain clerical skills, participation in large-group athletics, performance in music and art, conformity with routine regulations as to group behavior. Pupils on the point of leaving school possess a relatively high measure of ability in most of these fields, as judged by such tests and observations as the Inquiry was able to conduct.

The majority of high schools give little or no place to the development of other types of competence, in which leaving pupils are notably deficient. They do not teach pupils directly and systematically about their local communities, or encourage them in any penetrating thinking about fundamental social problems, or get them to participate, by reading or listening to the radio, in out-of-school discussions of controversial matters. Most of the schools pay no direct attention to the development of social conscience. They seldom concern themselves systematically with such fundamental skills as reading, correct speech, and ability to deal with simple numerical problems, though many pupils enter the high school lacking a dependable mastery of these skills. They devote much less attention to the kind of literature with which pupils will be surrounded outside of school than to the academic classics. They usually give no consideration at all to the radio and the movies. Though they provide for the development of vocational skills in clerical occupations and in homemaking, in the one instance they offer training which is frequently out of line with actual business requirements and in the other instance they reach only a handful of pupils. These items and others like them add up to a considerable total of attitudes and abilities directly related to civic, leisure time, and vocational competence, and largely neglected by all but a few high schools.

It seems fair to conclude, in the light of what the schools do not teach, that *a major reason for young people's lack of success in meeting out-of-school problems is that the secondary schools give them insufficient chance to master important abilities which the out-of-school world will require of them.* What the schools actually teach they teach with reasonable effectiveness, but they fail entirely to teach many significant things which boys and girls are quite unlikely to learn except as the schools do teach them.

POSSIBILITY OF MORE EFFECTIVE INSTRUCTION

The fact that most schools now fail to teach certain things does not mean that these things are unteachable. The pupils who leave some of the New York State high schools are demonstrably better prepared for what lies ahead of them than are the pupils going out into the world from the average school. Careful study of the curricula of the exceptional schools makes it evident that *many desirable traits and abilities which high schools in general fail to develop in their pupils can be developed by methods which certain schools are already using*. If high schools were to address themselves directly to that end, there is ample reason to believe that boys and girls could be given a far higher degree of social competence than most of the young people now leaving school possess.

One illustration of what can be done in this respect is provided by the specialized vocational schools. The unusually successful vocational adjustments made by the graduates of these schools cannot be attributed entirely to the vocational school curricula. Vocational pupils have made up their minds even before they enter the specialized curricula to be satisfied with occupations relatively low in the economic scale. Moreover, vocational schools ordinarily assume responsibility for placing their graduates in jobs,[8] a service which academic high schools rarely provide. Both these factors help to explain the out-of-school histories of vocational graduates. But giving such factors all the weight properly due them, there can still be little question that the direct teaching provided in the vocational schools—the realistic experience offered in shops and related classes, the dealing with problems thoroughly meaningful to the pupils, the emphasis on preparation for a future which boys and girls themselves know that they are facing—plays a highly important part in the development of superior competence. Teaching of a similar sort, were it to be provided for the thousands of young people who are at present unable to take advantage of the vocational school program, would almost certainly add to the effectiveness of the average secondary school.

A further example of a type of competence which a few schools are already effectively developing is ability in reading.

[8] See Chapter IX.

It will be recalled that 10 per cent or more of the seniors in the average high school tested in the Inquiry failed to pass an eighth grade reading test. In one school all the seniors passed. This particular school was a small rural school, no more fortunately circumstanced than are most of the rural schools which the Inquiry investigated. It provided a plan of teaching, however, which was notably different from that of the typical high school. Its teacher of English administered to each entering ninth grade class a diagnostic test of reading ability. To pupils found to be low in ability she gave separate instruction in reading. She had these pupils read to her individually, so that she could be sure of the nature of their difficulties. She helped them to get from the local library, for leisure-time reading, books of a kind they liked, not too difficult for them to read easily and with enjoyment. She went over with them their reading assignments in other classes, helping them to find the meanings of unusual words and discussing with them the sense of what they read. Through these methods—methods, it should be noted, that are practicable in any high school—a school not greatly different from the average in other respects developed one form of competence which placed its pupils in the front rank of all those whose similar competence was measured.

The extracurricular program, as well as the formal program of studies, offers examples of unusually effective practice. Schools in which the social conscience of pupils—their willingness to "put themselves out" for the common good—was found to be definitely more active than the average were all of them schools in which the pupils were given a large measure of responsibility for certain phases of school life. They were not necessarily schools whose pupils came from unusually favored homes, or schools in communities with a tradition of good citizenship among the young people. One school whose pupils showed an especially strong sense of social obligation was, in fact, a school enrolling pupils from an economically poor rural district, in which a few years before it had been the custom for high school pupils to defy the teachers, abuse school property, and make themselves generally a nuisance. The change in the pupils' attitudes was reported to have been brought about by entrusting the pupils with complete authority and responsibility for certain school activities in which they were vitally interested. They were allowed to raise money by selling sandwiches and organizing "benefits," and to spend the money as they saw fit on projects which concerned the school as a whole. They took complete charge of the enforcement of certain school rules. Their growth in social concern and in healthy social attitudes owed much, it is clear, to the personal influence of one or two farseeing members of the school faculty. But the activities through which they had a chance to grow were activities which any secondary school can introduce if it will.

These particular examples are drawn from schools which have added distinctly new elements to their programs. Illustrations of effective teaching are not lacking, however, within the academic courses to which the high schools in general now give most of their attention.

In one school two programs in the social studies were being offered simultaneously at the time of the Inquiry. The program enrolling the larger number of pupils consisted of a relatively conventional arrangement of courses in ancient and mediaeval history, modern European history, and American history. An experimental program, in which more than a third of the social-studies pupils in the three upper grades were enrolled, provided for a study of world history in the tenth grade, of contemporary social problems in the eleventh grade, and of "the United States in the world, emphasizing domestic and foreign problems" in the twelfth grade. Scores in the tests given by the Inquiry showed that the achievement of the experimental-program pupils did not greatly differ from that of the larger group at the end of the tenth grade, but that at the end of the two succeeding grades the pupils taking the new program were increasingly better equipped than were those taking the old, in their information about current affairs, their knowledge of their own community, their acquaintance with social terms, and their attitudes toward democratic principles. The gains thus achieved had been brought about entirely within the framework of the academic curriculum.

Again, it has been noted that certain of the New York State high schools are doing unusually successful work, at least with their abler pupils, in the teaching of English composition. The key to the success of these schools seems to lie in the fact that instead of merely assigning topics for compositions which are written outside of school and checked up on in class, the teachers of English encourage much writing and developing of ideas in the classroom. Pupils are led to talk in class about their out-of-school experiences; they are helped to see the interest or significance of what has happened to them personally; they are then encouraged to write about their experiences in ways which will make their expression as vivid and concrete as possible. The results are clearly evident in the maturity and originality which the writing of these boys and girls displays.

The emphasis placed in these schools on their pupils' immediate experience suggests one further example of unusually effective teaching in an academic field that has already been mentioned—the social studies. The survey tests given in one of the centralized schools, which was some forty miles distant from the nearest city, showed extraordinarily high attainment by the pupils in acquaintance with current affairs and in understanding of social concepts. Most of the schools as remote as this one from urban newspapers and urban influences in general seemed to be seriously handicapped in developing social competence of this sort. The specialist who visited the school discovered in the methods of teaching used by the teacher of history the apparent answer to the question of how this particular school brought about an achievement so much above the average. "There was recitation and discussion aplenty in the class," he reported, "but there were also many extended and well-received explanatory 'lectures' by the teacher. The chief characteristic of these explanations was the fact that invariably they translated abstractions into concrete terms. Generalities about prices and price-fixing were dealt with in terms of the cost of the bottle of ink on the teacher's desk. The cow in a pasture which could be seen through the classroom window became the center of an explanation of economic aspects of dairying in particular and of agriculture in general. The teacher's flair for reducing abstractions to concrete terms seemed to be the basic explanation of her pupils' high achievement."

These examples are not intended to illustrate all the qualities which may enter into effective teaching.[9] Their purpose is to show the possibility of equipping boys and girls, not just in a few schools, but in many, with important attitudes, abilities, and understandings which they now lack. They will perhaps serve to suggest the kind of teaching which may result in a far greater contribution to social competence than most schools now make. That kind of teaching is fortunately neither unknown nor untried. It consists, first, in a recognition of pupils' own experiences and interests as a primary basis for successful learning. It consists, second, in direct and unremitting attention to the particular habits and abilities which a school wants its pupils to have. *Nonacademic habits and abilities are seldom achieved merely as a result of the teaching of academic subjects. They can be achieved in very considerable measure by defining the qualities which boys and girls ought to possess, and by aiming as directly toward those qualities as schools now aim toward academic achievement.*

[9] For an extended analysis of such qualities, and for further illustrations of promising methods and materials of teaching, see the separate Inquiry reports on special fields of teaching.

IMPROVEMENT IN THE CURRICULUM

The differences between the average school and schools which are attaining exceptional results do more than illustrate the specific methods by which competence may be developed. They suggest certain conditions which must be established before general improvement in the curriculum can be assured.

If schools in general are to provide as effective teaching as certain individual schools now provide, it is evident that they must break the academic mold in which most of their programs have been cast. The Inquiry discovered no single school making a better than average contribution to its pupils' social competence which had not departed in important respects from the usual program of secondary education. Successful departure from the conventional program has not thus far meant, and ought not to mean, an abandonment of academic courses. Almost certainly, however, it must involve extensive changes in the content of those courses, together with the addition of subject matter and methods of teaching which now find small place in the average school.

If schools in general are to add effectively to their pupils' social competence, *it is clear also that they must give much closer attention than most high schools now give to pupils' out-of-school needs.* The usual academic curriculum is only remotely related to the pressing out-of-school concerns of the great majority of boys and girls. The subject matter which it includes has been selected because of tradition, or because educated people a generation ago were familiar with that subject matter, or because a few young people will find use for it in college courses. The academic curriculum as a whole rests its claim to general value on faith that it will be effective, and not on any pragmatic testing of its outcomes. Even the vocational curricula, which have been derived from more straightforward scrutiny of pupils' out-of-school needs, have not been consistently sensitive to those needs. Vocational schools obviously ought not to overtrain certain pupils and undertrain others; they ought not to prepare pupils for jobs which are not merely lacking at present but unlikely to materialize in the future; they ought not to educate boys and girls in such a way as to make them resistant to normal occupational changes. Any curriculum, vocational or general, which is to make a maximum contribution to young people's social competence must be continuously sensitive to social needs and must change as those needs change.

Finally, if schools in general are to provide more effective teaching, *it is evident that there must be continual trial of promising methods and subject matter under conditions which allow for pragmatic testing of their effectiveness.* The Inquiry has identified certain methods of teaching which are of demonstrable value. All these methods have been the outcome of intelligent variation of the curricula of individual schools. It would be idle to assume that they are the best methods that can ever be devised, or the only methods by which desirable goals may be reached. If the high school curriculum is to be kept alive to changing needs, and if it is to be responsive to the best means that can be discovered for meeting those needs, it must have room in it for continued variation. With that variation ought to go what few high schools have yet attempted—provision for the conscientious testing of new procedures in terms of the actual competence which they develop in boys and girls.

Departure from convention, realistic attention to pupils' out-of-school needs, and a pragmatic attitude toward the results of teaching are not unattainable in New York State. The readiness of the schools to profit by just these conditions is evidenced by the attitudes of school officers toward the present high school curricula. At the outset of the Inquiry each of the high school principals of the State was asked to describe in writing the problems which had recently given him most concern in the administration of his school. The responses to this request emphasized repeatedly the restricted nature of the local programs of studies. Of more than six hundred principals who replied, 74 per cent listed one or more problems growing out of a need for expanding or revising the curricula in their schools. Later more detailed inquiries brought forth specific comments on the limited contributions of certain academic subjects (most notably foreign languages and mathematics), and on the need for extending the local programs to include a greater amount of subject matter which would be useful in everyday life. It is safe to say that school officers already widely recognize the major weaknesses of the present high school curriculum, and are deeply concerned to see a more effective program established.

SUMMARY

Hence the principal conclusion to be drawn from this analysis of the curriculum—that high schools are not now making the contribution to their pupils' social competence which they might make, chiefly because they do not address themselves directly or systematically to that goal—does not mean that the schools are altogether blind to present defects in the curriculum. The conventional high school program has much to answer for in its neglect of the out-of-school problems of boys and girls. The conventional program is even now being modified to great advantage in individual schools. Its widespread improvement will obviously depend in part on the invention of new methods of teaching and new instructional materials. Of more immediate importance than new invention, however, is the adoption by schools in general of numerous thoroughly practicable kinds of teaching which have already demonstrated their value.

CHAPTER IX

Educational and Vocational Guidance

No MATTER how rich its curricular and extracurricular program may be, a school cannot do all it should do for its pupils unless it sees that each boy and girl gets from its program the kind of teaching that he especially needs.

This means that the school has a number of responsibilities beyond the mere offering of courses. The school ought to know what the individual needs of its pupils are. It ought to make its teaching flexible enough so that boys and girls studying the same subjects may profit from them just as fully as their individual capacities and interests allow. It ought to assure itself that each pupil selects the particular subjects most likely to be of benefit to him. It ought to see that when a pupil leaves school he gives himself a fair chance to make use of what his school work has taught him. Failing provision for any of these matters, the school program is bound to be only partially and casually effective.

ACQUAINTANCE WITH INDIVIDUAL PUPILS

To discover how far the New York State schools know what their pupils' needs are, the Inquiry gave particular study to the reports submitted by the schools on their individual leaving pupils. These reports contained information as to the school history of each pupil, his home background, his exceptional personal qualities if he had any, his readiness for vocation and citizenship, and his activities after leaving school. The great majority of the reports had been filled out with obvious care. This fact, and the circumstance that most of the reports were voluntarily prepared by the schools which submitted them, justify considerable reliance on them as genuine indications of how well school authorities are acquainted with boys and girls who have recently withdrawn from school.

Analysis of the reports showed that *high schools in general know little about many of their pupils beyond the facts implied in records of school marks.* Information as to what had become of individual pupils after they had left school proved especially difficult for the schools to supply. Lacking also in the reports on many pupils was information about one phase or another of the pupil's home life: the language spoken in his home, the occupation of his parents, the economic status of his family, the general goodness or badness of his home background. For surprising numbers of pupils the schools could give no information about distinctive personal qualities. The only facts which every school was able to supply about practically every leaving pupil were his name, age, color, and sex, the grade which he had last attended, the curriculum in which he had been enrolled, and the marks he had obtained during the year in which he had left school.[1]

The schools supplied more information about certain types of pupils than about others. A study of the reports for various groups of pupils suggested that *high schools know most about boys and girls from well-to-do homes, who graduate from the college-preparatory curriculum; they know least about young people from economically poor homes, who leave school without graduating.* The fullest information that the schools gave about any single

[1] Visits to a large number of the schools which submitted leaving-pupil reports disclosed few which kept individual-pupil records pertaining to anything but school success. Even the data on school success tended to be limited to teachers' marks and Regents' Examination ratings; more objective data were usually lacking. Of sixty-two academic high schools whose records were examined, only twenty-nine had intelligence test ratings for all their pupils. Only two out of twelve specialized vocational schools had such ratings. Fewer than a third of the academic high schools and only one of the vocational schools reported any systematic use of standardized achievement tests.

group of pupils was given about the boys and girls who had spent an extra year in high school as postgraduates in the college-preparatory curriculum. This is the group, it will be recalled, which stands at the top of the academic hierarchy. From this group down, the schools reported less and less completely about each lower group in the hierarchy—general, fine arts, commercial, vocational. Furthermore, whatever the curricula which the pupils had followed, the schools knew less about young people whose homes stood low in the social scale than about those whose homes stood high; less about pupils who had received school marks below average than about those whose work had been better than average.

There was only one noteworthy exception to the tendency for the schools' information about pupils to be meager in direct ratio to the pupils' lack of academic success. Among pupils withdrawing before graduation the schools were better acquainted with those who left early than with those who left late—a fact which suggests that the schools go out of their way to investigate the backgrounds of pupils who have become special problems.

The schools do not systematically investigate the backgrounds of most of their pupils. School officers who cooperated in the preparation of the leaving-pupil reports frequently commented that the data called for in the reports had never before been systematically gathered for their schools. It was apparent from the reports themselves that most of the background information which the schools possessed about individual pupils had come to the schools because the pupils or their parents had brought it of their own accord. Thus, much fuller reports were submitted for boys and girls who, after graduating or withdrawing, had voluntarily returned to school for advice, than were submitted for pupils who did not come back to the school. The inference may fairly be drawn that the burden of keeping the schools informed about their pupils' personal qualities and out-of-school circumstances rests more heavily on the boys and girls about whom the schools ought to be informed than it does on the schools themselves.

No one type of school tended to supply consistently full information about its pupils. Comparisons of the reports from various kinds of schools indicated, nevertheless, that *small schools, and schools with definite programs of educational and vocational guidance, are somewhat better acquainted with their pupils than are high schools in general.*

Reports from large schools, unless these schools had systematic guidance programs, were likely to be especially meager. One such school offered an explanation of the gaps in its data: "We graduated more than six hundred pupils from this school last June. Unfortunately the teacher who knew those pupils is now on sabbatic leave." Very small schools, in contrast, often added detailed comments to their reports on individual boys and girls, attesting the intimate personal acquaintance of principals and teachers with at least some of the pupils in their charge.

As a means of testing the effectiveness of organized guidance programs in increasing the schools' recognition of individual needs, a number of schools providing especially well-developed arrangements for guidance were identified for the Regents' Inquiry by the State Education Department. The leaving-pupil reports submitted by these schools were separately analyzed. The analysis made it clear that these schools knew more than did the average school about the backgrounds of their pupils. But the analysis showed also that their advantage was limited to their acquaintance with their graduates. They offered little more information than the average school about pupils who withdrew before graduation. Moreover, their acquaintance even with graduates was frequently meager. The question of whether the boys and girls reported on had any exceptional personal qualities, for example, was not answered by these schools for one-eighth of the pupils to whom they had presented high school diplomas. As an indication of how many pupils are likely to be unknown and overlooked in even the best-informed schools at the present time, this fact is of obvious significance.

In the light of the reports in general, the fundamental question as to whether the high schools know what their pupils' individual needs are must be answered very largely in the negative. The great majority of schools are obviously not well enough acquainted with the backgrounds and personal qualities of large numbers of their pupils, even by the time these pupils leave school, to adapt school work to their particular needs. They know least about the boys and girls who most need help. Though certain schools may recognize that such-and-such proportions of their pupils are on relief, or come from broken homes, or have various personal handicaps, they frequently do not know what particular boys and girls are thus affected. At best, therefore, their educational programs must be planned in terms of averages, rather than in the light of the special needs of individuals.

ADAPTATION OF TEACHING
TO INDIVIDUAL NEEDS

How widely the needs of pupils are likely to differ has been demonstrated by such a multitude of surveys and special studies, both in New York State and elsewhere, that this point hardly needs further discussion here.[2] For present purposes the range of individual differences among pupils studying the same subjects in New York State schools may be adequately illustrated by a single example. Tests of ability to read, given to pupils as a part of the special study of the teaching of English, showed that as many as seven years of attainment in reading

[2] Detailed data on individual differences among pupils in New York State high schools may be found in Ruth E. Eckert and T. O. Marshall, *When Youth Leave School*, Regents' Inquiry, 1938.

commonly separate the best from the poorest pupils in high school classes as they are usually organized. Add to differences in ability to read the no less extreme differences in other types of specific school achievement, in general scholastic aptitude, in home advantages, and in personal interest or ambition, and the result offers a fair measure of the assortment of individual teaching problems which confronts the high school teacher who tries to deal in any one class with a representative group of pupils even from a single grade.

The fact that few schools take systematic steps to find out what the differences in their pupils' needs actually are offers an obvious handicap to whatever efforts the schools may make to meet those needs. Nevertheless, the schools' provisions for individual differences are worth reviewing.

To help teachers to cope with the wide range of differences among pupils in any single grade, *approximately a fourth of the high schools of the State have adopted some plan for grouping pupils according to ability.* Grouping of this sort is most common in the junior high schools. Nine junior high schools out of ten provide one scheme or another for subdividing pupils within single grades for instructional purposes. Under the plans most often used, the pupils enrolled in a given grade are classified as slow, average, or rapid learners, and are assigned on this basis to separate class-sections in their major subjects. The classifications are made in terms of scholastic aptitude ratings, achievement test results, marks in courses, teachers' judgments, or some combination of these criteria. Subdivision of pupils in this way within a single grade is obviously possible only in relatively large schools, if class sizes are to be kept at the usual standard of twenty-five or more, a circumstance which partly explains the more extensive use of grouping by junior high schools than by schools in general, since most of the present junior high schools have comparatively large enrollments. Even in large schools ability-grouping must be limited to subjects enrolling many pupils—usually English and social studies. Consequently the use of grouping as a regular administrative practice is ordinarily restricted to schools in city systems.

Ability-grouping may reduce the range of individual differences with which the teacher has to deal in any one class. Numerous experiments have shown, however, that ability-grouping is unlikely to be attended by much better results than the usual plan of classifying pupils merely by grades, unless differentiated subject matter and methods of teaching are systematically provided for groups of high, average, and low ability. It is therefore significant that *in the New York State high schools ability-grouping is seldom accompanied by the provision of systematically differentiated curricula.*

Junior high schools again display the most active concern for individual differences. Approximately a third of these schools, as contrasted with fewer than four in a hundred of the other secondary schools, report both ability-grouping and differentiated curricula. But the converse of these figures is especially striking: two-thirds of the junior high schools and more than 96 per cent of the four-year and senior high schools report no systematic differentiation in subject matter or teaching method.

Significant also is the fact that *the few plans of differentiation which have been developed are designed chiefly for the benefit of the least able pupils.* The group of pupils whose special needs most often receive attention are the so-called "non-Regents' " pupils—boys and girls who lack either the academic ability or the willingness to work which would enable them to pass the Regents' Examinations after the usual class instruction. For these pupils some schools provide supplementary help or special coaching in the regular academic subjects; other schools offer separate "non-Regents' " courses. The latter consist for the most part of conventional work scaled down to the abilities of slow pupils, and not designed to lead to Regents' diplomas. Few schools have developed essentially new courses for low-ability pupils.[3] Only a handful, so far as the Inquiry staff could discover, have arranged special courses for pupils of exceptionally high ability. Differentiation at present therefore consists chiefly, first, of recognizing two or three major groups of pupils—those who can meet the Regents' requirements easily, or at least barely, and those who cannot; second, of letting the pupils who can meet the requirements take the standard program; and third, of providing a diluted program along the same lines for pupils who cannot or will not follow the standard program.

With plans for differentiation limited in this way, and with differentiation restricted to a small minority of the secondary schools of the State, the burden of providing for pupils' individual differences in aptitudes, needs, and interests rests in most cases almost wholly on the individual classroom teacher. Various plans of teaching can be used, even in a heterogeneous class, to adjust class work to individual differences. Teachers in certain schools have found it possible to devise differentiated assignments for their pupils, or to adopt a "job-sheet" method under which pupils work individually on tasks adapted to their needs, or to divide single classes into recitation sections according to an arrangement long in use in elementary schools. Ordinarily, however, the high schools sponsor none of these plans officially, so that whether any such plan is put into effect rests entirely with the individual members of the teaching staffs.

Observations of hundreds of classes throughout the State indicate that teachers rarely adopt any of these plans of their own accord. *Lacking the guidance of course outlines which suggest needed differentiations, the majority of teachers make no definite provisions for pupils' individual abilities and needs.* Teachers of vocational courses and of some of the courses in art represent an excep-

[3] The introduction of one such course, in "economic citizenship," has been expressly encouraged by the State Education Department, but the course has thus far found a place in the programs of only a minority of the high schools.

tion to the general rule; these teachers frequently conduct their classes in such a way that pupils may progress rapidly or slowly as their abilities warrant, or may vary their work according to their interests or talents. Teachers of other courses commonly deal with each class as if it were an indivisible unit, no matter how wide a range of individual differences it may present. All pupils are required to study the same assignments; all are expected to take part in the question-and-answer procedure which makes up the usual recitation; all are subjected to the same tests. In classes in which pupils are not grouped by ability, the assignments and recitations tend to be aimed at the slowest pupils who can reasonably be expected to meet the Regents' requirements. In ability-groups the pace is likely to be adjusted to the capacities of the average pupils, or of those who are slightly below average, in each particular group; but the teaching is still largely uniform for all the pupils who happen to be grouped together. The brighter pupils in any of these classes can ordinarily "keep up" at the cost of a relatively small amount of effort; if they do more than that they do so of their own accord, or under the stimulus of higher marks, rather than because the plan of teaching holds them to a standard commensurate with their abilities. The slower pupils are normally obliged to work harder or longer than the others, to avoid being left behind. The only pupils whose abilities are directly and continuously taken into account tend to be those who are academically just about passable, which is to say, mediocre.

Thus, common practice in the New York State high schools clearly does not provide any such flexible teaching as the wide range of differences among individual boys and girls would seem to demand. Attention to individual needs has been limited for the most part to a thinning-out of the standard program in order to bring that program down to the level of the least capable. Even this kind of modification has been systematically attempted only for a minority of the schools. The majority supply for their pupils merely a series of uniform exposures to a fixed array of subjects, varied for individual pupils solely as the pupils may elect some subjects and pass others by. As test results show, the pupils profit from these subjects in widely varying degrees. But whether each individual pupil profits in proportion to his own real abilities and needs is a matter over which few of the schools seem to exercise any marked control.

EDUCATIONAL GUIDANCE

Whatever their classroom teachers may do about pupils' individual needs, most high schools ostensibly make some provision for individual differences through their offering of elective courses. Their success in providing for individual differences in this way must necessarily depend on the extent to which boys and girls select, or are guided into, the elective courses most appropriate for them.

As part of a report which was requested of all the secondary schools in the State, high school principals were asked by the Inquiry to name the subjects included in the programs of their schools which they believed to be exceptionally valuable for their pupils. They were asked likewise to name those subjects which seemed to them to be producing meager or otherwise unsatisfactory returns. Nearly six hundred principals replied. In answer to the first question they reported that home economics for girls, English, social studies other than history, science, typewriting, and introduction to business were in many schools yielding excellent results for all types of pupils; that these subjects and music, art, and mathematics were often producing superior outcomes for better-than-average pupils; and that home economics and industrial arts were especially valuable for below-average pupils. In response to the second question they reported serious dissatisfaction with the outcomes of work in foreign languages, and almost equal dissatisfaction with the outcomes of work in mathematics for other than superior pupils.

Even a cursory examination of pupils' elections shows that there is little relation between the popularity of courses as indicated by the numbers of pupils who take them, and the value of the courses as judged by the high school principals. The discrepancies are sufficiently great, in fact, to justify the statement that *high school pupils tend to elect the subjects which, in the judgments of school officers, are least likely to yield valuable educational returns, and not to take the subjects which are likely to be most fruitful.* Enrollment in the disapproved subject of foreign languages accounted in 1937 for one-eighth of all subject enrollments in New York State high schools. Among the subjects reported as yielding especially valuable outcomes, only English, a required subject, had as large an enrollment. Mathematics, the second disapproved subject, attracted one-twelfth of all the enrollments. Among the more valuable subjects, only science, with one-tenth of the total, was elected as often. Enrollments in the highly rated subjects of home economics and introductory business amounted in each case to approximately one-fiftieth of the total; in typewriting, to less than one-twentieth; and in social studies other than history, to barely one-sixteenth.

These enrollments are, of course, to be explained in part by the fact that certain of the subjects rated highly by the principals are less frequently included in the present school programs than are foreign languages and mathematics. It is doubtful that the small enrollments in the reputedly more valuable subjects can be completely explained on this basis. A factor that has obvious effect on subject enrollments, quite apart from the mere presence or absence of particular courses, is the advice which the schools give or fail to give to pupils who are choosing elective work.

As a means of gauging the influence which advice from the school has on pupils' choices, the two thousand pupils who were interviewed after they had left school were asked who had advised them to take the curricula which they had elected.

No doubt some of these pupils did not wish to tell where they got advice, but the replies of graduates and nongraduates, girls and boys, agreed so closely that their answers would seem to have considerable reliability. Judging from the reports of these young people, *more than half the boys and girls who go through the secondary school choose their courses without having received definite advice from anyone.* One in seven of the young people who were interviewed said that he had been helped by his parents or by other members of his family. One in about twenty-five reported that he had had advice but could not recall from whom. Hardly more than one in four could remember having been advised by anyone connected with his school—teacher, counselor, or principal.

That these statements do not exaggerate the present situation becomes apparent when one considers how little the average New York State high school does about educational guidance. In the course of visits by members of the Inquiry staff to the seventy-four schools included in the general testing program, the officers of these schools were asked to describe in detail their arrangements for helping pupils to choose appropriate courses. The replies made it clear that *the majority of high schools throw the burden of educational choices almost entirely on the pupils and their parents, offering little or no assistance beyond an explanation of the alternatives among which the pupils may choose.*

Under the present course-of-study requirements, the crucial choices for most pupils come at the beginning of the ninth grade. Here each boy or girl is expected to decide on his program for the remainder of his stay in school: college-preparatory, general, commercial, industrial, home economics, or other, depending on the offerings of the local school. In preparation for this choice, the high school program of studies and the requirements for the various high school diplomas are usually explained to the pupils just before they enter the ninth grade. Ordinarily this is done by means of mimeographed or printed bulletins, supplemented by oral explanations by classroom teachers. Having had the possible choices indicated for him, each pupil is asked to fill out, either by himself or with his parents' help, a card showing what curriculum he expects to follow and what subjects he plans to take. This card must be signed by the pupils' parents and returned to the school within a specified time. The cards are then examined one by one, first by the elementary school principal or teachers and later by someone acting for the high school, to make sure that no pupils with poor elementary school records have chosen courses in which they are certain to fail. Pupils who seem likely to succeed in the work they have chosen are assigned without more ado to the classes they have selected. The pupils who have elected courses beyond their ability are ordinarily called in for a special conference with the high school principal, and are persuaded, or sometimes flatly required without persuasion, to change their elections. Thereafter, for as long as he stays in school, each pupil is expected to abide by the choice that has been approved for him, unless he fails in his work or becomes discontented enough so that he voluntarily seeks a change in his program.

Under such a plan as this, it would be surprising to find that any large number of pupils made well-considered decisions. A ninth-grade boy or girl is ordinarily about fourteen years old. Neither in eight years of elementary school experience nor in his experience outside of school while he has been an elementary school pupil can he have gained enough maturity or knowledge of the world or acquaintance with the values of education to choose wisely for himself among various possible fields of specialized training. If his parents are exceptionally intelligent and well informed they may be able to help him in his choice. Most parents, however, have had less schooling than their sons and daughters are now getting, and many of them, particularly among the immigrant populations in the cities, are not well enough acquainted with school requirements or school opportunities to give appropriate advice. Unless the schools step in to help, the decisions which most pupils make must therefore be the casual decisions of children, with or without such relatively uninformed advice as their parents are able to give them.

Yet the typical high school stands largely aloof. It rarely shows boys and girls how to choose among the various programs open to them; it informs them merely about the subject requirements in those programs, and tells them that some courses prepare for college, others for business, and still others for industry, homemaking, and agriculture. It seldom leads boys and girls to think about their own financial circumstances as determining the kind of high school education they should elect, or about the out-of-school demands for various forms of specialized training, or about the specific educational values of the high school courses. It gives boys and girls no chance to try themselves out in specialized courses before making their decisions. And it seldom offers advice to individual boys and girls, except when those boys and girls have made egregiously inappropriate decisions or have become school failures.

The outstanding exceptions to this policy of aloofness are the junior high schools and the minority of other schools which have introduced systematic guidance programs. The junior high schools, unlike most of the schools organized on the eight-year elementary and four-year high school plan, commonly provide seventh or eighth grade tryout courses in business, industrial arts, home economics, art, and music (but not in agriculture), as a means of helping pupils to decide on appropriate specialized programs beginning in the ninth grade. The schools with guidance programs (and these include most of the junior high schools) ordinarily designate one or more members of their staffs as counselors. The counselors assume responsibility for examining pupils' earlier school records, finding out about their home backgrounds, securing information as to their special abilities and interests, and checking their school progress to make sure that educational choices have been wisely made. Counselors usually confer individually with pupils who are having difficulty with their school work; they confer also with the pupils who are most in need of help in their election of further school work. The small number of counselors ordinarily assigned to any one school and the multitude of duties which each counselor is expected to perform seriously handicap most counselors in seeing that all necessary individual adjustments are made. Nevertheless, the designation of any one person whose major concern it is to look after such adjustments represents a positive step toward responsibility on the part of the school for its pupils' success or failure.

This step has not been taken by most New York State high schools. The schools give boys and girls a chance within such limits as the school program may afford, to decide what they will study. But the schools do not systematically see to it that individual boys and girls decide wisely, nor do they undertake in any thoroughgoing fashion to provide their pupils with the experience and the knowledge which alone would make well-considered decisions possible.

VOCATIONAL GUIDANCE AND PLACEMENT

If the high schools stand aloof from the decisions which their pupils make with respect to school work, they stand even more aloof from any concern with what pupils do after they leave school. Yet the activities in which a boy or girl chooses to engage, or even happens to engage, after he is out of school are at least as important in determining the value of his education as are the interests and abilities he has acquired in school. Except as his out-of-school activities give him a chance to grow in what he has learned, his education may turn out to have been very largely futile.

Interviews with boys and girls who had recently left school showed that for the majority of these young people the problem of getting and keeping a job is paramount. The fact that certain boys and girls failed to get appropriate jobs seemed to account as much as any other single factor for cases of maladjustment and misguided or antisocial behavior. But if the guidance programs reported by the sixty-two academic high schools visited by the Inquiry staff furnish a fair sample of those throughout the State, *nine-tenths of the academic high schools assume no active concern for their pupils' vocational adjustment when they leave school.*

In explaining the high school program of studies to entering pupils, school officers frequently mention the fact that the choice of specialized curricula implies some sort of vocational decision. A few schools, most often junior high schools, offer eighth or ninth grade occupational-survey courses dealing with such topics as the distributions of wage earners in the United States, the advantages and disadvantages of various occupations, the traits and abilities needed by workers, and the dignity of labor. Certain schools ask their pupils periodically what their vocational plans are, with the obvious implication that high school pupils ought to have vocational plans. Beyond the "guidance" that may be inherent in such practices as these, the great majority of academic high schools let their pupils' vocational problems strictly alone. In some instances the school officers are frankly defeatist about such problems: "How can we offer vocational guidance when we can't be sure what kinds of jobs will be open?" Others see no need for vocational guidance: "All these kids are going to work in the mills anyway. Better let them take what jobs they can get."

The academic high schools do even less about helping pupils to get jobs than about helping them to make up their minds as to the kinds of jobs they want. When a pupil leaves school, his going is usually the end of the matter so far as the school is concerned. The law requires each pupil to stay in school till he has reached a certain chronological age. It does not, however, require him to complete any well-rounded program; and nearly twice as many pupils drop out of school without having completed any such program as remain to graduate. Yet it is the rare school which makes any systematic effort to find out just when each of its pupils is likely to leave, or what he will do when he gets out of school. Not knowing when pupils will leave, the school is in no position to make sure that it has done all it can do for a given boy or girl before he goes. And not looking to see what happens to its pupils after they leave, the school is neither ready to help them make a satisfactory adjustment outside of school (except as it may occasionally give some former pupil's name to an employer who telephones for a boy or girl to fill a particular job), nor is it prepared to judge from their experience whether its educational program has been appropriate and effective.

Again there is one group of schools which represent a consistent exception to the usual practice. These schools, however, are not ordinarily the junior high schools, nor indeed any special group of the academic high schools. The study of arrangements for guidance made by the Inquiry showed that *only in the specialized vocational schools can a boy or girl be reasonably sure that the school will try to see that he gets a chance for employment after he completes his secondary school program.*

The vocational schools do not assume responsibility for the vocational adjustment of all their pupils. Most of them are apparently as unconcerned as the academic high schools about pupils who leave before graduation; they allow these pupils to go without any systematic check on their plans or their subsequent fortunes. Nor do the vocational schools hold themselves altogether responsible even for their graduates. Lacking any well-defined standards for admission, and not offering the preliminary educational guidance which would help pupils to choose their specialized vocational programs wisely, these schools frequently graduate pupils whom the schools know to be unprepared for satisfactory vocational adjustment. But the vocational schools do ordinarily consider it a part of their responsibility to place their graduates in appropriate jobs if the jobs are anywhere available. With few exceptions they maintain systematic contacts with employers; they keep records of former pupils' success or failure in the jobs which the pupils secure; they try to encourage pupils who have lost their jobs to return to the school for guidance or further training. In all these respects the vocational schools display a concern for the out-of-school consequences of their educational programs which seems altogether lacking in most of the academic high schools.

GUIDANCE AND PROVISIONS FOR INDIVIDUAL DIFFERENCES

It would be painting an extreme picture to say that New York State high schools pay no attention to their pupils as individuals. Many young people who have left school, as well as many of the boys and girls who are still in school, can testify to the direct and personal interest in their needs that teachers and school officers have shown.

But the conclusion can hardly be avoided that few of the schools take any systematic account of their pupils' individual or personal problems. The average school knows little about the boys and girls who come to it year after year beyond what it sees of them during the school day, and even then it looks at them chiefly in terms of their ability to meet academic standards. It puts its pupils through the academic round class by class, dealing with all the pupils in a class in much the same way. It leaves to each pupil and his parents the problem of deciding what sort of education the pupil shall expose himself to. It instructs pupils while they are in school, but it does not regularly concern itself with how long any one of them will stay in school, nor does it look to see what happens to him after he leaves. In short, except in the case of some pupils who make trouble and others who happen to attract the interest and attention of particular teachers, it contents itself with offering courses in which pupils may enroll, and allowing the pupils to get out of these courses as much as they can.

The schools' practice of leaving to boys and girls the task of discovering and taking care of their own particular needs explains many of the defects in social competence among the boys and girls just out of school. Most obviously it explains why large numbers of these boys and girls flounder aimlessly and ignorantly in their first contacts with out-of-school problems. The schools have not shown them how or where to look for employment; consequently they hunt for jobs at random, and get jobs that often bear little or no relation to their abilities or their interests. The schools have not shown them how or where to go on learning. They rarely take advantage, therefore, of the chances to learn which their work might offer them, and outside their jobs they fall easy prey to the first proprietary school salesman who talks to them positively and with assurance about the kind of training that will be good for them. The schools have paid little attention to their varying opportunities for recreation and leisure, and their varying problems of getting along with family and neighbors and community. Accordingly they occupy themselves with whatever activities first come to hand, without any considered plans for making the most of their own particular circumstances. The most helpless among them, it will be recalled, are the boys and girls who leave school before graduating; and these boys and girls the schools are especially prone to ignore.

The schools' present practice goes far to explain also why exceptionally able boys and girls do not get all they might get out of their high school education, and why these pupils often fail to continue their education in appropriate higher institutions. Adapting its teaching chiefly to pupils of average or below average ability, the high school is usually content to demand from the abler pupils work which is merely somewhat better than the average. If these pupils drift instead of making active progress, the school may notice and regret that fact. It provides little individual stimulation, however, for the boy or girl who is not making the most of his ability. Nor does the school ordinarily take any decisive part in the educational planning which its abler pupils need to do. It asks each pupil and his parents whether or not he intends to go to college and what college he has chosen. If the college which the pupil selects is one for which the school can prepare him, the school sees that he gets the necessary preparatory work. But the high school does not often venture to direct a pupil to any particular kind of college, nor does it usually take the initiative in seeing that every boy or girl who is likely to profit by college work makes any thorough canvass of the opportunities for entering college.

Finally, the schools' present practice offers a clue, though only a partial one, to the notable differences in achievement between girls and boys. Except in the courses in home economics for girls, most of the high schools now offer substantially the same programs for all their pupils. Historically, these programs were planned for boys. They are the outgrowth of a scheme of education influenced by the requirements of men's colleges; they have been accepted without protest as good programs for girls largely because of the notion that to show themselves intellectually equal to boys, girls must study the same subjects as boys, in the same way. Yet the interests characteristic of high school girls, as those interests were reported by the pupils questioned by the Inquiry staff, are quite different from the interests of boys. What is even more revealing, though the boys' interests tend to change during the secondary school period in such a way that the boys express more and more liking for the kinds of subject matter emphasized in the school program, the girls' interests remain much the same from grade to grade. In holding all their pupils to the same academic program, it seems probable that the high schools are in effect providing a boys' education for girls and boys alike.

The schools' lack of concern for their pupils' individual needs thus offers a further reason for the unreadiness of many young people to meet out-of-school problems. There is room for debate as to how far schools can wisely go, and how far public interest requires them to go, in smoothing the way for individual boys and girls. Certainly the schools ought not to hold every boy or girl by the hand till he has met and conquered all his difficulties. One of the chief purposes of schools is presumably to help put enough courage and good sense and knowledge into young people so that they can meet their own problems with a minimum of leaning on other people or on society. But schools can accomplish this purpose only if they are willing to stand beside individual boys and girls long enough and sympathetically enough to find out what the major problems of those boys and girls are likely to be. They can accomplish it only if, in addition, they are concerned enough about individual pupils to take some responsibility for their welfare. And few New York State high schools at present do either of these things.

MORE EFFECTIVE PROVISIONS
FOR INDIVIDUAL NEEDS

In spite of the schools' general lack of concern for their pupils' individual differences, *programs by which individual pupils and certain special groups of pupils may be more adequately prepared for out-of-school problems are already in the making in various New York State schools.* The one major problem of individual differences on which the Inquiry could discover no demonstrably successful attack was the problem of appropriately differentiated instruction for girls and boys. The seriousness of this problem has apparently not been widely enough recognized, either in New York State or elsewhere, to bring about extensive efforts to deal with it. On other types of problems growing out of pupils' individual needs a number of schools are making notably successful beginnings.

Possibly the most striking plan for meeting the special needs of one particular group of pupils is that which has been adopted in one of the moderate-sized cities of the State. The school budget in this city provides for educational counselors and a vocational placement officer. Starting with no equipment except a desk and an office, no data on vocational opportunities, no detailed records of individual boys and girls, the placement officer began his work by asking the junior and senior high school counselors to send him the names of the pupils in their schools who were getting along badly in school and who were most in need of jobs. He talked with each of these boys and girls. From them and from the counselors he found out all he could about their school records, their interests, their abilities, and their family circumstances. He then proceeded to hunt for a job for each of them individually, telephoning to employers who might have work which the particular boy or girl could do, describing the pupil he was trying to place, and asking for suggestions as to openings elsewhere if the employer with whom he was talking had none to offer. As a result of these telephone contacts and of visits to various business concerns he not merely placed the first group of pupils in jobs but he built an initial list of the kinds of jobs most likely to be available to boys and girls in the local community.

Most of these jobs called for unskilled labor, such as washing cars, changing tires in a garage, doing miscellaneous work in homes, sweeping floors in stores and factories, waiting on table or washing dishes in restaurants or cafés. The boys and girls who were being helped to find employment were for the most part pupils who were not intelligent enough or not skillful enough with their hands to hope for much higher forms of work. Despite the small amount of skill called for in such work, it became apparent that preference in employment usually goes to boys and girls who have already had some experience in the kind of work a given employer wants done, and who can be counted on to be courteous, neat, and dependable on the job.

Accordingly, the schools made arrangements for short-unit courses in the kinds of work for which there was most frequent demand. These courses were taught by certain of the shop teachers and teachers of home economics. They were so conducted that they not only gave pupils practice in the limited skills which the jobs required, but developed the pupils' pride in doing each job as well as it could possibly be done. To make the training thoroughly realistic, the schools obtained orders for work from members of the school staffs, charging a small amount for such work and paying the boys and girls who performed it.

The schools insisted that the pupils who enrolled for these courses should enroll also for certain other courses. One of the latter was a course in English, in which the pupils were given special instruction in how to talk pleasantly and correctly with other people as they would have to talk on their jobs, in how to write business letters, in how to read, and in how to use the library. A second was a course in arithmetic, which placed chief emphasis on keeping accounts, making out bills, and managing personal finances. A third was a course in social studies, in which the pupils had a chance to discuss problems of employment, the duties of citizens outside their jobs, and the personal problems which they themselves were facing in school and outside. The school work for all these pupils was given a frankly vocational outlook, but an outlook in which the pupils' preparation for jobs became much more than training in technical skills.

The results of this program showed themselves partly in the unusual success of these boys and girls in making a beginning outside of school. They found and kept jobs while similar pupils from other schools drifted aimlessly. But certain further results were apparent while the pupils were still in school. Many of these boys and girls had previously been a positively bad influence on the morale of the school as a whole. Their enrollment in the job-training courses did not change them all, nor change any of them overnight, but it did give most of them a motive which was reported to have notably improved their whole attitude toward the school.

This particular school system had the advantage of a special staff in dealing with problems of guidance and placement. At least two schools with only a principal and half a dozen teachers each were found to have been making a similar, though necessarily more limited, effort to deal conscientiously and realistically with the needs of individual boys and girls. In one of these schools the principal tried to discover each year which boys and girls were planning to leave school in the course of that year or at the end of it. Early in the year he talked with pupils who were spending their last year in school, trying to arrange for them as valuable a final year's program as his school could afford. Sometimes a boy or girl "got away before he expected it." He hunted up every such pupil, found out why he had left school and whether he had a job, helped him so far as he could to get the best kind of job that was available for him.

The principal of the second school had had the advantage of living for many years in the local community, and had made it a point to become personally acquainted not merely with his pupils but with one or both of their parents. Like the first principal he was not content merely to ask his pupils about their educational and vocational plans; he assumed it to be part of his work to help them make their plans and to see that they were in a position to carry them out. In addition, he encouraged his teachers in schemes for providing special kinds of work for pupils who had special individual interests. Pupils who displayed little interest or ability in academic work were given individual programs which allowed them to spend much of their time on independent projects in agriculture, shopwork, or home economics. Pupils of exceptional academic ability were expected to elect the usual academic program, but the school made a strong effort to enlist their interest in extracurricular clubs which would put them on their intellectual mettle. Typical of these clubs was a group organized by the principal himself, which devoted spring and fall week ends to an intensive study of local archaeology. A number of boys from this group later went to college for the particular purpose of finding an outlet for the interest in archaeology which they had developed in high school.

The effort which this small school made to provide a suitable education for boys and girls of unusual ability has taken the form in larger schools of separate curricula for the more able pupils. A few schools have established special programs for pupils unusually gifted in art or music. More often the separate curricula have been designed to recognize superior intellectual ability rather than unusual artistic talent. They ordinarily differentiate between intellectually gifted and average pupils in one or two subjects—English, history, science, or mathematics—rather than in the secondary school program as a whole. The curricula for the more able pupils tend to go far beyond the usual syllabus outlines in the breadth and substance of the reading, observation, and thinking which they require; they put more than ordinary emphasis on class discussions as distinguished from "recitations"; they give an important place to independent study and research on problems of particular interest to individual pupils or to the class as a whole; they encourage use of the classroom as a laboratory in which pupils may find books, exhibits, and all necessary working materials in particular fields of study. Nearly all these curricula are at present frankly experimental. Their results as observed in the Inquiry nevertheless justify a considerable measure of confidence in them as a means of providing more effective education for academically able boys and girls.

OBSTACLES TO IMPROVEMENT

It is evident from these examples that a school need not have elaborate and expensive administrative machinery before it can make a beginning at caring for its pupils' individual needs. The two small schools referred to were accomplishing better results in preparing individual boys and girls to meet out-of-school problems than were many larger schools which the Inquiry examined, including several schools which reported far more intricate administrative arrangements for educational and vocational guidance.

Schools in general, however, cannot accomplish all that certain individual schools have been able to accomplish in their attention to pupils' individual needs, so long as they suffer under a number of handicaps which are widely prevalent. *Serious obstacles both to effective guidance and to flexibility in teaching are presented by the widespread lack of adequate instructional equipment.* The schools' acquaintance with their pupils is frequently restricted by the lack of diagnostic testing materials. The range of elective subjects through which the schools can meet pupils' varying needs is as narrow as it is in many schools, partly because of insufficient funds to provide for special courses—particularly vocational courses, which demand special machinery, tools, and supplies. The teaching in the subjects which the schools do offer is often similarly restricted. Libraries are notably deficient in many of the schools; classroom equipment is often meager or outworn; teaching materials in class after class are frequently limited to a single basic text, with one copy for each pupil. If the schools deal with their pupils chiefly in the mass, one reason for their doing so is the fact that they lack the wherewithal to provide more effective teaching.

A further obstacle to adequate provision for individual boys and girls is the restriction which present teaching schedules often place on teachers' time. *Teachers are frequently obliged to deal with so many different classes of pupils, if not with so many different boys and girls, that they have small opportunity to consider the needs of any single boy or girl as a person.* One teacher wrote to the Inquiry:

In the —— High School, I teach four hours of French and one of Civics each day; the sixth hour is given over daily to the supervision of a study hall.

As a teacher of Civics, I answered a week or two ago a questionnaire on social sciences. I wish to apologize here for the rather hurried way in which that questionnaire was filled out. I was so rushed with papers and lesson plans the two days it was in my hands that no other course was possible.

The way I filled out that questionnaire is the way I've had to do any kind of extra or broadening professional work while school is in session. Usually I do none at all. Worse than that, in planning the next day's work, a 50-minute class period has to be planned out in ten minutes, or less, and the work of that period suffers accordingly. With no free period during the day, I have to see any slow students, or those for make-up work, after school. Result: in the two years I have been teaching, I have been in the school library a total of perhaps three or four hours if that much. How can you assign or suggest reading for the faster pupils when you can't find time to investigate the material on hand for them to use? Any odd free moments are taken up by the accounting process of marking cards, keeping registers, and the like, and by the guidance work incidental to supervising a homeroom.

What I'm trying to point out is not that teachers are overworked. I was in business for four years in a New York bank, and in a year of teaching I put in about the same amount of routine and drudgery as I did there in a year, if you count the evening hours spent correcting papers. But teachers have in general a schedule too loaded full to give the best of themselves to those whom they teach. Furthermore, week ends and summers are breathing-spells spaced too far apart to insure that a teacher enters each class with a clear idea of what's going to be done in the next fifty minutes, and why. This business of motivating and then teaching youngsters is not like adding a column of figures. You can't toss it off while you think of something else. Each class period is a special problem, a complex one, that ideally should be preceded by a few minutes' deep consideration and planning.

The difficulties which this teacher describes are fairly typical of those which present teaching schedules impose on many high school teachers. Teachers who have fewer assigned class periods than did this particular teacher may often have duties which he does not list—responsibility for extracurricular activities in addition to their class teaching, or for the supervision of pupils in the corridors or the cafeteria or on the playground. Whatever the nature of any one teacher's assignments, his work with boys and girls as individuals must ordinarily be done in the time left after he has completed his work with his pupils in the mass.

As with defects in the program of studies, a large proportion of the high school principals of the State are fully aware of the weakness of present provisions for pupils' individual needs. Nearly half the six hundred principals who reported their major problems to the Inquiry listed problems growing out of the wide range of individual differences among their pupils. Twenty per cent reported themselves concerned with the development of programs of guidance. That there has been little progress in dealing with these problems may be attributed in considerable measure to the handicaps of inadequate equipment and crowded schedules under which the schools now suffer.

SUMMARY

Consideration of what the schools know about their pupils as individuals, and of what they do for them as individuals, makes it clear that the limited scope of the high school curriculum is not alone to blame for young people's lack of social competence. Boys and girls often fail to profit as fully as they might even from the present curriculum, because the schools have no consistent plan for seeing that individual pupils get what they need from their class work.

The adjustment of the school program to individual needs is now largely haphazard. The teaching does not systematically recognize individual differences, with the result that pupils who are less able academically than the average are often overlooked, and the abler pupils are seldom challenged to make the most of their ability. The absence of well-considered educational and vocational guidance lessens the value of the school program for many pupils, irrespective of their ability.

There can be no cure for this situation merely in urging teachers to give a greater amount of direct attention to individual boys and girls. Lack of material equipment and the pressure of classroom routine stand in the way of effective provisions for individual differences in many schools. But there can be no cure for the situation, either, merely in the provision of more equipment and the rearrangement of teachers' schedules. Of fundamental importance, if pupils' needs are to be adequately met, are an active concern on the part of the schools for what becomes of individual boys and girls, and a willingness to take responsibility for their pupils' educational and vocational plans.

CHAPTER X

The Regents' Examinations

THE nature of the curricula in local schools, the provisions which the schools make or fail to make for the individual needs of their pupils, and the extent of the schools' concern for pupils' educational and vocational plans, go far toward explaining why boys and girls leave school well equipped in some respects and meagerly equipped in others. Local school programs, however, are largely conditioned in any state by general state policy. In New York State the amount of control which the State exercises over its secondary schools, through the Board of Regents and the State Education Department, is probably greater than in any other state in the Union. A comprehensive accounting for educational results must therefore look behind local programs to the nature and methods of state regulation.

ORIGIN OF REGENTS' EXAMINATIONS

One of the chief instruments which New York State uses to assure an appropriate state-wide program of secondary education is its system of Regents' Examinations. This system culminates, so far as it affects the secondary schools, in a series of high school leaving examinations which determine the standing in major subjects and the eligibility for diplomas of the pupils enrolled in the schools.

The system began not with a plan of leaving examinations but with a plan of entrance examinations. An early provision for state aid to local schools called for the distribution to public academies of money from the so-called Literature

High School and Life

Fund. The numbers of pupils enrolled in individual academies were considered in determining the amount of aid to which the schools were entitled. To discover who were *bona fide* academy pupils, the Board of Regents in 1864 established admission examinations which had to be taken by those wishing to attend the academies. These examinations were prepared by the State Education Department but were at first both given and rated locally. A scheme was soon adopted, however, under which papers rated as passing by the local schools were required to be individually reviewed and accepted by the Department before state aid could be allotted for the pupils concerned. The system of Preliminary Examinations thus set up determined for many years practically all promotions from the eighth to the ninth grade, and with various modifications is operative in some schools at the present time.

The plan of uniform and impartial entrance examinations commended itself, in general, to the school men in charge of the academies. Moreover, the colleges saw in the plan the promise of a scheme by which greater uniformity of preparation and higher standards of training could be assured among the academy pupils who were being prepared for higher institutions. A number of resolutions, largely motivated by the interests of the colleges, were accordingly introduced at University Convocations in the years following the establishment of the Preliminary Examinations, looking toward the extension of the plan to the level of high school graduation.

In 1877 the Legislature enacted a bill empowering the Regents to establish a further system of examinations which should "furnish a suitable standard of [secondary school] graduation . . . and of admission to the several colleges of the State"; and in June, 1878, under the provisions of this act, the Regents administered the first of the so-called Academic Examinations.

A review of their recent history indicates that *the Preliminary Examinations have had a waning influence in recent years.*

Tremendous increases in the numbers of pupils seeking entrance into the secondary schools, the establishment of junior high schools which admit pupils to certain branches of secondary school work at the end of the sixth grade, instead of at the end of the eighth, and the more and more dependable arrangements adopted by local school systems for supervising pupil promotions, have led to rulings by the State Department which make state examinations for admission to the secondary schools compulsory only in certain rural districts. The Preliminary Examinations now tend to be given chiefly in the small school systems. While they are still prepared by official state committees, they are both administered and scored entirely by the local schools. As a factor of decreasing importance in the educational control exercised by the State, they may be expected in the future to have no very marked effect on the outcomes of secondary education.[1]

In contrast with that of the Preliminary Examinations, *the influence of the Academic Examinations continues to be pervasive and important.* These examinations, like the Preliminary Examinations, are drawn up each year by committees under the chairmanship of members of the State Education Department. Since 1906 the examination committees have been appointed by a State Examinations Board, itself appointed by the Board of Regents and composed of twenty members divided equally among representatives of the State Department, the colleges and universities, the high schools, and the superintendents of elementary schools. Through the general rules laid down by the Examinations Board and the examinations set by its subordinate committees, the Board of Regents

---

[1] Until 1937 the examination system also included so-called "grade examinations," prepared by committees of district superintendents for use in determining promotions within the rural elementary schools. These examinations were printed by the State Education Department, but were not prepared under the official sponsorship of the Department, and were used entirely at the option of local schools.

determine who shall receive the official high school diplomas which the Regents are authorized by law to grant.

ADMINISTRATION
OF ACADEMIC EXAMINATIONS

To make clear the present effects of the Academic Examinations on the secondary schools and thus on the outcomes of secondary education in the State, particular attention needs to be given to the way these examinations are now administered.

Originally the Academic Examinations were offered only in subjects which prepared for college. Each year of high school work in these subjects was separately tested, so that a pupil was obliged to present himself for examination in four successive years in order to earn a state high school diploma. The increasing variety of high school subjects led, however, to a widening in the range of the examinations; at present there are Regents' Examinations not merely in college-preparatory subjects but in certain subjects in practically every field in which high school instruction is offered, including fine arts, music, commercial work, vocational industrial and vocational technical work, home economics, and agriculture. With the increase in the range of subjects tested has come a gradual abandonment of the plan of testing every pupil every year. Regents' Examinations are now required only in the last two years of the high school program, and are often so framed as to apply to the results of three or four years of work rather than to the results of the year which the pupil has just completed.

The original plan for scoring the papers has also been gradually modified. The tremendous number of examinations given annually (1,698,950 papers were printed in 1936–37) has made it practically impossible for all the papers passed by the local schools to be reviewed separately in Albany. Accordingly, sample examinations only, from the total number of papers forwarded to the State Education Department, are systematically rechecked. Examinations in any one subject may not be reviewed at all in a given year; or the ratings from certain schools may be accepted without question, while those from other schools are reviewed in detail. Though each school finally receives from the Department a notice of the official acceptance or modification of the examination scores of its individual pupils, the present scoring procedure means that thousands of examinations every year are rated only by the teachers in the schools in which they are given.

The present system is one in which the Board of Regents assumes responsibility for the passing or failing of hundreds of thousands of individual boys and girls every year, solely on the basis of written tests only some of which are actually reviewed by any central authority. The system is open to a number of important questions. Is the plan fair to the individual boys and girls directly affected by it? Does its administration serve to bring about more effective teaching in the schools? Can it be so used as to promote a better preparation of young people for the activities which lie ahead of them outside of school?

RELIABILITY OF THE EXAMINATIONS

Almost from the beginning, the examinations have been subject to criticism from the standpoint of their fairness to the individual pupils concerned. It is an evidence of the conscientiousness with which the examinations have been administered that this criticism has been as strongly voiced by members of the State Department as by any one less closely connected with the examination system. Commissioner Draper found occasion to analyze the whole plan of Regents' Examinations at the University Convocation of 1907; Commissioner Graves has more than once pointed out serious flaws in the examination system; and in recent years various members of the Department have conducted a number of searching studies of the values of the examinations.

The principal criticisms of the examinations from the point of view of their fairness have emphasized the fact that *the examinations are subjectively made, subjectively weighted, and subjectively scored.* There can be no denying that in all these respects there is much room for improvement in the present system.

The committees which prepare the examination papers take their work with much seriousness, and make definite efforts to frame examinations which will serve the best interests of the pupils. The usual procedure, however, does not allow for any advance trial of the examinations, so that whether a given examination will be difficult or easy for pupils to pass, and whether it will measure the abilities which the committee wants it to measure, must be guessed at on the basis of the experience of the committee members.

The examinations tend to follow stereotyped forms. In preparing examinations for a given year each committee ordinarily uses as its guide the examinations of the year before, devising parallel questions, and usually the same number of questions, for the new examination. Each question is arbitrarily given a certain number of credit-points; the possible credits always total 100, and the passing mark is always fixed at 75 for college-preparatory pupils and 65 for most others. Again, in determining how much credit to allow for particular questions, subjective judgment of the committee members must be relied on.

In the main the examinations are confined to topics which are reasonably sure to have been "covered" in the secondary school courses. Occasionally, however, committees insert questions of a kind not included in previous examinations, for the purpose of stimulating the teaching of particular topics. Introduced as alternatives, such questions may provide flexibility in the examinations, but they obviously risk the causing of serious injustice to pupils whose school work does not happen to have included the topics with which they deal.

Though the committee members themselves devote careful attention to the kinds of answers which they expect the examination questions to call forth, they do not prepare keys for the use of the teachers who are to score the papers. Instruction sheets sent out by the State Education Department offer for the most part only general directions for rating the papers. As a result, answers which may be acceptable to a given committee may be rejected by overconscientious teachers, or the same answers may be variously rated by different readers. Papers which are reviewed by the State Department are uniformly scored through the use of keys drawn up by the official readers, but the present system allows wide variations in the scoring of papers which are not reviewed.

The consequence of the present methods of preparing and rating examinations is that the Regents' Examinations are not the dependable indices of pupils' achievement which they are intended to be. Their unreliability is clearly shown by the variations which occur each year among the proportions of pupils passing and failing particular examinations. The quality of instruction probably does not vary greatly from one academic subject to another in the high schools of the State; nor do the groups of pupils examined in each of the academic subjects differ in average learning ability from subject to subject. Yet in a given year a much larger proportion of pupils may fail in one subject than in another. In 1935, for example, 27.3 per cent of the pupils who were examined in mathematics failed in that subject; 17.8 per cent failed in Latin; only 10.2 per cent failed in modern languages. The proportions passing and failing in any one subject likewise vary from year to year to such an extent that examination committees frequently consider, in making out each new examination, whether the previous examination in their subject has been unduly hard or easy.

Fluctuations in the difficulty of the examinations may work serious hardship on pupils who are near the borderline in achievement. Criticisms of the examinations have been largely concerned with the injustice likely to be done to such pupils. But the examinations may work hardship also on able young people whose examination scores determine their eligibility for college scholarships or for admission to particular higher institutions. The state scholarships and the Cornell scholarships awarded by the Regents are allotted on the basis of the pupils' average examination scores; and certain colleges, notably the State Teachers Colleges, refuse to admit candidates whose scores fall below a predetermined average. If fluctuations in the difficulty of the examinations make it hard for pupils to earn a high school diploma one year and relatively easy to earn it the next year, these same fluctuations may obviously mean the difference between high grades and mediocre grades for pupils who are trying to achieve honors. In addition, it is entirely possible that an examination which is easy to pass may be one in which it is hard to achieve honors, or that an examination which is hard to pass may be an easy one in which to achieve honors if a pupil is above the passing level. The brighter pupils may thus, in effect, be subject to quite as much jeopardy as the average pupils under the examination system as it now operates.

EFFECTS OF THE EXAMINATION SYSTEM

The question of how far the examination system affects the work of the schools is more difficult to answer in terms of thoroughly objective data than is the question of whether the examinations are fair to individual pupils. Nevertheless, informal evidence of the responsiveness of the schools to the examinations is abundant. In scores of visits to schools and in conferences carried on by the Inquiry with classroom teachers, school officers, and members of the State Department, it was everywhere apparent that the Regents' Examinations are decisive influences with respect to local educational policies and methods.

Because of the prestige of the Board of Regents and the conscientiousness and impartiality of the examination committees, the examinations have earned widespread respect. Their unreliability as measures of individual achievement has not been generally recognized. What has been recognized is that they are impersonal and obviously fair in intent; that they emphasize scholarship; that they are ordinarily difficult enough to pass so that a satisfactory rating means positive achievement. In the eyes of most laymen and many school people, therefore, *success in preparing pupils for the examinations is held to be of prime importance in appraising a secondary school.* Individual teachers as well as individual schools are judged on this basis. The teacher who succeeds year after year in getting a large proportion of his pupils "past the Regents'" regards himself, and is commonly regarded, as a good teacher; and while it is recognized that there may be extenuating circumstances in the case of a teacher many of whose pupils fail, few teachers will allow themselves, if they can help it, to be put in the position of having to apologize for their Regents' records.

The importance attached to success in preparing for the examinations has been increased by the uses which the State Department has made of the examination results. The proportions of pupils passing and failing from each school in the State are published each year. Moreover, the Department often uses the examination scores as a basis for its supervisory inspections of individual schools. Supervisors from the Department analyze the examination records of a given school before making a visit to that school, and frequently discuss the work of the school with its principal and teachers in the light of those records. As a natural consequence, schools which have average or better-than-average examination records generally consider their programs satisfactory; schools which fall below the average make strenuous efforts to raise their standing.

Since the examination records are commonly regarded as measures of good teaching, *the teaching in high schools everywhere in the State tends to be focused on preparation for the Regents' Examinations.* Few schools fail to devote at least a month or six weeks at the end of the year to coaching the pupils who are to take the examinations that year. Many schools base their last two years' work almost entirely on "Regents' material." Some organize their work, from the ninth grade on, with an eye to drilling pupils in the types of questions that the examinations are likely to ask.

Preparation for the examinations is made easier by the existence of a considerable body of printed material which teachers can use as guides to class work. Early in the history of the examinations the State Education Department undertook to furnish outlines of the subject matter on which the examinations were to be based. Textbook makers were persuaded, as the numbers of pupils in the New York State high schools grew, to issue their books in special editions paralleling the state syllabi and thus facilitating direct preparation for the examinations. In addition to these more legitimate aids, a commercial organization has for years published a widely used series of Regents' review books, in which are presented, subject by subject, lists of questions from past Regents' papers, so arranged as to make possible a concentrated drill on the kinds of questions most likely be asked. Thus the basic curricula in the schools have been largely shaped to meet the examination requirements.

The school programs have been negatively, as well as positively, influenced by these requirements. Specialists from the Inquiry visiting high school classes were told by many teachers that the classwork did not include certain topics because those topics were not likely to be met in the examinations. High school principals explained the lack of particular subjects, especially subjects designed to meet the needs of the less able pupils, by the fact that those subjects were not "recognized" by the Regents. Subject matter which is known to be called for in the examinations is almost certain to be included in the program of every school, large or small. Subject matter not touched on in the examinations is ordinarily found only in schools with teachers and principals of exceptional courage and vision.[2]

The tendency of the examinations to discourage marked deviations from the standard program is apparent. Partly as a consequence of this tendency, partly because of the way in which the examinations are prepared, *the effect of the examination system has been to keep the work of the schools largely static.*

The syllabi which have supplemented the examinations as guides to teaching have been very infrequently revised. In the beginning, it was the announced plan of the State Department to issue new syllabi every five years. Later the Department decided to make revisions "when needed." Few new syllabi have been published within the last decade.

---

[2] From a comprehensive study of the influences of the Regents' Examinations in chemistry, Dr. Warren W. Knox, now Acting Director of the Examinations and Testing Division of the State Education Department, drew the following conclusions:

Teachers emphasize topics in chemistry largely in accordance with the emphasis given these topics on past Regents' examinations. . . . The implied teaching emphasis seems to be independent of syllabus considerations. . . .

The introduction and continued emphasis of a comparatively new topic on Regents' examinations is followed by corresponding teaching emphasis. . . .

Regents' examinations in chemistry influence teachers to greatly extend the amount of time normally given to general reviews. Such review or drill procedures are characterized by the use of old Regents' examination papers and Regents' review books. . . .

Regents' examinations influence teachers to employ the state syllabus in the general planning of their courses in chemistry. When the teachers are released from responsibility for examination results, the majority tend to emphasize those sections of the course that may be described as the chemistry of everyday life. . . .

There is cumulative evidence that Regents' examinations in chemistry influence teachers to adapt their instruction to the inferior pupil. . . .

See W. W. Knox, *A Study of Some of the Influences of Regents' Examinations in Chemistry.* (Unpublished dissertation) Teachers College, Columbia University.

· 197 ·

The present syllabus for civics was prepared in 1923; for economics, in 1924; for general science, in 1925; for physics and chemistry, in 1926.

The examination committees, in an effort to be fair to teachers and pupils, have not merely restricted the examinations to subject matter outlined in the syllabi, but have used routine topics and routine types of questions much more often than they have introduced new items or new types of questions. Examinations in the making are usually checked against the appropriate syllabus to make sure that no question is asked to which the answer is not included in the field prescribed by the syllabus. Even a question covered by the syllabus may be rejected on the ground that "They will not be expecting that," or "They have never had a question like that." The result is that the examinations, instead of leading the way toward better teaching, have often tended merely to perpetuate the kind of teaching to which a majority of the teachers have become accustomed.

EXAMINATIONS AND OUTCOMES
OF SECONDARY EDUCATION

Quite apart from the question of the reliability of the Regents' Examinations, it is evident that *the present examination system is largely responsible for the kind of educational equipment with which boys and girls now leave the secondary schools.* What the schools teach, the ways in which they teach it, and the extent to which they concern themselves with individual boys and girls, are definite resultants of the examination requirements. The curriculum in the majority of schools faithfully reflects the content of the examinations. If that curriculum does not prepare boys and girls to meet the problems which they must face outside of school, the fault lies partly in the fact that the examinations have little bearing on such problems. Teaching methods in most classrooms are those which will train boys and girls in the abilities which the examinations demand. If the methods consist largely in drill on memorized facts and skills, and if they provide for little attention to pupils' individual abilities and needs beyond the coaching of pupils who are slow to learn, it is because memory is a principal factor in success on the examinations, and because individual pupils can be successfully "crammed" without attention to their particular needs or desires. The schools' chief concern about their pupils is that as many of them as possible shall pass the examinations. If the schools take account of pupils' educational plans only to the extent of seeing that individual boys and girls do not elect courses in which they cannot succeed, and if the schools largely ignore what happens to boys and girls outside of school, it is because the criterion of educational success established by the examinations calls for no vital consideration of boys and girls as persons.

In their effect on the schools and hence on the educational achievements of high school pupils, the lack of reliability of the present examinations plays only a minor part. The factor of chief significance is the attitude of the schools toward the examinations. *As long as the schools use the examinations as they now use them, no mere increase in the reliability of the individual tests is likely to bring about much change for the better in the schools' programs.* Any constructive plan for improving the examination system, therefore, must give major attention to the nature and scope of the system as a whole, and to the way it is used, rather than to the details of examination procedure.

INCREASING THE RELIABILITY
OF THE EXAMINATIONS

Present defects in the reliability of the examinations are nevertheless a legitimate cause for concern. Fortunately, *steps looking toward the correction of various weaknesses in the examination procedure are already being taken by the State Education Department.* Before considering what needs to be done with respect to the examination system in general, it may be well to consider what can be done and what is being done to remove these weaknesses.

Experimenting actively with new types of examinations during the last fifteen years, various examining bodies have developed methods for trying out new examination questions in advance of their actual use in rating pupils. One such method consists of adding to each regular examination a series of trial questions which are studied and revised in the light of pupils' responses to them. This procedure makes it possible for each new examination to be composed of questions of which the difficulty is already known; it thus goes far to eliminate the guesswork involved in the attempt to formulate fair, and at the same time searching, questions in advance of actual trial. A plan for using questions which have been tried out in advance is now being experimentally employed in connection with certain of the Regents' Examination papers.

Investigations carried on by many specialists in educational measurement have demonstrated the practical value of examinations which can be objectively scored, as contrasted with examinations in which ratings must be based largely on subjective judgment. The objectively scored examinations do not serve all the functions of the older, essay type examinations which form the basis for most of the Regents' papers. Consisting of large numbers of relatively brief questions, each of which can be correctly answered in only one or two predetermined ways, they give less opportunity than the essay examinations for pupils to set forth on paper an original exposition of a complicated process of thinking. They allow, however, a much wider sampling of pupils' knowledge and skills than do the essay type of examinations, so that what they sacrifice in one respect they make up in another. In their fairness to individual pupils they may be much superior to the usual essay examinations, because of the reliability with which they can be scored even by inexperienced readers.

Their effective use calls for a training in test construction which few members of the present Regents' Examination committees possess. Under the guidance of specially trained members of the State Department, however, objective type questions are being increasingly relied on in certain of the Regents' papers. Their value has been especially demonstrated in connection with the Regents' Preliminary Examinations in English.

The preliminary tryout of examination questions and the use of objective rather than essay type questions may eventually make possible a system of standardized Regents' Examinations which can be uniformly scored for all pupils alike. The adoption of standardized examinations and the use of scoring devices now available would, in fact, allow the scoring of all papers by the State Education Department itself, at no greater cost than is now involved in reviewing sample papers. So far as the technique of examining is concerned, the major criticisms directed at the present examinations may thus be almost completely met.

IMPROVED ACHIEVEMENT THROUGH EXAMINATIONS

Assuming that the examinations can be made reliable tests of the achievement of individual pupils, can the examination system be so used as to promote a better preparation of young people for the activities which lie ahead of them outside of school?

The repressive influence which the Regents' Examinations now exercise on the secondary schools does not indicate that examinations as such are bad. On the contrary, the very strength of that influence demonstrates how much can be done to shape the educational program of a whole state, through a system of examinations respected as the Regents' Examinations are respected. Hence, *the question which faces New York State is not the question of whether to retain or to abolish the Regents' Examinations; it is the question, rather, of how to make those examinations contribute effectively to the kinds of educational outcomes with which the schools ought to be chiefly concerned.*

The fact that the Regents' Examinations are now retarding influences, rather than instruments of progress, would seem to be due principally to three circumstances.

First, the examinations are now designed chiefly to measure ability of the sort required for successful work in college courses. It is this circumstance which has been principally responsible for the development of "non-Regents'" courses in the secondary schools. The Academic Examinations were introduced, it will be recalled, largely at the instigation of the colleges, at a time when preparation for college was the major function of the secondary schools. Despite changes which have been made in the high school syllabi, the examinations still retain a predominantly college-preparatory character. Furthermore, the examinations in most of the academic subjects—English, mathematics, foreign languages, science, the social studies—are the same for all pupils who are seeking credit in those subjects. Unusually able pupils and pupils who are of mediocre or below-average ability, pupils who are planning to use the subjects as a foundation for further scholarly training and pupils for whom the subjects represent the general-education content of business or technical training—all must pass these examinations if they are to be eligible for Regents' diplomas. With only one official measuring instrument which they can use to gauge school achievement, certain schools have been forced, for the sake of their own records as well as in the interests of their pupils, to exempt considerable numbers of boys and girls from the Regents' requirements. In some instances these schools merely refuse to admit to the examinations pupils whose daily classroom work is unsatisfactory or whose records on unofficial tests show that they are not likely to succeed. In other instances the schools assign all pupils with poor academic records to special classes in which no attempt is made to prepare for the examinations.

The present system is satisfactory neither for the college-preparatory pupils nor for those who are not "college material." On the one hand, the effort to maintain thoroughly scholarly standards among pupils who are going on to college has resulted in a kind of examination inappropriate for large numbers of boys and girls who will not go to college. On the other hand, the effort to make high school diplomas available to pupils who are not proficient in academic scholarship has threatened a relaxation of scholarly standards for the college group.

The remedy lies in recognizing that standards of academic scholarship cannot be satisfactorily maintained by examinations which must serve a multitude of other functions as well. The ability demanded for successful scholarship is in many respects a product of specialized training—training as distinct from that which should be provided for all boys and girls as is the training which leads to unusual competence in music, for example, or competence in fields involving highly developed vocational understandings or skills. This being the case, *scholarly ability ought to be tested by examinations separate from those which are used as measures of general high school achievement.* Examinations of the latter sort—that is, tests of the attitudes and understandings which high schools should properly expect of all their leaving pupils—should be given alike to young people planning to go on to college and to those who are ending their full-time school work in the high school. The college-preparatory pupils should be tested, in addition, for their possession of the specialized abilities which continued academic work will demand of them. If separate examinations designed to test these particular abilities can be established for the college-preparatory group, the standards of scholarship for this group may be made as exacting as the demands of college work require. If, at the same time, there can be provided appropriate tests of the attitudes and abilities which should be a product of high school education in the case of every boy and girl, the types of competence which the present academic examinations largely neglect may be given direct attention.

A second circumstance which has made the present examinations a restricting influence in the schools is that the examinations are limited to pencil-and-paper tests; they demand no other evidence of pupils' abilities or attitudes. This has meant that only those outcomes of school work have been emphasized which can be readily measured by written examinations. What boys and girls know can be fairly accurately tested in writing; what they think or are interested in is very difficult to test in this way. Written tests, moreover, are likely to give evidence only of what boys and girls can or will do on demand; they offer slight evidence of what boys and girls will do of their own accord, though the latter is obviously the more important. So long as written examinations are used as the sole means for judging pupils and schools, there can be only a partial measurement of the possible outcomes of a school's work, even though different examinations may be provided for different types of pupils.

If the Regents' Examinations are to serve the constructive purpose which they may well serve, *the examination system needs to be broadened to provide for the collection of all possible pertinent information about pupils' educational growth.* Certain of the data through which the Inquiry has sought to judge the work of the schools illustrate the kinds of information that may be revealing. Inventories of pupils' interests, pupils' statements of their plans for the future, accounts of what pupils do outside of school, observations of pupils' successes or failures in their hobbies or their jobs, may be even more significant in appraising school work than the pupils' written answers to questions on a formal examination. Much of this information must be gained by other means than what, properly speaking, are called examinations. No doubt some of it will come too late to help in determining whether a particular pupil should receive a high school diploma. Yet all of it may contribute so directly to the fundamental purpose of improving the work of the schools that it ought not to be neglected in any scheme of educational appraisal which the Regents may sponsor.

The final circumstance which detracts from the value of the present examinations is that they are used in such a way as to relieve local schools of responsibility for the out-of-school success or failure of their pupils. This circumstance has been perhaps more to blame than any other for retarding progress in individual schools.

Long tradition has accustomed both the public and the school people of the State to the notion that the high school marks and diplomas that count are those that "come from Albany." The public values the prestige which a Regents' rating gives; local marks and local diplomas are usually looked on with comparative suspicion. The school people are often grateful for the protection from local criticism which the Regents' system affords to individual teachers and school administrators. Relying on the prestige of the Board of Regents, teachers can use the Regents' ratings either as a defense against parents who believe that their children have been unjustly marked, or as an evidence of effective teaching. Principals can cite examination results to support existing or proposed course offerings, nonpromotion or refusal of diplomas in the cases of individual pupils, renewals or terminations of appointments of teachers. The examination system as it now operates thus offers the schools a constant temptation to shift the responsibility for important decisions to an impersonal agency remote from the local situation.

If a centralized examination system provided, or could provide, means for judging accurately all aspects of a pupil's individual growth, this situation would not need to cause concern. But no remote and impersonal agency can dependably offer the kind of judgments of individual pupils which the Regents' ratings are assumed to represent. The present examinations are not reliable enough to justify unquestioning acceptance of their results.[3] Made as reliable as they could possibly be made, they still could not safely be used to determine the fate of individual boys and girls unless there were added to them the knowledge possessed by people competent to fill in details which the examinations could not reveal, to reconcile conflicting results, to interpret examination scores in the light of an intimate acquaintance with persons and circumstances. People able to interpret the examination results in this way cannot be found in an office in the state capital. They must always be lacking in the State Department, not because able people are not available for State Department service, but because no one at Albany can expect, except by chance, to know an individual pupil in a distant school well enough to be his educational judge.

For the sake of justice to individual boys and girls, therefore, *pupils' ratings on State Department Examinations need to be combined with the best judgments of local school people as a basis for promoting pupils from grade to grade or for awarding them their high school diplomas.* No centralized examining agency ought to bear sole responsibility for determining what happens to individual pupils in these important matters.

But justice to pupils is not the only argument for making the schools finally responsible for decisions about their pupils. It has been pointed out in an earlier chapter that the schools cannot be expected to do what ought to be done for the boys

[3] As has been suggested earlier, the State Education Department itself is under no illusions in this matter. A letter addressed to the Supervisors in the Examinations and Inspections Division on February 2, 1937, by the Acting Director of the Division, contains the following statement: "Reliability is especially important as far as our examinations are concerned since many pupils in this State are passed or failed on the basis of the marks they make in the Regents' examinations. In my opinion, this practice is an abuse of the examination system. We must admit that as far as reliability is concerned, the Regents' examinations are in a defenseless position."

and girls whom they are educating, unless they are sensitive to their pupils' needs. So long as the State Department acts as sole arbiter of the success of each pupil's education, that sensitiveness will often be lacking. The schools will not be obliged to think for themselves beyond the lines which the Department lays down. They will not have to consider what else they might have done for particular young people, or whether what they have actually done has been of value. If it is to stimulate local planning and local initiative, any examination system which the State maintains ought to avoid taking the responsibility for this sort of thinking away from the local schools.

The further development of the Regents' Examinations needs to be planned in the light of all these considerations. *What the examination system can valuably do is to provide a variety of objective evidences on which judgments about pupils and schools may be partially based. What it ought not to do is to furnish a sanction for the use of partial and unreliable data as the sole means for deciding young people's educational fates.* The examinations need lose none of the respect which has been accorded them by becoming a source of information to the schools, rather than an umpire for the schools. To the degree to which they can be made a source of more varied and more reliable information than at present, their fundamental value may be greatly increased.

SUMMARY

In their present form the Regents' Examinations are keeping the schools from equipping boys and girls with much of the knowledge and many of the abilities which secondary school work ought to give them. The young people directly affected are not merely the least able boys and girls, but the ablest and the average as well. Yet the examinations have unquestionably helped the schools also, in the thoroughgoing respect they have built up for scholarly achievement.

The unique values of the examination system ought by all means to be preserved. The system has been modified in the past to meet new educational conditions and requirements, and it is currently being changed in various respects. Certain of its defects are being remedied by new methods of preparing the examinations and by improvements in their content. Further thoroughly practicable modifications in the scope of the examination system, and in the way in which the data that it may provide are used, should make the system as a whole a highly constructive part of the State's educational machinery.

CHAPTER XI

Secondary School Organization and School Enrollments

THE influence of the Regents' Examinations explains certain general shortcomings in what the New York State secondary schools do for their pupils. It fails to account, however, for the fact that large numbers of schools offer much less extensive programs than the State Education Department has sought to encourage. This further limitation on the schools' accomplishment is to be explained in part by the small enrollments in many of the schools, and by the plan of organization under which the schools now operate.

PREVALENCE OF SMALL HIGH SCHOOLS

In 1937, some 55 per cent of the high school pupils in New York State went to schools which enrolled over two thousand pupils each. Most of these pupils lived in New York City; the rest attended some one of a score of large schools in other cities. Undoubtedly many of these schools present extremely difficult educational and administrative problems because of their size. Available evidence, however—test results, reports from the schools, interviews with leaving pupils—tends to show measurably greater educational achievement on the part of pupils from these large schools than on the part of pupils from small schools. In the light of this evidence it seems fair to conclude that, for the average New York State boy or girl, going to high school means attending a school big enough in terms of the numbers of its pupils to be able to provide an extensive and varied program of secondary school work.

But in this same year some twenty thousand upstate New York pupils were in high schools which enrolled fewer than a hundred pupils each. Thirty-six thousand more were attending schools enrolling more than a hundred but fewer than two hundred pupils each. Another twenty-five thousand five hundred were in high schools of between two hundred and three hundred enrollment. These three groups of pupils—approximately eighty-one thousand five hundred in all—were attending nearly six hundred different schools. The schools to which they went constituted almost two-thirds of all the public secondary schools in the State.

The significance of these facts becomes apparent when it is realized that a high school enrolling fewer than approximately three hundred pupils cannot, without undue expense, offer a comprehensive and flexible educational program; and the farther a school's enrollment falls below this figure, the more limited its program is likely to be. High schools in New York State are commonly thought of as very large schools. Actually, *a majority of the secondary schools in New York are too small to provide either the range of subjects or the thoroughness of teaching that an effective program of secondary education requires.* The kinds of programs which these small schools do manage to offer, the effect of the current plan of school organization on their work, and the efforts which have been made to establish a better educational program for the boys and girls now enrolled in such schools, all need to be considered in accounting for present educational results.

PROGRAMS OF SMALL HIGH SCHOOLS

The programs which small high schools manage to provide are determined in considerable measure by convention. One feature of current convention is the expectation that except in the large cities, every individual secondary school, regardless of its size, will serve as a comprehensive high school. A few of the cities have established separate schools offering specialized academic, fine arts, and vocational programs to meet the needs of special groups of young people. In the majority of school systems programs of this sort, if they are offered at all, are provided in one general secondary school which must be responsible for all high school pupils in the local school system.

The pressure to be comprehensive means that each general high school sets out to offer a program which will cover a variety of fields. Convention again dictates that it shall begin with an academic program. If, having supplied enough academic subjects to meet most college-entrance requirements, it has teaching time left over, it then adds a number of business-training subjects. Provided it can expand still further, it may offer some form of training in practical arts; but it ordinarily gets to the latter only after it has arranged for a considerable list of purely academic credits. The academic tradition is usually so strong that *systematic planning in terms of particular local needs seldom plays a part in shaping the high school program*, as is shown by the 60 per cent of agricultural communities whose high schools offer no work in agriculture, and the still larger proportion of industrial communities which provide no industrial training.

Nor does cooperative planning on the part of a number of schools in a given area enter in to relieve any single school of its obligation to offer a full program. The complete lack of cooperation among the small high schools is especially noteworthy. While each small school is making up its own program by the process of adding piecemeal bits to a list of more or less miscellaneous academic subjects, the high school in the next town, perhaps less than five miles away, is going through the same procedure. *No matter how near one another a group of small high schools may be, the schools' programs merely duplicate one another instead of supplementing one another.* Hence thousands of secondary school pupils now living within practicable traveling distance of three or four secondary schools, each have only Hobson's choice as to what their high school work will be.

This method of arranging the high school program partly accounts for the overwhelming predominance of college-preparatory courses in the smaller high schools of the State. Though proportionately fewer pupils from small schools than from large schools actually go to college, it is only among schools of more than three hundred pupils each that a majority of the schools offer as many as three major fields of specialization, namely, business training, industrial arts or agriculture, and home economics, in addition to a purely academic program. In schools enrolling fewer than three hundred pupils, more and more of the nonacademic work is likely to be missing with each decrease in the size of the schools.

The effort to be comprehensive is also reflected in the incompleteness of the academic programs of many small schools. The smallest schools cut their programs at the top: as many as one-third of the New York State schools enrolling fewer than one hundred pupils are "M1," "M2," or "M3" schools, that is, schools chartered by the Regents to offer only the first one, two, or three years of a four-year high school program. Even apart from the "M" schools, large numbers of small schools offer headless courses. For example, though practically all small schools make it possible for pupils to start the study of high school mathematics, the total amount of mathematics usually offered by schools enrolling fewer than two hundred pupils is limited to five semesters (two and one-half years) in a four-year high school program. Again, most of the high schools with enrollments below one hundred offer work in two foreign languages, namely, Latin and French; but more than half provide only beginning work in one or both of these languages. Courses in business training and practical arts in the small schools are still more likely to consist only of very elementary work. The program of studies characteristic of the majority of these schools gives pupils a chance to piece together enough diverse subjects to satisfy the requirements for an academic diploma. In few of the schools, however, is it likely to provide for the continued study of any single subject except English. Furthermore, though the program may show courses labeled "elective," a small-school pupil must often study almost every subject his school offers if he is to accumulate enough credits to graduate.

Were the small high school programs characterized merely by incompleteness, the effect on pupils' achievement would be unfortunate enough. To this characteristic, however, must be added certain others growing out of the fact that *the pressure to offer comprehensive programs forces many small schools into various makeshift expedients.*

To avoid the necessity of omitting subjects altogether, certain schools adopt the device of pairing various subjects and offering each subject in a pair in alternate years only. Thus, a school may offer physics one year and chemistry the next, beginning again with physics the third year; or it may alternate first-year French and second-year French, or algebra and first-year Latin. This practice is undoubtedly preferable to the plan of not offering one of the subjects which are paired. Nevertheless, it introduces very apparent difficulties, in that pupils from two or three grades must be combined in each alternated subject, and orderly programs are often almost impossible to arrange.

Whatever the school may do to extend its program of studies, the number of teachers which a small school can afford is necessarily limited. Practically all small schools, therefore, are sooner or later forced into the expedient of requiring each teacher to teach a variety of subjects, in some of which the teachers may have no adequate educational background. As a result, teachers trained in European history are to be found teaching English and foreign languages; home economics teachers are called on to teach fine arts; teachers trained in business subjects or Latin may be required to "take care of" a class in civics. In New York State this practice seems most seriously to affect the teaching of the social studies. Classes in this field are admittedly assigned by the principals of many small schools as program-fillers to teachers trained in other subjects.

Again the schools try to escape one makeshift by adopting another. As a means of avoiding a wide spread of teaching assignments to any one teacher, small schools often provide more teachers than an economical pupil-teacher ratio would suggest, keeping instructional costs down by employing inexperienced or meagerly trained teachers at the lowest possible salaries. This device is practically forced on schools enrolling fewer than one hundred pupils, no matter what other expedients they may adopt. Wherever it is used, it obviously allows an approach to a comprehensive program only at the sacrifice of skill and maturity in teaching.

All these devices merely emphasize the handicaps either of restricted offerings or of inferior teaching, or both, against which the small school must work. Moreover, the small school's disadvantage when it is compared with the large school is not limited to its formal program of class teaching. In proportion to the number of its pupils, the expense of heating the school building, keeping it in repair, and providing necessary janitorial service is much greater in the small school than in the large. As a result, the small school ordinarily has less to spend on all sorts of supplementary educational service. Its teaching materials—books, classroom supplies, maps and pictures, models and apparatus—must be kept to a minimum. It can offer only a limited range of extracurricular activities. It can afford less expense for guidance services than can the large school. Its principal must devote most of his time to teaching; its teachers therefore lack the direction and the constructive help that a well-planned supervisory program could give. In all these respects the small-school program is of necessity a distinctly narrow program, barren of many of the opportunities for learning with which a high school ought to provide its pupils.

This does not mean that there can be no good small high schools. Excellent instruction was observed in various small schools by members of the Inquiry staff. A number of examples of such instruction have been cited in the preceding chapters; they were drawn from small schools which were doing outstanding work in the teaching of particular subjects, in individual attention to certain types of pupils, in the development of certain kinds of extracurricular activities.

But it would appear almost inevitable that *no school with an enrollment of much fewer than three hundred pupils, unless it be an unduly expensive school, can be good in more than one or two phases of its program.* Except for one small school which was, in fact, enormously expensive, the Inquiry staff discovered none with an enrollment of less than three hundred that ranked consistently high in such measures of achievement as the Inquiry staff found it possible to use. If the usual small school excels in one field of instruction, it must of necessity pay inadequate attention to other fields of equal importance. If it includes in its staff one teacher of exceptional experience and ability, it necessarily employs four or six or eight others who are gaining their first teaching experience, or who, at the other end of the scale, have lost their enthusiasm for growing in their work. The great majority of small schools do not stand out even in special parts of their programs. Forced to do their best under conditions which keep that best from being really good, they may do an honest and conscientious job, but almost invariably it must be a narrow and formal one.

This fact goes far to explain certain of the outcomes of the present educational program. The small schools in New York State are predominantly rural and village schools. It will be recalled that rural pupils are at a marked disadvantage, as compared with city pupils, in most of the abilities which the

Inquiry was able to measure. *That rural boys and girls are less well educated when they leave school than are city boys and girls, and that they take up fewer out-of-school activities which will add to their education, must unquestionably be attributed in considerable part to the narrow and incomplete programs especially characteristic of the small schools from which these boys and girls come.*

CURRENT PLANS OF SCHOOL ORGANIZATION

Beyond the small size of the majority of its high schools, a circumstance which has had a further limiting effect on the secondary school program is the fact that the great majority of high schools in New York State have clung to the conventional four-year organization.

Outside New York State, the junior-senior high school organization has been rapidly supplanting the conventional four-year high school in many school systems. Junior and senior high schools began to be widely established in the United States about 1910. Under the plan of grade-grouping which accompanied their establishment, the traditional eight-year elementary program was usually reduced to six years, and two years were added to the period of secondary education. Most of the reorganized secondary schools became either separate three-year junior and senior high schools, or six-year junior-senior high schools; the six-year organization in particular has spread widely in recent years. Over the country as a whole, reorganization proceeded so rapidly in the twenty years after it began that by 1930 half the secondary school pupils in the United States were enrolled in reorganized schools.

Numerous investigations have shown that it is entirely possible to accomplish in a modern six-year elementary school the educational task which used to take up the first eight years of a pupil's school life. As to the effects of reorganization in the upper grades, the recent National Survey of Secondary Education made it evident that the two years thus saved have in general been profitably incorporated in the secondary school program.[1] The Survey demonstrated that reorganized secondary schools tend to provide distinctly broader educational opportunities for their pupils than schools of corresponding size organized on the conventional basis. Though the junior-senior high school organization does not in itself cause improved school programs, there is ample evidence that it makes such programs easier to arrange and to administer.

The advantage of a departure from the conventional organization, especially when that departure consists in the adoption of a six-year high school program, lies in a number of factors. With six grades instead of four in which to offer their work, secondary schools can make greater use of survey and tryout courses as a basis for guidance. Their larger staffs make possible a more varied offering of extracurricular activities. By bringing together greater numbers of pupils in a single school unit, they can provide for more economical and flexible use of specialized classrooms, equipment, and teachers.

These various advantages are important to large schools and small schools alike. Particularly important from the standpoint of small schools is the larger teaching staff which reorganization allots to the secondary grades. A six-year junior-senior high school, offering a program in which its teachers are responsible for the teaching of their subjects in the seventh and eighth grades as well as the four upper grades, can afford half again as many teachers who are specialists in various high school subjects as can the four-year school which it displaces. It need be under much less pressure than the conventional high school, therefore, to assign to its teachers subjects in which they are not adequately prepared.

Despite these advantages, *New York State has been notably slow to adopt the junior-senior high school plan.* Rochester was one of the first cities in the United States to explore the advantages of reorganization; its example has had marked influence on

[1] National Survey of Secondary Education, Monograph No. 5: *The Reorganization of Secondary Education.* U. S. Office of Education Bulletin, 1932, No. 17.

practice in other states. New York City has established sixty-two junior high schools. Elsewhere in New York, reorganization has been confined chiefly to the larger school systems, and for the last fifteen years has proceeded at the rate of no more than four or five schools a year. Among a total of nearly a thousand secondary schools in the State, it is probable that the number of schools which are now organized either as junior or senior high schools or as combined six-year schools is less than one hundred fifty.[2]

How far the failure of New York to organize its schools on a junior-senior high school basis has affected the outcomes of its program of secondary education is difficult to estimate. Reorganization does not insure a better educational program; it merely makes that program more readily possible. But coupled with reorganization have tended to go more direct attention to the needs of individual pupils, more comprehensive provisions for guidance, and a broader and more flexible program of studies. Certain of these features have been noted as particularly characteristic of the junior high schools in New York State.[3] It is probably fair to conclude that *failure to adopt some form of the junior-senior high school plan has meant, in large and small schools alike, a less positive contribution than the schools might otherwise have made to their pupils' general and individual competence.*

CENTRALIZED SCHOOLS AS A REMEDY FOR PRESENT DEFECTS

In the light of gains which might be made through reorganization there is ample reason to urge a change in the conventional eight-four plan under which most of the New York

[2] Exact figures on the extent of secondary school reorganization in New York State are exceedingly difficult to secure. On the one hand, the State Education Department sometimes recognizes and separately identifies junior high schools in school systems which do not have separately organized junior high schools. On the other hand, considerable numbers of secondary schools which are designated by their own officers as six-year high schools or junior-senior high schools are listed by the Department merely as four-year schools.

[3] See Chapter IX.

State high schools now work. But as between this general change and the more radical change which will be necessary in order to provide the boys and girls who attend small high schools with the educational opportunities they ought to have, the latter is of far more pressing importance. It will therefore be appropriate to devote the remainder of this chapter to a discussion of what can feasibly be done to free the small schools from their present handicaps.

New York State has for some years been encouraging local districts to combine several small schools into one centralized school. Observation of the State's experience with the plan of centralization suggests a number of considerations which should play an important part in any state-wide program for reorganizing rural high schools.[4]

First, *improvement in rural secondary education does not necessarily require the immediate substitution of large school units for all the present small high schools.* Many of the existing small schools are excellently housed. To abandon their present buildings and to construct new buildings which would accommodate pupils from several existing schools would represent a gross extravagance. The essential element in centralization ought to be the centralization of educational planning and supervision, rather than the mere physical bringing together of large numbers of pupils, though in most cases the latter will eventually be important. Under a centralization of planning and supervision, small high schools in several present districts might remain for the time being as separate high school units in one larger district. Instead of competing with one another as now, however, these high schools ought to supplement one another. Thus, while one might emphasize college-preparatory work as its particular field of specialization, a second might provide an extensive program of business subjects, and a third might offer specialization in home economics, agriculture, or industrial

---

[4] Recommendations for the general reorganization of school districts in New York State are presented in Luther H. Gulick, *Education for American Life,* Regents' Inquiry, 1938.

arts—the separate schools exchanging pupils according to the particular types of specialization which individual boys and girls most need. Duplication of certain basic offerings would necessarily remain, but each school, by restricting its program, could do well what it set out to do, and the programs of all the schools together might represent for a given area a comprehensive and well-coordinated educational offering.

Second, *any new school units which are established as a result of the combination of existing districts ought to be as large as they can practically be made.* There is little danger that new schools in the rural areas of the State will be too large for effective administration. Studies of school organization point to the increasing educational effectiveness of schools with larger and larger enrollments up to at least three hundred pupils in each grade;[5] and for maximum economy in providing plant and equipment, a school probably needs a total enrollment of not less than twelve hundred.

Much greater than the danger of schools which are too large is the danger that new schools may be established which, though larger than the schools whose places they take, are still too small. This has unfortunately been the case in a number of the existing centralizations. A study of small schools in general suggests that except as a matter of absolute necessity, no high school ought to be permitted to continue with fewer than one hundred pupils. Certainly no new school with so small an enrollment should be established. Occasional high schools with enrollments below two hundred in the four upper

[5] Lest it be feared that individual pupils might be lost sight of in a school of this size, it should be noted that the National Survey discovered that large schools in general offered more thorough and comprehensive arrangements for studying pupils' individual needs, for adapting class work to individual differences, and for providing systematic guidance to individual pupils than did schools of smaller enrollments. Systematic provision for pupils' individual needs is so rare in both large and small schools in New York State at the present time that no general comparisons can now be made within the State, but the National Survey evidence clearly indicates that large schools need not neglect individual boys and girls.

grades may properly become specialized units in a centralized administrative district, but no such school ought to remain, if there is any way of avoiding it, as a comprehensive high school serving all the pupils of a district. Even as a specialized school, a high school ought normally to have an enrollment of more than two hundred. The smallest school which can safely be recognized as a comprehensive school is one which enrolls not less than three hundred pupils, either in four grades on the conventional plan or in six grades organized as a junior-senior high school.[6]

[6] These estimates of necessary minimum size are in keeping with the clearly observable effects of limited enrollment on small schools. They have, however, a theoretical as well as a practical basis.

To be economically administered, every high school needs to organize its pupils in class groups as large as its individual teachers can manage effectively, at the same time keeping the average pupil-teacher ratio small enough to allow teachers a fair opportunity to become acquainted with individual boys and girls. In general practice, an average class size of approximately twenty-five pupils is assumed to meet this criterion. If a school organized in terms of a four-year program is to maintain classes of this size even in required subjects without combining pupils from two or more grades in each class, the school must obviously have a total enrollment of at least one hundred pupils.

Considerably more than one hundred pupils are necessary, however, if the school is to provide economically for a reasonable program of elective work. Every elective class which the school offers results in a subdivision of pupils, and accordingly, unless pupils from several grades are taught in the same class, in a lessening of the average class size. Investigations have shown that to assure the minimum number of elective classes which a comprehensive high school program ordinarily demands, with separate classes for each grade, the school's enrollment must be equivalent to not less than two class groups in each grade. Thus a four-year high school which is to offer a reasonable minimum of electives must have a total enrollment of not less than two hundred pupils.

Other considerations than those of economical class size alone make a larger enrollment highly desirable. The program of studies in a comprehensive high school ought to include a dozen different fields of instruction: English, social studies, mathematics, science, foreign languages, fine arts, music, business education, industrial arts, agriculture, home economics, physical training. The demands of these fields are such that a competent teacher in any one of them must have had specialized training in that particular field. To offer a program embracing all these fields a high school ought, therefore, to be able to command the services of at least twelve different specialists. In practice, it can rarely have

Third, *centralized schools, whether new or old, ought to take full advantage of the possibilities of the junior-senior high school plan of organization.* Most of the present centralized schools, though they enroll pupils in all twelve grades, seem to have continued the conventional eight-four organization. The opportunities which the junior-senior high school plan offers for adding to the scope and flexibility of the secondary school program are so well established that there is small excuse for a retention of the older form of organization.

Finally, *each reorganized school district ought, if possible, to form an educational unit large enough to employ teachers, supervisors, and administrative officers equivalent in rank and responsibility to the corresponding members of the staffs of city school systems.* One reason for the present low estate of rural education is that an able and enterprising teacher or principal can find no permanent career in rural schools. Advancement means almost always a change from a country school to a school in a town or city. Though the low salaries offered by rural schools have much to do with this fact, low salaries are not the sole cause of the desertion of these schools by able school personnel. Organized in small school units and small districts, the rural schools now offer little opportunity for a skillful teacher or administrator to rise to a position of wide influence or responsibility. There are few department headships in rural districts to which unusually competent teachers can be promoted; the principalships seldom compare with city-school principalships in the scope which they give to an able administrator; the superintendencies offer limited opportunities for educational leadership. Until rural districts can be made large enough in area, and comprehensive enough in the scope of their educational programs, to

all these specialists, even on a part-time basis, unless it can afford a staff equivalent to at least this number of full-time teachers, which means that to provide a comprehensive program and at the same time to have classes averaging twenty-five pupils to a teacher, a four-year high school must enroll not less than three hundred pupils.

furnish within themselves a road for promotion to positions of recognized professional importance, few rural schools will be able to command the professional ability which they badly need.

FINANCIAL WASTE
IN THE PRESENT SMALL HIGH SCHOOL PLAN

No state with as scattered a population as that in certain areas of New York can hope to provide for all its pupils even in moderately large high schools. New York must undoubtedly expect always to maintain certain schools which are necessarily so small that they can offer effective educational programs only at a considerably greater than average cost. But *the great majority of small high schools which now exist in New York State represent both a needlessly ineffective type of educational organization and a needlessly wasteful one from a financial standpoint.*

In 1935, the latest date for which usable figures are available, the average number of pupils for each teacher in village high schools was 22.62.[7] If the small high schools in the villages could have been reorganized in such a way as to bring the average class size for all such schools to twenty-five, the annual saving in teachers' salaries in terms of current salary schedules would have been $420,000.

Far greater savings might have been accomplished in the case of small high schools in the rural supervisory districts. In these schools the average number of pupils per teacher was 17.24. Assuming that the average class size could have been increased by only five pupils (that is, to 22.24), the saving in annual salaries would have been $1,600,000. If the average class size in the district high schools could have been brought to twenty-five, the annual saving in these schools alone would have been $2,200,000.

[7] This figure and those which follow are based on data provided by the cost study of the Inquiry. Since the data form part of the special report on school costs, they are not here presented in detail. See Alonzo G. Grace and G. A. Moe, *State Aid and School Costs*, Regents' Inquiry, 1938.

Savings of this magnitude can obviously not be made immediately. Against them, when they are made, will have to be balanced eventual capital outlays for new buildings and equipment, and possible increases in costs of transportation (though a study of current plans for transportation suggests that duplication of routes and competition among school districts are now producing excessive costs here also[8]). Yet the figures offer a fair estimate of the financial waste of an educational program in which small high schools play as prominent a part as they now play in New York State. Even more important, they furnish a measure of the resources which the State can readily command to provide better teaching, more adequate equipment, and a broader educational program for rural boys and girls.

SUMMARY

In terms of the relative numbers of pupils whose education they directly affect, the six hundred small high schools now a part of the New York State school system are probably not so important in the State's educational program as are its larger schools. For thousands of boys and girls every year, however, these small schools provide an education which in most cases is exceptionally narrow, academic, and superficial. The lesser competence of rural young people at the time they leave school, as compared with that of young people in the cities, unquestionably goes back in large measure to the restricted programs of these schools.

Marked improvement in the high school education offered to rural pupils is entirely possible without the immediate abandonment of any but the smallest and least efficient of the existing schools. The most important step which could be taken toward such improvement would be a reorganization of the present school district system to bring about better

[8] Alonzo G. Grace and G. A. Moe, *State Aid and School Costs*, Regents' Inquiry, 1938.

coordination of local school programs. A plan of unified supervision applied to several adjacent small schools would make it possible for these schools to supplement one another, instead of competing with one another as they now do. Better internal organization would allow these same schools to make more effective use of their own staffs and equipment. If to these improvements can be added the gradual substitution of larger schools for those too small to do independently effective work, much can be accomplished toward eliminating the educational inequalities which now bear heavily on rural boys and girls.

CHAPTER XII

The State Education Department

IT HAS already been said that New York State maintains an unusual degree of centralized control over its schools. The administration of the Regents' Examinations by the State Education Department represents only one method of state control. Hardly less important in determining what New York State boys and girls learn in the secondary schools are certain other phases of the work of the State Department.

ACTIVITIES AFFECTING
SECONDARY SCHOOL PROGRAM

The State Department has included a number of divisions and bureaus[1] which have been directly or indirectly charged with regulating and improving the secondary school program.

The most immediate and widespread contacts of the Department with local secondary schools have come through an Examinations and Inspections Division, which has had a professional staff made up of a group of specialists in the teaching of academic subjects and of art, music, and commerce, together with one general supervisor of secondary school work. Though this division has nominally been part of a Secondary Education Division under an Assistant Commissioner for Secondary Education, its Director has actually

[1] On July 30, 1937, the Board of Regents approved a reorganization of the State Education Department which will be commented on later in this chapter. Since the reorganization was not in effect at the time the schools were engaged in the work whose results the Inquiry has attempted to measure, direct accounting for those results must consider the earlier organization and activities of the Department.

exercised more or less independent responsibility in many matters affecting the administration of the Regents' Examinations and the supervision of high school work. The members of the Division have headed the committees which have prepared the Regents' Examinations, and have been responsible for drawing up syllabi in their particular fields. In addition, they have traveled widely throughout the State, holding conferences with groups of teachers and school officers, visiting schools, and discussing local problems with individual school people. Their visits have furnished a principal means for insuring local compliance with Department regulations, as well as for offering supervisory help to the local schools.

Apart from the staff of the Examinations and Inspections Division, the Secondary Education Division has had a professional membership composed only of the Assistant Commissioner for Secondary Education and a supervisor in charge of work with junior high schools. The Secondary Education Division has therefore attempted no such extensive visiting of individual schools as that undertaken by the Examinations and Inspections Division. It has, however, cooperated actively in the professional work of various organizations of secondary school people, perhaps most notably that of the Associated Academic Principals, and has offered widely sought advice and suggestion through correspondence, through conferences in Albany, and through various bulletins and reports on the secondary school program.

The State Department has also maintained direct contact with the secondary schools through a Vocational and Extension Education Division, under an Assistant Commissioner coordinate in authority with the Assistant Commissioner for Secondary Education. The Vocational Education Division has had charge of all programs in industrial arts, home economics and homemaking, vocational industrial and technical education, and agriculture. Its staff has included one or more supervisors for each of these fields. The Division has not had charge of programs in business training, which have been supervised by a member of the Examinations and Inspections Division. The authority of the Vocational Education Division to pass on the eligibility of local school programs for federal aid under the Smith-Hughes Act has given it firm control over vocational work in the schools. It has been exceedingly active not merely in supervising existing vocational courses, but in promoting the establishment of new courses in conformity with the provisions of the Smith-Hughes Act.

These three divisions are the branches of the Department which have been most immediately concerned with the secondary school program. In addition, an Elementary Education Division has indirectly influenced the secondary schools through its supervision of the preceding elementary grades; a Rural Education Division has exercised independent responsibility for supervising high school as well as elementary school programs in rural schools; an Attendance and Child Accounting Division has dealt with reports from the schools on individual pupils, and with the administration of the compulsory-attendance laws; a Health and Physical Education Division has concerned itself with its own particular phase of the school program; a Library Extension Division has furnished books to the schools on loan; a Visual Instruction Division has supplied lantern slides and other visual aids, likewise on loan; and an Educational Research Division has conducted certain studies of secondary school problems.[2] None of these latter divisions has been a part of the three whose major responsibilities have centered in the secondary schools. Excepting those three, the division which has maintained the closest contact with individual high schools has been the Rural

---

[2] Though other divisions—notably a Teacher Education and Certification Division, a School Buildings and Grounds Division, a Law Division, and a Finance Division—have been incidentally concerned with the work of the secondary schools, those listed are the divisions which seem to have had most definite influence on local secondary school practice.

Education Division. The Director of this Division and his assistants, working with district superintendents of schools throughout the State, have given much attention to specific local problems. The work of the other divisions has for the most part been conducted in Albany, but through letters to individual schools, bulletins of suggestions, and participation in professional meetings, the members of these divisions have made their influence widely felt.

There is abundant evidence that representatives of all these divisions have played a constructive part in determining educational practice in individual secondary schools. New York has been fortunate in attracting to the educational service of the State an unusual number of able and experienced men and women. Reports from teachers and school officers throughout the State emphasize the fact that *members of the State Department have assisted in developing local school programs, in suggesting constructive solutions for local problems, and in keeping before school officers various broad educational goals*. The visits of members of the Department to the schools have been welcomed by the local school people, and their criticisms and suggestions have in general been conscientiously acted on.

POLICY OF THE STATE DEPARTMENT WITH RESPECT TO SECONDARY EDUCATION

Despite the help which its individual members have given to local schools, the work of the State Department has been less positively constructive than it might well have been. A number of circumstances have limited the effectiveness of the Department.

Perhaps most important among these circumstances has been the fact that *the Department as a whole has had no coordinated program for the development of secondary education in the State*. Its several divisions have frequently planned their work without due regard for the plans of other divisions, and have, in fact, sometimes worked at cross-purposes with one another.

A striking example of incoordination appears in the programs which have been separately fostered by the Elementary Education, Secondary Education, Examinations and Inspections, and Vocational Education Divisions. These four divisions have approached their work from notably different standpoints. The Elementary Education Division has encouraged the adoption of the so-called activity program, in which formal school subjects are subordinated to informal projects based on children's "natural" interests. The Secondary Education Division has apparently not favored any such extensive use of projects, though it has encouraged experimentation with new subject matter and the introduction of extracurricular activities. The Examinations and Inspections Division, at least in its examinations, has placed thoroughly conventional emphasis on pupils' mastery of academic subject matter, organized on a formal course basis. The Vocational Education Division has sought to focus attention on the development of practical understandings and abilities, through a program which has had little in common with the general academic program.[3]

All four of these divisions have been concerned with parallel groups of pupils, sometimes with exactly the same pupils. Seventh and eighth grade pupils have been under the charge of the Elementary Education Division if they were in elementary schools, of the Secondary Education Division if they were in junior high schools, of the Examinations and Inspec-

---

[3] The policy of the Vocational Education Division has been partly dictated by the requirements of the Smith-Hughes Act. In New York State this policy has had the effect of separating the vocational schools from the general high schools to such an extent that requests for information addressed by the Inquiry to "secondary school principals" frequently went unanswered by vocational school principals because, some of the latter explained, they thought that only the principals of academic high schools were meant. As a further result of this policy, the programs for pupils enrolled in business training courses, which have been supervised by a member of the Examinations and Inspections Division, have undergone a very different development from the programs in other vocational fields.

tions Division if they were preparing for the Regents' Preliminary Examinations, and of the Vocational Education Division if they were taking work in industrial arts or in home economics. Though upper-grade pupils have not been subject to the Elementary Education Division, they have been affected by the programs of each of the other divisions.

The differing policies of the four divisions have inevitably caused confusion and misunderstanding. The way in which these policies have been interpreted by school people in the field is well illustrated by the comment of more than one superintendent and high school principal to members of the Inquiry staff: "If you have a question that you need a ruling on from Albany, you can get any answer you want provided you know whom to go to." That all members of the Department should think exactly alike is, of course, neither to be expected nor to be desired. Constructive action by the Department as a whole, however, would seem to demand fundamental agreement on a general program, exceptions to which might be recognized as exceptions and treated on their merits. No such fundamental agreement has thus far been apparent among the branches of the Department most immediately concerned with the secondary schools.

Lack of coordination has been evident also in the failure of the Department to make systematic provision for certain important school problems. One such problem is that of junior high school reorganization. As long as school systems have remained organized on the conventional basis, the Elementary Education Division has supervised the work of the first eight grades and the Secondary Education Division that of the last four grades. After a school system has adopted the junior-senior high school plan, the Elementary Education Division has given up its responsibility for the seventh and eighth grades and the Secondary Education Division has added these grades to its charge. Neither Division, however, has felt itself responsible for encouraging school systems to undertake a reorganization. The junior high school supervisor attached to the Secondary Education Division has given assistance and advice to school officers planning a reorganization if he has been directly asked to do so, but the initiative has ordinarily rested with the school systems concerned. Moreover, even after reorganization has been accomplished the Department has not taken full account of the problems involved in the change from a four-year to a six-year secondary program. It has continued to require principals of reorganized schools to make various reports on forms designed for eight-year elementary schools and four-year high schools. Its syllabi have paid scant attention to a six-year secondary school program. Though the Secondary Education Division has expressed its general approval of the junior-senior high school plan, neither this Division nor any other has made a systematic effort to further the adoption of the plan or to help schools take full advantage of it once it has been put into effect.

One further type of incoordination deserves mention. This is the spreading of responsibility among several members of the Department in such a way that a consistent program of action is difficult to achieve. Incoordination of this last type is apparent in the complete separation of the Vocational Education and the Secondary Education Divisions. It is evident also in the Department's provisions for the development of guidance programs in the schools. A supervisor of vocational guidance attached to the Vocational Education Division has had nominal responsibility for this field. At the same time guidance problems connected with attendance, the use of pupil-records, the issuing of employment certificates, and the interpretation of the compulsory attendance laws have been the responsibility of the Attendance and Child Accounting Division. Members of the Department attached to each of these Divisions have made numerous contributions to the development of a guidance program, but under the separation of responsibility which has prevailed, the furthering of a consistent and comprehensive program has been practically out of the question.

In brief, the State Department as it has been organized has made available to the schools a variety of specialized services. Many of those services have been constructive because the individual members of the Department have been able and interested people. Yet the aggregate of service has been far less impressive than it might have been, because the Department as a whole has had no unified plan of action.

EDUCATIONAL RESEARCH

A further circumstance which has lessened the value of the Department's work has been the failure of the Department to base its supervisory program on any comprehensive program of research.

The Department has required from the schools extensive annual reports on a variety of matters: attendance, the enrollments of pupils in separate high school subjects, school expenditures, the observance of the Education Law, and the like. The data from these reports it has summarized year by year in a printed report of its own. For the most part the data thus collected have not been sought as a means of defining or dealing with specific educational problems, but have been gathered as a matter of routine. As a result, they have often been inaccurate, contradictory, or inconsequential.

The Department has also maintained an Educational Research Division. The reports which this Division has prepared have in many instances been timely and illuminating. Recently, for example, it has sponsored a comprehensive study of changes in the occupational pattern of New York State, and has been engaged in a critical examination of the school district organization in one of the rural counties of the State. From time to time it has reported on various problems of high school administration, teacher preparation, or examination procedures. But the Research Division, unfortunately, has seldom worked in any integral relationship with other divisions; its research activities have consisted for the most part of detached investigations of somewhat miscellaneous problems. Furthermore, the Research Division has been meagerly staffed, and has had few clearly defined responsibilities; its work has therefore been parenthetical. Other divisions have neither made a practice of calling on it for assistance in dealing with their problems, nor used its findings in any systematic way.

The remaining research activities of the Department have been those which have been more or less spontaneously and independently engaged in by its various individual members. Like the work of the Educational Research Division, these activities have tended to be detached and miscellaneous. Members of the Examinations and Inspections Division have made a number of studies of the reliability of the Regents' Examinations. The Acting Director of this division has recently completed an analysis of the programs of small high schools in the State. Supervisors of academic and vocational subjects have sponsored occasional experiments with new subject matter or methods of teaching. Members of several divisions acting in cooperation have conducted school surveys at the request of local school officers. All these research activities together, however, have produced only scattered additions to present knowledge either of how schools in general should be run or of the problems which face New York State schools in particular.

The result is that *the State Department has at its command no comprehensive or substantial body of facts through which to determine the best educational program for New York.* It has not rigorously investigated the particular educational needs of the various kinds of communities of which the State is composed. It has no detailed information as to the kinds of boys and girls who live in those communities. Except as its supervisors have recently visited certain schools, it knows little about the programs of individual high schools.[4] It cannot point to any extensive measures of the values of particular methods of teaching, gained through objective testing of those methods. Though it can supply the examination marks of every boy and girl who has ever taken the Regents' Examinations, it does not know whether these young people turned out well or badly after they left school, nor has it ever systematically examined the connection between pupils' school work and their out-of-school success or failure.

Lacking information of this sort, the program of the State Department has been based chiefly on professional rule-of-thumb. Its members have assumed that certain curricula or methods of teaching would be "good," and have urged schools to adopt them. Other methods have been frowned on for the opposite reason. Subjective judgment, rather than thoroughly objective study of educational needs and opportunities, has furnished the principal basis for the Department's regulations and for its supervisory activities.

RELATION OF STATE DEPARTMENT TO SCHOOLS

The nature of the Department's relations with the schools has also been an important factor in restricting the value of the educational leadership which the Department has supplied.

So far as the secondary schools of the State have been concerned, *the Department has devoted more attention to passing on the achievements of individual pupils and inspecting the work of individual teachers than to developing the high school program as a whole.*

The Examinations and Inspections Division has been making particular effort in recent years to deal constructively with general secondary school programs. In 1936–37 it sent its members on a series of carefully planned visits to small high schools, in an attempt to improve the organization and administration of these schools. Also, the Division has regularly

[4] The Secondary Education Division reports, for example, that no file has ever been kept of permissions granted individual high schools to substitute special curricula for the curricula outlined in the syllabi published by the Department.

invited applications from all the schools in its charge, for visits which would allow the study of particular local problems.

But the principal work of this Division has had to be that of making, administering, and scoring the Regents' Examinations, and of guiding the schools in their preparation for the examinations. The school visits which its members have made have been largely colored by efforts to "bring up" the schools' Regents' ratings. Its special-subject supervisors have quite naturally looked at the schools first of all from the standpoint of individual teachers' work in preparing for the examinations.

Furthermore, this Division and the other divisions immediately concerned with the secondary schools have been handicapped by a lack of staff members fully competent to work with high school principals on broad problems of educational policy. As contrasted with eight or nine subject supervisors, the Examinations and Inspections Division has had on its staff only one person qualified by special training and experience to deal with the planning of class schedules, the organization of a comprehensive curriculum, the administration of extracurricular activities, or the arrangement of special programs to meet the needs of individual pupils. For dealing with such general problems the Vocational Education Division has had not even one qualified person among some twelve supervisors of vocational subjects. Though the two members of the Secondary Education Division have been competent to deal with such problems, these two, with the one general supervisor from the Examinations and Inspections Division and one or two members of the Rural Education Division, have constituted a staff hardly large enough to furnish needed assistance to the principals of nearly a thousand secondary schools.

Consequently the help which the Department has been able to give on problems of general school management has been limited in the extreme. Supervisors of special subjects have made conscientious efforts to deal with such problems in their visits to the schools. Most of the supervision offered by the Department, however, has necessarily been focused chiefly on classroom procedures in particular subjects, rather than on the relation of those subjects to one another or on the relation of the whole program of subjects to pupils' needs.

Even in special fields of teaching, moreover, the State Department has seldom offered extensive guidance to teachers and school officers. Except in the Vocational Education Division, the number of supervisors has been small in relation to the number of schools to be supervised.[5] The pressure of the supervisors' work in connection with the Regents' Examinations, and of their schedules of visits to widely scattered schools, has no doubt largely accounted for the infrequency with which certain of the subject syllabi have been revised. Other than the syllabi and occasional supplementary bulletins, the Department has had no systematic means of bringing good educational practice to the general attention of schools throughout the State. The Department has issued few extensive aids to teachers in the form of detailed outlines or teaching materials, nor has it published lists of schools where especially promising work might be observed. The help it has offered has come largely in the form of suggestions based on the experience of individual

[5] The numbers of supervisors assigned to the various secondary school subjects have had little apparent relation to the numbers of schools, teachers, or pupils concerned with those subjects. One supervisor each has been allotted to ancient languages, modern languages, science, mathematics, music, drawing, commercial work, social studies, and English under the Examinations and Inspections Division. Under the Vocational Education and Extension Division a Bureau Chief and one supervisor have been assigned to an Agricultural Education Bureau, a Bureau Chief and two supervisors to a Home Economics Education Bureau, and a Bureau Chief and four supervisors (not including a supervisor of industrial teacher training) to an Industrial Education Bureau. The extension activities of the latter Division and its responsibility for certain schools above the secondary level may account for some of the disparities in personnel between the two divisions, but it is apparent that the Vocational Education Division has been in a far better position to offer direct assistance to individual schools than has the Examinations and Inspections Division.

supervisors, made in the course of brief visits to particular schools or in letters after the visits. Forced often to consider a multitude of questions in addition to those of improving instruction in their own fields, the supervisors of academic subjects in particular have obviously been able to do little more than touch superficially and somewhat at random on the problems which they have happened to encounter.

Furthermore, *the State Department has been handicapped by its remoteness from many of the schools in the State.* Other branches of the state government have divided the State into administrative districts and have placed resident representatives in each district. The Education Department has continued to carry on almost all its work from Albany. It has thus been kept from the continuous contacts with various sections of the State which would be necessary if it were to undertake educational planning in terms of regional or local needs. Coupled with its preoccupation with the Regents' Examinations and with routine reports and inspections, the distance of the Department from the schools has made it chiefly a regulating agency in the minds of many high school principals and teachers.

The Department's relations with the secondary schools have also been affected by the fact that *the Department has tried to perform various necessary services for the schools which the schools might better have been helped to perform for themselves.* This tendency has been especially apparent in the supervision of teaching carried on by the Department, and in the programs of the Visual Instruction and Library Extension Divisions.

The supervisory program of the Examinations and Inspections Division, as it has applied to small schools in particular, has been chiefly a substitute for a type of supervision which ought to be available locally. Large school systems commonly provide their own subject supervisors or department heads, and in these systems the supervisors from Albany have usually worked with the local supervisory officers rather than directly with the teachers. Small school systems provide few supervisors of any sort. In small schools, therefore, the State Department supervisors have had to accomplish what they could through visits to individual classrooms. Their work with individual teachers has undoubtedly been of some immediate advantage to the schools concerned, but the practice has also unquestionably had serious disadvantages. It has called for an inefficient use of the supervisors' time, in rare visits each year to scores or hundreds of separate classes. More important, it has substituted necessarily inadequate supervision by the State for the local supervision which rural schools must have if they are to approach the effectiveness of city schools, and which they can eventually have if rural school districts are made large enough to be sound administrative units.

The State Department has even more clearly been doing for certain schools what all schools probably should have been doing for themselves, through its Visual Instruction Division. Experiments with lantern slides as an aid to teaching were begun by the Department some twenty years ago. There is no question that the policy of experimenting in this field was thoroughly justified. Nor is there any question that the Department's effort to encourage the use of visual aids has been justified. But much of the experimenting has long since virtually stopped; the Visual Instruction Division has recently been engaged chiefly in administering a state loan library of slides. If these slides are actually important enough in teaching to warrant the provision of many sets of them at state expense, they are important enough to be part of the regular teaching equipment of the schools. They are not now used as regular teaching equipment, and the policy of the Department keeps them from being so used. They are not regularly used because individual schools find it difficult, under one centralized loan system, to get the slides they need when they need them. Moreover, the fact that the Visual Instruction Division keeps these slides on loan relieves most schools of any sense of responsibility for providing them on their own account.

Though not every school system could afford to buy all the slides it needed for its individual use, groups of schools, or, again, large administrative districts, could economically own such slides,[6] and must eventually do so if they are to use them effectively.

A similar criticism may be made of the policy underlying the Department's Library Extension service to schools. That the State should acquire and lend to the schools unusual books, or exhibits too costly to be reproduced in quantity, is understandable and appropriate. That it should try to palliate the barrenness of small-school libraries by sending them for temporary and occasional use a few boxes of books each year, sometimes including dictionaries, only emphasizes the inadequacy of the present educational program.

It is not to be inferred from these comments that the State ought to refrain from helping individual schools to secure adequate supervision or visual aids or books. On the contrary, one of the major functions of a State Education Department ought to be to make certain that schools have all necessary aids to effective teaching. But the surest way to bring about the schools' possession of such aids (including adequate local supervision) probably is not to dole them out on loan from a central supply. In so far as these aids are actually essential to a sound educational program, the State should move as rapidly as possible to a plan of administrative organization and of financial support for local districts which will allow local schools to have at their own command whatever aids they may need for at least a minimum basic program. The present arrangements for supervision of individual teachers by the Department, for the supplying of visual aids on loan, and for the furnishing of basic library and reference books, prevent

[6] Considerable numbers of schools in the Middle West, and a few in New York State, are already buying and using motion pictures on a cooperative basis. For a further discussion of the use of visual aids in the New York schools, see Elizabeth Laine, *Motion Pictures and Radio—Modern Techniques for Education*, Regents' Inquiry, 1938.

rather than further any fundamental improvement in the lot of the schools.

The State Department's relations with the secondary schools have been marked, finally, by the Department's unwillingness to enforce penalties for noncompliance with important regulations. *Though the Department has insisted that schools meet minimum standards as to plant, equipment, and program before they are chartered by the Regents, it has not systematically required them to maintain those standards after charters have been granted.* In 1937, according to an estimate supplied to the Inquiry by the head of the Examinations and Inspections Division, probably one-fourth of the secondary schools of the State would not have been eligible for new charters if their old charters had been revoked.

There now appear on the statute books of New York State a number of laws relating to details of the educational program. In several instances, particularly in connection with the teaching of citizenship and temperance, the Legislature has established minimum requirements in terms of content, grade levels, and periods of instruction. These requirements are difficult to administer and of doubtful value. Though their intent is usually excellent, their effect in most cases is to perpetuate the kind of teaching which does no more than "cover" a specified subject. The Department has nevertheless paid systematic attention to their enforcement, requiring schools to attest compliance with all legal provisions in the annual applications for state aid.

The Department's hesitance to enforce appropriate standards has appeared not so much in connection with the statutes as in the matter of its own regulations. Before a school can offer a sound secondary school program it must of course have an adequate building and appropriate equipment and supplies. The Department requires certain minimum facilities as a condition for chartering new schools. In the case of many established schools, however, members of the Inquiry staff concerned both with the teaching of particular subjects and with the secondary school program as a whole were impressed with the lack of essential equipment. Schools were found to be operating without any reasonable semblance of a school library, or with miscellaneous books locked in almost inaccessible storerooms. Classes in woodworking were being taught with only a few odd pieces of wood to work with. The only wall maps available for history and geography classes in some instances antedated the World War. Gymnasiums, lunchrooms, or toilet facilities in the older buildings were frequently overcrowded and unsanitary.

Where the improvement of physical facilities would demand large capital outlays, there has undoubtedly been reason for the Department to temper a strict interpretation of its rules. Many of the present lacks in the schools, however, could be cared for through the expenditure of relatively small sums. Moreover, the Department's requirements have not been unreasonable so far as physical equipment has been concerned. They have certainly called for no more than a community should reasonably be expected to supply if that community is to have a high school at all. Yet even in cases in which the absence of needed facilities could have been easily corrected, the Department has apparently contented itself with letters of criticism, followed perhaps by stronger letters if no improvement was made. It has practically never availed itself of its legal right to enforce minimum standards by withholding state aid. Its use of this extreme penalty would, of course, have resulted in a temporary denial of educational opportunities to pupils in the communities affected. Its failure to use it has meant that school officers have lacked the support that the Department might have given in communities which have become indifferent to educational needs, and that pupils in many schools, year after year, have been deprived of the kind of educational program to which they were entitled and which could have been provided for them.

Considered as a whole, the relation of the Department to individual schools has been largely that of a somewhat paternalistic inspection agency. The Department has given advice to the schools when they have asked for it, or in connection with its supervisors' visits. It has dealt only here and there with general educational planning, because it has had relatively few supervisors experienced in meeting the broad problems which underlie such planning. It has supplied for some schools services which the schools were too poor or too unconcerned to supply for themselves. It has nominally insisted on the fulfillment of certain minimum requirements as to buildings, equipment, and programs. The penalties it has imposed, however, have been the indirect penalties of pupils' failure in the Regents' Examinations—failure which chiefly affects boys and girls who have had nothing to do with nonobservance of the regulations—more often than they have been the direct penalties of withdrawal of financial aid from communities which have not done their fair share in maintaining a sound educational program.

EFFECT OF POLICIES ON PUPIL ACHIEVEMENT

Lest it seem that this analysis of the Department's activities leads to nothing but adverse criticism, it should be repeated that individual members of the Department have been of outstanding service to the schools. Because of the help which they have given, the Department is deservedly respected by the school people of the State. But the conclusion is inescapable that *the Department has functioned in the past as a collection of individuals rather than as an integrated organization engaged in furthering a well-considered and soundly established educational policy.* Its divisions and bureaus have not been related to one another in such a way as to promote a comprehensive and consistent program. It has gathered no such body of information concerning educational needs and educational results as would allow it to plan its program objectively. It has dealt with the schools in ways which have often failed to place the long-range educational program of the State on a substantial footing.

As a result, the Department has exercised no very aggressive or dependable leadership toward a program which would add to the social competence of the young people of New York State. *In some instances the Department has encouraged educational developments which, in the light of an impartial review of present needs, would seem to be quite inappropriate.* This has been especially the case in the field of vocational education. The Vocational Education Division has actively fostered highly specialized vocational training. As the analysis of vocational curricula has shown,[7] the Division has approved courses which in some instances have overtrained their graduates, in other instances have left graduates without the kind of training necessary to make them employable at beginners' wages, in a great many cases failed to produce appropriate vocational adaptability. The plans of the Division have apparently been largely opportunistic. It has furthered the kinds of training for which employers asked or for which federal funds could be secured or for which the Division judged there might be a demand, in centers where such training could be most easily established. As a basis for its program it has made no extensive surveys of vocational requirements or of opportunities for employment; its plans have apparently rested almost entirely on subjective estimates of fitness or need.

More often than it has encouraged inappropriate new programs, however, *the State Department has failed to take constructive action with respect to inadequate existing programs.* In the matter of training for citizenship or leisure-time activities schools have been left to do largely as they would, because of the Department's chief concern for academic accomplishment. The development of vocational training, except business training, has been hindered in academic high schools by the separa-

[7] See Chapter VIII.

tion within the Department of the Secondary Education and Vocational Education Divisions; and the business training programs, having been dealt with on an almost entirely academic plane, have been allowed to become largely sterile. Systematic attention to educational and vocational guidance has failed to materialize out of the division of responsibility with respect to problems in this field. The schools' provisions for individual differences have received hardly more notice than the Department has been forced to give in view of the obvious disparities between certain pupils' abilities and the Regents' Examination requirements. With respect to none of these matters has the Education Department as a department formulated any positive program, though individual members of the Department have no doubt often had such matters in mind in their work with local schools.

These are all matters in which the current school programs are notably weak. The Department's failure to pay well-considered attention to them unquestionably accounts for many of the defects in the education of the boys and girls now leaving the high schools of the State. Except in the field of vocational education, the official program of the Department has thus far been one which has accomplished little more than to maintain the established school offerings for these boys and girls. If certain schools have improved on the conventional high school program, either of their own accord or as a result of suggestions from individual members of the Department, their doing so would seem to have been only an incidental accompaniment of the Department's activities. In all too few instances can any such improvement be attributed to the Department's constructive leadership.

REORGANIZATION
OF THE STATE EDUCATION DEPARTMENT

It is fair to expect that the State Education Department should be more than simply an elaborate regulating agency.

If the Department is to exercise the constructive influence that may properly be demanded of it, it cannot continue to let such leadership as it offers grow out of the incidental activities of its various members. Systematic coordination of its program, responsible planning based on comprehensive factual evidence, and a relationship with local schools which will both enable and encourage the schools to offer the kinds of education particularly appropriate in each locality are all essential to the Department's thorough justification of its work.

Looking forward to some such new emphasis in the Department's program, the Board of Regents instituted in 1937 a number of changes in the plan of organization under which the State Department had been working up to the time when this Inquiry was begun. Not all those changes need be reviewed in this report,[8] but the features of the new plan which most directly affect the development of secondary education deserve at least brief attention.

The new plan of organization approved by the Regents removes a number of defects which have thus far kept the Department from consistent leadership in secondary education. The plan provides for greater coordination of the Department's work with the schools, by bringing together under one assistant commissioner for instructional supervision several related divisions and bureaus which were originally not closely connected with one another, notably the Divisions of Elementary Education and Secondary Education, the Division of Examinations and Testing (formerly Examinations and Inspections), the Division of Health and Physical Education, the Bureau (formerly Division) of Child Accounting and Attendance, and a Bureau of Radio and Visual Aids. It establishes a Bureau of Business Education under the Division of Vocational Education,

[8] The new plan of organization is outlined in the University of the State of New York Bulletin, No. 1118 (predated June 15, 1937): *Organization and Functions of the New York State Education Department, As Approved by the Board of Regents, July 30, 1937.* For a discussion of the plan as a whole, see Luther H. Gulick, *Education for American Life,* Regents' Inquiry, 1938.

thus putting specialized business education on the same plane with other vocational courses. It gives greater substance to the research activities of the Department by providing an assistant commissioner for research, whose division is to be "responsible for administering and improving the statistical services of the Department," and who is to "[initiate] such studies as are needed by the Commissioner and the Regents for the formulation and evaluation of policies." As a means of insuring more thoroughgoing attention to the curriculum, the plan adds a Bureau of Curriculum Development under the Division of Secondary Education, to serve as "a clearing-house for the building up of curriculum and instructional materials" for reorganized secondary schools as well as for schools operating on the conventional four-year high school basis. It clarifies the field service functions of the Department by creating a new Bureau of Instructional Supervision charged with the visits to schools which in the past have been made by supervisors from the Examinations and Inspections Division; and it limits the functions of the Division of Examinations and Testing to the preparation and administration of state-wide examinations In all these respects it offers a promising remedy for shortcomings which have been pointed out in the original plan of organization.

The new plan of organization does not provide, however, for certain services and relationships which are highly important if the Department is to give adequate direction to the State's program of secondary education.

The new plan still separates vocational education and general secondary education, placing the one under an assistant commissioner for vocational and extension education and the other under an assistant commissioner for instructional supervision. The fruits of this separation in the past are apparent in the fact that the two types of programs are almost completely dissociated from each other in New York State. The vocational courses, fostered independently of the general high school courses, have offered a program which has largely ruled out any continuance of general education for the boys and girls seeking vocational training. The academic high schools have persisted, as one vocational educator expressed it, in "telling their pupils that the vocational school is the place where all bad little boys and girls go after they die— educationally." Until vocational education for boys and girls who have never held jobs[9] is recognized and administered as a phase of a unified program of secondary education, there is small likelihood either that the present overspecialized vocational programs will be brought within reasonable bounds, or that the hundreds of academic high schools which now lack essential vocational courses will introduce such courses.

The new plan makes no better provision for the development of guidance programs than that existing under the former organization. It retains a Bureau of Guidance (dropping "vocational" from the title) under the assistant commissioner for vocational and extension education; it places the Bureau of Child Accounting and Attendance under a Division of School Administrative Services (formerly the Rural Education Division) whose director is responsible to the assistant commissioner for instructional supervision. The need for a well-considered and comprehensive guidance program in the secondary schools has thus far not been met partly because of this division of responsibility. It is not likely to be met except as the Department recognizes that guidance, like vocational education, ought to be a phase of secondary education in general. Nor will it be met so long as pupil accounting is thought of merely as a statistical service, having nothing to do with pupils' educational needs and educational plans.

[9] This statement is not intended to apply to specialized vocational education for persons who have already made a vocational beginning in actual employment, and who are seeking "upgrading" courses. It applies simply to initial vocational training. For a discussion of vocational education on the higher level, see Floyd W. Reeves, T. Fansler, and C. O. Houle, *Adult Education*, Regents' Inquiry, 1938.

Though the new plan separates the functions of examination and supervision, placing the one in a Division of Examinations and Testing and the other in a Bureau of Instructional Supervision, it makes no explicit provision for any other kind of supervisory assistance to local schools than that which they have received in the past. The plan provides chiefly for supervisors of special subjects. It leaves the supervisors as remote from the schools as before. The Department cannot be fully effective in building up local school programs until it includes more staff members than at present who are competent to deal with general secondary school problems and who can stay close enough to various sections of the State to become well acquainted with the particular needs of those sections.

The new plan makes no change in the arrangements for supplying special aids to the schools, namely, supervision of teachers in small schools, lantern slides on loan, books in the form of traveling libraries. It does nothing, therefore, to eliminate a form of dependence on the State Department which is now pauperizing the small-school programs.

Nor does the new plan promise any change in the Department's policy for insuring the provision by local communities of the physical facilities which they should provide for their secondary schools. The Department's concern with educational leadership ought not to relieve it from a concern to see that every secondary school has the means of achieving essential educational goals. The Department should insist, and it should back up its insistence with financial penalties when necessary, on the continuous provision by every school system of suitable buildings, equipment, and supplies, and of an adequate and properly qualified staff.

That these defects in the new plan of organization should be remedied is highly important. The new plan is likely to prove more effective than the old plan has been, but the fundamental leadership which the State Department ought to exercise can be much advanced through a scheme of organization that the present plan does not fully provide.

SUMMARY

Having grown by a process of adding new officers and new functions, as any expanding organization must, the State Education Department has presented until recently a dis-united collection of individual divisions, bureaus, and staff members. As a Department, its influence on the secondary schools has been chiefly that of a regulating and inspecting agency. Though its members have given valuable guidance and help to many individual schools, the Department has lacked both the coordination of policy and of organization, and the basic information about educational needs, which would have allowed it to exercise constructive leadership.

The failure of the Department to maintain a position of constructive leadership has largely accounted for serious defects in the general program of secondary education. It has accounted, in particular, for the infrequency with which the general high schools of the State have looked beyond a routine program of academic subjects in providing for their pupils' needs. The Department has been aggressive in the field of vocational education, but in this field its policy has been essentially opportunistic. It has promoted vocational educa-tion quite apart from general secondary education. The separation of the two programs, together with the lack of any detailed or comprehensive study of vocational needs, goes far to explain the limited opportunities which the State provides for vocational education at the secondary level, and the frequent lack of connection between those opportunities and actual vocational requirements.

Reorganization of the Department, toward which the Board of Regents has already taken a first step, needs most of all to emphasize the Department's responsibility for fundamental research and planning. Leadership based on research and coordinated planning may, and should, make the Department a far more constructive influence on the secondary school program in New York State than it has been in the past.

CHAPTER XIII

Contribution of the Schools to Social Competence

B ECAUSE this study has been concerned with what the Board of Regents, the State Education Department, and the individual secondary schools of New York State may do to improve the education of New York State boys and girls, it has given chief attention to the formal school program. Behind and around the schools lies always the adult community. What adults outside the schools do to and for boys and girls, either directly or by example, is at least as important as what the schools themselves may do.

Any conclusions as to why boys and girls have the traits and abilities which they do have when they leave the secondary schools must be tempered, therefore, by the knowledge that the schools are only partially responsible for what these boys and girls are like. Decent homes and neighborhoods, honest government, clean newspapers and magazines, a chance to have wholesome fun outside of school, opportunity for jobs when jobs are needed, may counteract many bad effects of even the narrowest and most formal school program. The opposite influences may condemn the best school to an often hopeless effort.

But in so far as the schools themselves are responsible for what young people are like, the study of school programs and policies suggests a number of explanations for the present characteristics of boys and girls just out of the high school. It suggests likewise the major points to be attacked in any plan for widespread improvement in the secondary school program.

THE HIGH SCHOOL'S CONTRIBUTION
TO YOUNG PEOPLE'S ABILITIES

The average New York State high school is now geared to do one kind of job, and only one. It takes the boys and girls who are fed into it from the elementary schools, lets them sort themselves crudely according to their ability to master academic subject matter, and starts them on a four-year round of drill and memorization. Some pupils rebel against that round, or cannot keep up with its academic demands. These the school lets go as soon as the law will allow and as soon as they take it into their heads to leave. The rest it prepares for final examinations.

The examinations have little to do—directly, at least—with the abilities which boys and girls need outside of school. For the most part they consist of tests of the amount of academic subject matter which pupils remember well enough to use in response to written questions. Nor does the school's method of preparing for the examinations have any direct relation to out-of-school matters. The school does not, in fact, know much about its pupils' out-of-school concerns, nor does it look to see what happens to most of its leaving pupils after they have ended their school work.

Thus the average high school provides an educational mechanism which is unadjustable and relentless. The school does its work almost wholly within its own four walls. It fixes its attention on a kind of performance which has little meaning except in academic circles, and which is tested without reference to out-of-school standards.

Operating in this way, New York State high schools graduate many boys and girls who are proficient in academic subject matter. The graduates may occasionally be competent in other respects as well, but not usually because the schools have made them so. The graduates are the survivors of a rigorously selective school program—the ablest and most favored by circumstance of all the boys and girls who enter the secondary schools. What they know about nonacademic matters they have picked up for the most part outside of school in proportion to their intelligence, their opportunities for learning, and the keenness of their observation. The schools themselves can claim credit for little more than their pupils' ability to pass the formal examinations which give direction to most of the high school work.

This is admittedly an extreme picture of the New York State secondary schools. It may nevertheless point more sharply to the essential weakness of the present school program than would a carefully qualified description. That weakness consists in the narrowness of what the majority of the schools try to do. They fail to make their pupils ready even for definitely predictable out-of-school requirements and opportunities, chiefly because they do not systematically concern themselves with any such matters.

POSSIBILITY OF A MORE EFFECTIVE CONTRIBUTION

That the schools could contribute much more than they now do to their pupils' competence is apparent from the success attending the work of schools which have broken away from the conventional pattern. Here and there individual schools have tried realistically to find out what the needs of their pupils were; they have arranged subject matter and methods of teaching to accord with pupils' particular interests and abilities; they have followed boys and girls out of school to discover what happened to them and what their successes or failures might mean for the school program. As a result, certain of these schools have been able to develop in their pupils not merely academic ability, but the kind of social conscience which the great majority of high school boys and girls now lack. Some of these schools have helped their pupils to build up habits of discriminating enjoyment with respect to reading, moving pictures, and the radio. A considerable number, most notably the vocational schools, have succeeded in giving their pupils a common-sense appreciation of what it means to get and hold a job. The boys and girls whom these schools have helped, moreover, have not been merely the ablest. By working directly and realistically with the least able, various schools have assisted young people who would have gained little or nothing from the conventional academic program to face the world with some tangible preparation for what lay ahead of them.

It is not to be supposed, therefore, that a boy or girl who gets only a store of academic facts out of his school work gets nothing else because the school program cannot include anything else, or because he is incapable of learning anything else. Within fairly wide limits high schools can teach narrowly or broadly, superficially or intensively, according to what they set out to teach. The breadth and thoroughness with which certain individual schools have been able to teach give striking evidence of how much schools in general might do for their pupils if they were to make a point of doing all that could be done.

OBSTACLES TO A MORE EFFECTIVE PROGRAM

Tradition, lack of concern for fundamental improvement, preoccupation with day-to-day routine undoubtedly account for much of the narrowness and formality in the work of the average high school, as they account for similar qualities in any social institution. It is probable, however, that these matters play a smaller part in the work of individual schools in New York State than might reasonably have been expected. Teachers and principals in the high schools are in most cases keenly aware of the shortcomings of their schools and concerned to provide better educational programs. The present narrowness of the usual high school program is more directly accounted for by three major factors which stand outside the individual schools than by mere inertia within the schools themselves.

The first of these outside factors is the system of Regents' Examinations as that system is now administered. Designed originally to test academic ability, the examinations have unquestionably been more responsible than any other single influence for fixing the attention of the schools on a narrowly academic program. The purpose of the examination system is thoroughly sound, and the influence it has had on the schools shows how much may be accomplished through such a system to give constructive direction to secondary school work. But the present examinations need to be both extended in scope and adapted to the needs of pupils of varying interests and abilities before the schools can be free to do all that ought to be done for individual boys and girls.

The second factor is a plan of school district organization which keeps more than half the high schools of the State so small that they cannot, under normal circumstances, offer either a comprehensive or a thorough educational program. Until the present district plan is modified the smaller villages and towns in particular must choose between offering all their boys and girls only a partial education, or providing high school work which meets the needs of some pupils and largely ignores the interests and abilities of the rest.

The third factor is the lack of consistent leadership which has characterized the work of the State Education Department so far as the secondary schools have been concerned. Improvements in the secondary school program have come from independent experiments by school people in the field, more often than as a result of the organized activities of the State Department. Though the Department has welcomed promising experimentation by individual schools, its own attention has been largely devoted to maintaining a standard program of high school work and to testing the academic achievement of individual boys and girls who have been candidates for high school diplomas. If it is to help high school pupils get more than they now get from the secondary school program, the Department must give far greater attention than in the past to fundamental research on educational needs and educational outcomes, to the development of curriculum materials, and to the planning of a comprehensive and flexible program of secondary education.

RESPONSIBILITY OF THE PUBLIC

The three factors discussed above have to do with the organization and conduct of the schools. Whatever action is to be taken with respect to them, therefore, may properly be initiated by school people. But there is one serious limitation which needs to be recognized with respect to any improvement in the education of young people that school people as such can make.

A school cannot educate boys and girls to be much better than their elders are. It can equip young people with important information and valuable habits and skills; it can give them an intellectual understanding of happenings and problems outside the schools; it can do something to rouse them to a feeling of active social responsibility. Not even the ideal school, however, can overcome the tendency of young people to learn from the open example of their elders. If, therefore, the schools are to have any marked degree of success in developing healthy social attitudes in high school boys and girls, they must be able to depend on cooperation from the communities from which their pupils come.

This means that the attitudes with which young people leave school cannot be made all that adults would like to have them, merely by turning the job over to the schools and saying: "Bring us up a better generation." The schools, it should be repeated, can do more than they now do, but the task as a whole is one which calls for effort outside the schools quite as much as within. If New York State wants its young people to take social responsibility, its citizens cannot look tolerantly on disregard of social responsibility among adults, whether that disregard be expressed in outright graft or merely in the fixing of a traffic ticket. If the State wants boys and girls to enjoy themselves with decent amusements, it cannot be unconcerned about roadhouses, saloons, and gambling joints for adults. If it wants boys and girls to "stand on their own feet" and to "make their own way," it cannot be tolerant of a social order in which thousands of grown people are eager to shift their economic burdens to the shoulders of government. Nor can a remedy for these or similar matters take the easy form of merely legislating the undesirable activities of adults underground. Positive examples must somehow be substituted: respect for the rights of others and for one's own obligations; opportunities for wholesome, uncommercialized recreation; the chance for everyone to earn an honest day's pay by an honest day's work, and the spectacle of men and women doing just that.

To bring about these changes outside the schools is obviously a far more complex and difficult undertaking than to change the schools themselves. In such out-of-school changes, parents and citizens in general, rather than school people, must take the leading part.

There is likewise need for the help of parents and citizens in general in the internal reform of the schools. If the schools are to meet the educational needs of a new generation, their methods of teaching and the scope of the education which they provide must be radically changed. At the very least, the citizens to whom the schools belong must be willing to see such changes made, even though the schools become, as a result, different institutions from the academic high schools of a generation ago. The changes will be made more quickly, more surely, and more wisely if, beyond merely approving them, men and women outside the schools lend active support to planning and putting into effect a better educational program.

RESPONSIBILITY OF THE STATE DEPARTMENT AND OF THE SCHOOLS

In the internal reform of the schools, nevertheless, the school people of the State may and should lead. A better plan of district organization, a system of examinations through which the schools may gain both more information and more accurate information about their pupils' abilities and needs, and a program of aggressive leadership by the State Education Department—these are matters for which the State Department in particular must be responsible. Granted the help that the Department can provide, further responsibility for the education of individual boys and girls must devolve on the local secondary schools. It ought to be each school's responsibility to discover what kinds of education its pupils most need and to provide appropriate education for each of them. It should be a part of each school's concern, likewise, to stand beside its pupils long enough to make sure that they get as sound a footing as possible in the adult community into which they must go. Though the school can seldom create out-of-school opportunities, it can at least see that its boys and girls have a reasonable chance to take advantage of whatever opportunities may be open to them. In so doing, it may at the same time round out its contribution to the welfare of individual boys and girls, and provide itself with a continuing appraisal of its program more valid and searching than any examination system can ever give.

PART III

The Improvement of Secondary Education

CHAPTER XIV

Proposals for an Improved Secondary School Program

HIGH schools in New York State, like those in many other states, are now chiefly occupied with a more or less routine teaching of "subjects"—Latin and geometry and physics, and the rest of a standard list of academic studies. If the New York State schools are to serve the broader purpose which they ought to serve, that of helping young people grow in the varied interests, abilities, and knowledge which will give them as hopeful a start as society can give them toward satisfying and productive lives, the schools must eventually undertake an educational program different in many respects from their current program. It remains to suggest what sort of program the individual schools of the State most need to adopt, how the Board of Regents and the State Education Department can best further that program, and how an improved program of secondary education can be financed.

THE SECONDARY SCHOOL CURRICULUM

Analysis of the present high school curriculum has made evident one paramount reason for a lack of social competence among young people just out of high school. That reason consists in the schools' failure to give boys and girls a chance to acquire many of the abilities and attitudes which the out-of-school world will almost certainly demand of them. In any better program of secondary education a prime essential must therefore be a curriculum more directly focused on the kinds of competence which young people out of school will surely need.

To set forth all the details of a curriculum which will effectually prepare high school boys and girls for out-of-school living is at present impossible. Any thoroughly effective curriculum must grow in considerable measure out of planning on the part of each school that is to use it—planning which takes into account each school's resources in its plant and in the local community, which pays particular attention to the backgrounds of the school's pupils, and which capitalizes the special interests and abilities of the school's teachers. Moreover, the changes which need to be made in the curricula of most of the New York State high schools call for the introduction of methods and materials of teaching which have thus far been tried in only a few of the schools. Before these new methods and materials can be widely used there needs to be further experimentation with them under varying conditions. The comparative effectiveness of different plans for producing the same results needs to be carefully tested; subject matter needs to be systematized and put into a form in which it may be used by other teachers than those who first developed it; additional teaching materials need to be devised in fields in which present efforts have gone only far enough to show definite promise. Many of the details of an improved curriculum must therefore wait on progressive development over a period of years.

Furthermore, some of these details, once worked out, will undoubtedly have to be changed as conditions outside the schools change. Though a large part of any well-devised curriculum may be relatively permanent, a curriculum which is to center its attention on out-of-school problems and needs must be thoroughly responsive to new conditions. On this account also no complete prescription for a new curriculum can be offered.

Nevertheless, the broad outlines of a better curriculum can be fairly clearly distinguished.

Proposals for an Improved Program

As a major part of such a curriculum, *every secondary school ought to provide for those subjects of study and those forms of pupil-experience which promise fullest preparation for citizenship in the broad meaning of that term.* Education for citizenship is no less important in the case of boys and girls who are to go on to higher institutions than in the case of those who will complete their full-time schooling in the secondary school. In its provision for education of this sort the high school probably ought not to distinguish between the two groups of pupils. Both groups need to be made as ready as their abilities will allow, not merely for their formal duties in relation to government but for their informal day-by-day association with family, neighbors, and fellow workers.

The secondary schools cannot be expected to make boys and girls completely ready for citizenship in the sense that young people leaving the high school will possess all the knowledge and understanding and insight that an adult citizen may need. The schools can, however, inform their pupils both thoroughly and broadly about important phases of American community life: about the physical resources of the nation, the arts and occupations characteristic of America, the institutions on which American life depends, the agencies for ministering to human needs and raising the level of human wants, the means by which public opinion is shaped and used for individual or social ends. Furthermore, the schools can help boys and girls to understand something of the origin and significance of the major social problems which now confront America. In so doing, the schools can awaken the interest of boys and girls in current efforts to solve such problems, and can foster in these boys and girls an active concern to make democracy work. Through a program designed to achieve these purposes, young people may be prepared, by the time they leave school, to take advantage of the opportunities which adult citizenship offers them for becoming increasingly responsible and intelligent participants in American democracy.

The preparation for citizenship that is most likely to achieve these ends cannot be accomplished through teaching from books alone. Much of this preparation must be gained through young people's direct observation of the way in which government operates and the way people get along together, or fail to get along together, outside the school. It must include as much attention to social problems and social needs in the pupils' own communities as to the more remote problems of national and international affairs. And in order that this preparation may not be a mere talking about social problems, it must give young people immediate experience in dealing with problems of personal and group relationships within the school—experience of such a nature that the pupils may learn from their own success or failure in group enterprises which they themselves manage and which are important to them.

Nor can adequate preparation for citizenship be left entirely to teachers of current events, civics, and American history. It must grow in part out of teaching in fields that are now only occasionally dealt with from a social standpoint. For boys as well as girls, and for all pupils rather than a few, adequate preparation will include a realistic consideration of the problems of establishing and maintaining a home—problems now considered in only a few of the broader courses in home economics. It should draw upon the courses in science for an appreciation of the part which science plays in collective living, and for an understanding of the major applications of science to the problems both of the individual and of society. It should provide for study of certain economic problems—not the techniques of bookkeeping and formal business operations, but problems of earning and saving, investment, wise spending, and economical buying as these problems may affect the individual citizen and the social group. And it should include the development of habits of healthful living, and the study of fundamental problems of personal and social hygiene. Teaching which is to cover so broad an area plainly cannot be entrusted to a few members of the high school staff, but must be shared by teachers in various fields.

Perhaps most important, the schools' effort to prepare young people for citizenship should not stop with seeing that boys and girls "know the facts." Facts are essential to any constructive citizenship in a democracy. At least equally necessary, however, are respect for the rights which democracy guarantees, and a concern that democratic government shall succeed. Hence the schools' attention must be directed at the same time both to teaching young people the facts with which they need to be acquainted, and to awakening in them an active desire for social progress and a willingness to sacrifice immediate personal comfort or gain in the interests of justice and the general social good.

Thoroughgoing preparation for citizenship will demand more teaching-time than most schools now give to academic history and civics. Some subjects may need to be dropped from pupils' programs, or the schools' emphasis on certain subjects lessened, to make this time available. In the small high schools particularly, the schools' whole program of studies may need to be readjusted on this account. There can be little question that time may more justly be given to education for a citizenship in which all boys and girls must eventually play a part, than to training in purely academic subjects which will be valuable for a few only. If a school cannot provide effective training for citizenship and at the same time supply a full program of academic work, it may well sacrifice those academic subjects which seem to be offering least educational return to its pupils in general.

Beyond preparation for citizenship the secondary schools need to concern themselves with their pupils' readiness for continued learning. As a part of its basic curriculum *every high school ought to provide whatever teaching of reading, oral and written expression, and arithmetic may be necessary to give all its pupils at least enough command of the tools of learning so that they are able to learn through independent study.*

Merely because a boy or girl has been promoted from the elementary school, the high school cannot safely assume that he has adequately mastered the skills which he ought to possess in oral expression and in the three R's. Association with older pupils is often better for an overage elementary school pupil than is continued work in the elementary school environment; so that elementary schools may sometimes be justified in promoting to the high school pupils who have not mastered the tool skills.[1] Again, pupils who enter the high school with a minimum command of these skills may slip back unless they are given continued teaching which will make that command permanent. For both these reasons the high school needs to be continually alert to provide such elementary instruction as may be appropriate for certain of its pupils. It may do so in part through special coaching or remedial teaching; but every high school teacher ought to recognize his responsibility for teaching the special learning habits or skills that his particular subject may require.

Moreover, *every high school ought to see to it that each of its pupils knows where and how to go on learning most profitably after he*

---

[1] This fact does not warrant the abandonment by elementary schools of all standards of attainment. In the matter of reading especially, methods of teaching have been brought to a level of effectiveness at which it is entirely possible for an elementary school to guarantee a reasonable minimum of skill by the time even a somewhat dull pupil has spent six or more years in school, provided the school is willing to make a particular point of teaching its pupils to read. The tool skills are so important as a basis for continued learning that *it is to be strongly urged that elementary schools make a systematic and determined effort to see that on reaching the end of grade six every boy and girl of normal mental ability has reached an agreed-on minimum of competence in reading, English expression, and arithmetic.* Failing to develop this minimum in the case of any pupil, the elementary school ought to inform the high school of that fact, so that the high school may provide for special teaching.

leaves the high school. For pupils who are to continue their education in higher institutions, this means that the school should actively help each boy or girl both to choose the higher institution most appropriate for him, and to decide tentatively on his program of further study in that institution. For boys and girls who are to end their full-time schooling with the high school, the high school ought to provide realistic information about chances for part-time study. Such information can probably best be given just before individual boys and girls are about to leave school, rather than early in the high school program. In many instances it may perhaps better be furnished as a part of the guidance which the school offers to individual pupils than as a phase of any formal "subject." However it is given, the information should acquaint every boy and girl with the kinds of education that may be open to him after he leaves school; it should put him on his guard against exploitation by unscrupulous salesmen of proprietary courses; and it should help him to see what sort of further education is most likely to be profitable for him in particular.

The high school should assume responsibility, furthermore, for its pupils' growth in ability to learn independently. Only a minority of high school pupils need be limited by their meager scholastic aptitude to a mastery of the minimum skills of reading, expression, and arithmetic. The majority can, and should, make steady progress beyond any such minimum, in their command of the tools of learning. During each year of their stay in the high school they should become more proficient in obtaining for themselves information that may be useful to them; they should grow more skillful in analyzing what they read or hear or see; they should become increasingly aware of the part that studying may play in adding to particular kinds of individual competence. Above all, they should grow more and more accustomed to learning without having a teacher supervise all the details of their work.

Pupils' growth in these respects is not likely to be achieved merely by introducing a required course in how to study, or by insisting that pupils work without help. It must come largely through the teaching done by individual teachers, in their particular fields. To teach each boy or girl how to learn for himself, and to interest him in learning to such an extent that he will want to use some of his own time for learning, should be as important a part of every teacher's task as to teach any formal body of subject matter.

The secondary schools must concern themselves with their pupils' use of their leisure time for other purposes than studying. If secondary education is to have as much constructive influence as it may well have on the way young people spend their leisure, *every secondary school should provide teaching which will lead its pupils to enjoy the best types of recreation open to them after they leave school.*

To do what needs to be done in preparing boys and girls for a more wholesome use of their leisure, schools will need in part to modify their present teaching. Instead of teaching English literature with an eye chiefly to giving boys and girls an analytical knowledge of certain "standard" works, the schools will need to start with boys' and girls' present tastes in reading, and by introducing pupils gradually to better and better books—always making the reading of these books a pleasant experience—lead the pupils as far as possible toward a liking for the kind of reading that the schools would have them habitually do. Instead of paying little attention to pupils who have no talent for drawing or painting, the schools will need to awaken the interest of all their pupils in the art which they may have a chance to see and enjoy. And instead of placing chief emphasis on the coaching of bands and orchestras, the schools will need to give at least equal effort to fostering less formal musical activities, and especially to developing their pupils' appreciation of music from the listener's point of view.

In addition, the schools will be obliged to introduce some entirely new teaching. They cannot remain blind to the fact that moving pictures are quite as much a subject for enjoyment and appreciation as are the plays printed in books. Nor can they safely ignore young people's tendency to listen to the radio much more often than to listen to formal concerts or to go to the theatre. In the field of athletics the schools will need to recognize that small-group or individual sports— tennis, golf, swimming, hiking, and the rest—offer more frequent opportunities for out-of-school recreation than do football, baseball, track, and soccer. The recreations which boys and girls are practically certain to indulge in anyway will have to be definitely represented in any curriculum that is to do its full share in giving direction to young people's out-of-school living.

As with preparation for citizenship, the schools' attention to preparation for leisure-time activities may come into conflict with the teaching of purely academic subjects. The conflict must again be resolved in terms of the kind of teaching which will yield greatest returns to all high school pupils. A school too small to offer both a sound program for the majority of its pupils and specialized academic training for a few ought not on that account to shape its whole program for the few. Though it ought to protect the interests of the pupils who need intensive academic training by seeing that they have a chance to get such training elsewhere, the small school's first attention should go to the greater number of young people for whom it is responsible.

Finally, the secondary school curriculum should take positive account of the need on the part of most high school pupils to get and hold jobs once they are through with their schooling. *For every pupil who is to complete his formal education in that school, each secondary school ought to provide a necessary minimum of definite preparation for a vocation.* In the case of girls who do not expect to earn their livings outside the home, this minimum may perhaps be restricted to training in the management of a household. For other pupils it ought properly to include experience with the basic operations of various kinds of jobs, through which these pupils may become used to adapting themselves to differing requirements and accustomed to learning on the job; experience in getting along with fellow workers and superiors under job conditions; and enough specific training in a salable vocational skill to give each leaving pupil the chance for a foothold at the bottom of a recognized occupation. In addition the high school ought to provide young people with some fundamental understanding of the social problems inherent in vocational employment. No boy or girl ought to leave school without knowing, for example, about organized labor and the part which it plays in various occupations, or about the working conditions created by the growth of large-scale corporations and combinations of employers. With respect to skills and understandings both, the high school curriculum ought to furnish each boy and girl who is going immediately to work with the background which is clearly necessary for every beginning worker who is to be in any sense a master of his own vocational fate.

High schools ought not, however, to try to make boys and girls who have never had successful vocational experience into highly skilled craftsmen. The school's responsibility to vocationally untried young people is to give them a start, not to make them immediately ready to compete with experienced workers. Moreover, the school needs to recognize that, for beginners particularly, vocational adaptability is likely to be more important than highly developed specialized skill. It should therefore not train young people who have never held jobs to be electric welders, for example, though it may train them as electricians' helpers; nor should it try to make them into cafeteria or tearoom managers, though it may train them for counter service or as waitresses; nor should it attempt to make them full-fledged stenographers, though it may give them the basic skills in shorthand and typewriting; nor should it try to train them as specialists in horticulture, though it may make them competent to support themselves as general agricultural workers. Its training program for beginners should resemble in general the broader courses in industrial arts now offered in certain of the academic high schools rather than the specialized courses toward which most of the separate vocational schools have been tending.[2]

At the same time the secondary schools need to recognize the present lack of educational opportunities for young people who may properly enter various semiprofessional occupations. *Every secondary school whose resources permit it to do so should provide needed preparation for vocations requiring a more extended period of initial schooling than can be completed by the end of the twelfth grade, but demanding less training than that offered by established higher institutions.* The training in question should prepare students for beginning employment in such occupa-

---

[2] The degree of specialization which should be aimed at in the high school vocational courses must obviously be determined by the abilities required of beginning workers in particular fields. Requirements may differ from time to time, from one occupation to another, and even to some extent from one city to another. The vocational training program ought therefore to be developed on the basis of continuous surveys of local needs. For a more detailed discussion of these matters, see T. L. Norton, *Education for Work*, Regents' Inquiry, 1938.

It is to be understood that the proposal here made that the secondary school program should not aim at highly specialized training for vocationally untried pupils is not intended to rule out the provision of specialized training for experienced workers. The State's educational program ought to include more schools than at present, geographically well distributed and probably organized as separate vocational schools, which offer specialized vocational training. *Specialized training should be restricted, however, to persons who have demonstrated initial vocational competence under adult working conditions.* Training in electric welding or cafeteria management or stenography or horticulture may properly be offered as a part of this advanced program, even though such training should not be open to the vocationally inexperienced pupils who are receiving initial vocational education. Training for experienced workers has been recognized in the Inquiry as a phase of adult education rather than of secondary education. See Floyd Reeves, T. Fansler, and C. O. Houle, *Adult Education*, Regents' Inquiry, 1938.

tions as those of the laboratory assistant, the dental hygienist, the secretary (as distinguished from the typist or stenographer), the surveyor, the architectural assistant, the dietician. Admission to training of this sort should be restricted to pupils who have successfully completed a secondary school program extending through the twelfth grade, and who show definite aptitude for semiprofessional education. The work which the secondary school offers these pupils should not be merely a collection of technical courses piled on top of an undergraduate program. Neither should it be a program duplicating that of the first year or two of four-year higher institutions. It ought properly to consist of a carefully planned program in its own right, calling for from one to three years of training beyond the twelfth grade, as the nature of each occupation for which it prepares may require, and including continued general education as well as attention to specialized knowledge or skill.[3]

These various phases of the secondary school curriculum—preparation for citizenship, for continued out-of-school learning, for recreation, and for jobs—include the fields of teaching most in need of improvement in New York State high schools at the present time. They do not include formal

[3] It will be noted that this proposal does not contemplate any upward extension of the high school program in the form of an academic junior college. The desirability of establishing junior colleges has been canvassed in the study of higher education conducted by the Inquiry. The results of that study make it clear that high schools in New York State ought not to attempt to duplicate the work of the early years of the liberal arts colleges. New York is liberally endowed with colleges of high standing, so distributed throughout the State as to be geographically accessible to practically all young people. Boys and girls who can profit by a college education but who cannot afford the cost of college work can accordingly be better provided for in New York by an extension of the present plan of state scholarships than by the establishment of public junior colleges. Recommendations with respect to desirable increases in the number of state scholarships and in the stipends which they carry are presented in the Inquiry's general report. See Luther H. Gulick, *Education for American Life*, Regents' Inquiry, 1938; see also the recommendations with respect to scholarships in Chapter XV of the present report.

preparation for college. That part of the high school program has received so much emphasis in the past that it needs less immediate attention than do the nonacademic phases of the high schools' work. The young people who are preparing for college are nevertheless vitally concerned in the proposals here made. Many of these young people, like the boys and girls who will not go to college, are leaving the high schools deficient in the knowledge and interests and abilities which a sound general education ought to have given them. The most clearly necessary improvement in the high school program, for them as for the pupils who will have no further full-time schooling, lies in the development of a curriculum which will prepare all boys and girls for out-of-school living as successfully as the present curriculum prepares a minority for academic work in the liberal arts colleges.

RESPONSIBILITY FOR INDIVIDUAL PUPILS

Changes in the curriculum alone, however, will not enable the secondary schools to do all that is necessary in preparing boys and girls for social competence. Young people now leave school unready for what lies ahead of them partly because the schools have paid little attention to their individual needs. Beyond improving the high school curriculum, the secondary schools must therefore undertake far more systematically than at present, to recognize their pupils as individuals and to see that each pupil gets the kind of education appropriate for him.

If it is to do more than run its pupils through a mill, a secondary school cannot consider its work accomplished until it knows that each of its pupils who is on the point of leaving school is prepared as fully as his abilities allow for one of two alternatives. Either he should be ready to make a successful social and vocational adjustment to out-of-school conditions, or he should be prepared to continue his schooling successfully in an appropriate higher institution. The school's responsibility for insuring one or the other outcome for each individual boy and girl may occasionally need to be qualified in the case of pupils who present problems of delinquency or of inability to learn with which the public secondary school cannot properly deal. Such pupils will obviously have to be referred to other institutions. For the rest of its pupils the school's responsibility should be direct and positive.

In order to exercise this responsibility adequately, every secondary school must necessarily undertake certain duties which only a few schools now systematically perform. First, and most obviously, *every school must make it a point to learn as much about its individual pupils as may be necessary for a sound estimate of their abilities and needs.* No school ought to be content with what it discovers about its pupils merely from their class records or from the information that pupils and their parents volunteer. It ought to find out for itself, particularly in the case of boys and girls from the less privileged homes, about each pupil's general home background, about his interests and special abilities, about his major out-of-school activities and his hopes and plans for the future. Certain designated members of the staff should ordinarily be responsible for directing the collection and use of information of this sort. The school can probably learn most about individual boys and girls, however, not by assigning to one or two members of its faculty the task of trying to find out all that needs to be known about large numbers of pupils, but by making it a part of every teacher's responsibility to know certain pupils well. Dividing this responsibility among its teachers, the school may at the same time pool the judgments of various people as to each pupil's needs, and encourage greater sensitiveness on the part of teachers to young people's individual differences.

In the second place, *each secondary school ought to use its information about its pupils as a basis for systematically adapting its teaching to individual pupils' particular needs.* Most boys and girls probably gain more from having to learn in a group than they would gain from purely individual instruction, even though group teaching necessarily results in some slighting of individual interests. Group teaching, however, ought not to mean almost complete disregard of individual pupils, as it does in many high schools at the present time. The plans of homogeneous grouping and of differentiated teaching which certain schools have adopted may go far to prevent this disregard. Some such plan ought to be a part of the program of every school which enrolls pupils of widely varying abilities—not merely in order to prevent the slighting of pupils who have less ability than the average, but in order to hold the ablest pupils to a standard of work commensurate with their abilities. Especially in the case of teachers who have pupils of widely differing abilities in their classes, such plans should provide for relieving teachers as far as possible from purely clerical duties or routine administrative assignments, to allow the time that is necessary to make definite provisions for pupils' individual needs.

Every secondary school ought, moreover, to give its pupils positive educational guidance. Schools cannot rely on informed educational choices by most pupils or their parents. The schools themselves must take the initiative in seeing that pupils get the kinds of education most suitable for them.

If the guidance which the schools offer is to be dependable, each school will need to know more about its pupils' potential abilities than most schools now know or try to discover. On this account each school ought not merely to keep a systematic record of its pupils' school work and to use all its information as to pupils' out-of-school circumstances and interests, but it ought thoroughly to test its pupils' capacity to learn. In particular, it ought to give pupils a chance to try themselves out briefly in special fields of study before it requires them to choose among these fields in planning their specialized programs.

In the light of the information about each pupil which it may thus secure, the school ought to direct individual boys and girls away from programs which do not promise to lead to their social and vocational adjustment. Its concern should be quite as much for pupils who choose below the level of their abilities as for pupils who aim too high. Though it obviously cannot be sure of what may constitute the best educational choice in each individual case, it can certainly identify many of the seriously mistaken choices which pupils without guidance are likely to make. These it ought to use all its persuasion and influence to prevent.

Not every high school can offer a comprehensive program of secondary education. The best interests of certain boys and girls may require, therefore, that these boys and girls be directed to other schools in which they can secure a kind of education more appropriate to their needs. Individual high schools ought to have a conscience about all such pupils. No school ought, if it can help it, to allow a pupil to continue in a program which is clearly not the one that he needs. With young people who might better be transferred to other schools quite as much as with the rest of its pupils, every secondary school should take the initiative in seeing that each boy and girl discovers his own educational needs and finds a way of meeting them.

Each secondary school ought likewise to give those boys and girls who do not go on to higher institutions direct help in making their first out-of-school adjustments. If it is to assure itself that young people make effective use of what they have learned, the school will need to provide pupils who are about to leave school with realistic vocational guidance. It will need also to see that each boy and girl leaving school has a chance to make the out-of-school contacts which he most needs to make.

Vocational guidance which is to be thoroughly meaningful to high school pupils must deal with the vocational problems that boys and girls face at the time those problems are crucial.

Eighth grade or ninth grade surveys of occupations or of the problems involved in choosing a vocation are not likely to be meaningful for many pupils. Most boys and girls in these early grades are looking forward to staying in school. From their point of view the problem of getting a job is as yet a matter to be merely casually considered rather than a matter of vital and immediate concern. That problem becomes crucial for the majority of pupils only when they realize that they are on the point of leaving school. It is at this latter point that the vocational guidance which the school may offer is likely to make the most lasting impression, and it is here that the school's guidance can be of most direct assistance to individual boys and girls.

Each school, therefore, ought to single out as early as possible in every school year the young people for whom that year is likely to be their last of full-time schooling. For these pupils it ought to provide a survey of chances for jobs—not a remote study of occupations in general, but a canvassing of the actual job opportunities which are open to these particular boys and girls. It ought not to stop with talking about how to choose a job; beyond any such general discussion, the school should see that each boy or girl has a tangible plan for finding a job for himself, that he knows how to interpret help-wanted advertisements and how to approach a prospective employer, that he is familiar with local nonschool agencies—particularly government placement and welfare agencies—which may help him to find employment, and that he makes definite use of all this knowledge in getting work.

The school ought also to follow its pupils for at least a few months after they leave. It should do so not merely in order to give much-needed help to individual boys and girls, but in order to gain a pragmatic measure of the value of its own teaching. From the latter standpoint it will do better to ask all its teachers to share in the task of discovering what happens to individual pupils than to assign this task to one person;

though one person ought, no doubt, to be primarily responsible for directing each school's general follow-up program. In this program the school should not restrict itself to watching its former pupils' vocational success only. It should properly be concerned with all the activities of its pupils toward which the school has tried to contribute, namely, the pupils' relations with other people, the share they take in civic affairs, their recreations, and their further studying, as well as their work on their jobs.

Wherever possible the school should work through and with other agencies in its follow-up program. In many communities there are already organizations—state and federal employment agencies, welfare agencies of various sorts, and groups of citizens actively interested in helping young people—which are directly concerned with boys and girls outside of school. The school ought neither to duplicate the work of these agencies nor to compete with them. The school is, nevertheless, the only social agency now actively in contact with all boys and girls, and it is thus the only agency which can make sure that individual young people who are badly in need of help are not lost or forgotten. The school's responsibility should be to see that boys and girls who need assistance from other agencies get such help as those agencies can afford. Only when no organization exists or can be established in a community to furnish assistance to boys and girls outside of school ought the school to undertake the whole task of meeting these young people's needs.

Schools may properly undertake, however, to supply certain activities for out-of-school young people which are now all too infrequently provided. For one thing, *every school ought to make a systematic effort to supply wholesome recreational contacts for pupils just out of school.* Through clubs, dances, and organized sports, schools furnish such contacts for boys and girls still in school. Nevertheless most schools let their pupils leave school without any assurance that outside of school these pupils will have a chance to exercise the interests which the schools have been trying to develop. The experience of numerous schools has shown that out-of-school young people welcome the opportunity to continue at school the kind of recreation which the school can readily provide. Even though a school may not be able to open all its recreational facilities to former pupils, it may at least allow them to attend school dances, to use the school's playing fields when the fields are not occupied by boys and girls still in school, and to share in the school's dramatic and musical activities. Unless some such opportunities are made available to out-of-school young people, the schools' efforts to develop habits of wholesome enjoyment are destined to be largely futile.

Furthermore, *every school, so far as its resources permit, ought to see that work-opportunities are provided for beginners whose need for jobs cannot be met through normal employment*. Again the schools ought not to compete with established organizations— the National Youth Administration and the Civilian Conservation Corps in particular. The schools ought to make certain at the outset that all the young people who are eligible for the help which these agencies can give are brought in touch with the proper authorities. But the Youth Administration and the Civilian Conservation Corps provide for relatively limited numbers and kinds of young people, and are obliged to provide for them in ways which do not always meet individual circumstances. As a practical answer to the needs of many boys and girls in times when jobs are scarce, the schools can and should actively supplement the work of these agencies. They should assume responsibility, when there is the need, for enlisting the cooperation of local employers in providing opportunities for young people to do useful work. They should use to the full such possibilities for fruitful vocational experience as the operation of the school itself may provide: experience in routine clerical work, the keeping of records, the operation of the school cafeteria, the servicing of school busses, the making or repair of school apparatus, the decoration of the school building and grounds. Their faculty members may cooperate, as faculty members in various schools have done in recent years, to provide employment in the care of automobiles, the serving of lunches, or minor jobs about their homes. The work thus furnished should supplement that ordinarily done by adult workers, instead of making the employment of adults unnecessary. It should nevertheless be real work, and it should be paid for in terms of pocket-money, at least—both because it ought to be worth paying for, and because paid jobs rather than busy-work represent the real need of boys and girls who are through with their schooling.

For the school to take responsibility for finding such work for young people will not mean any change in the school's chief obligation. The school is primarily an educational institution and not a custodial or charitable institution, and it should remain so. With respect to jobs as well as to recreation, however, the education which the school provides may often be wasted if boys and girls who are through with their schooling get no chance to use what they have learned. In doing its utmost to discover temporary jobs for young people who cannot find work elsewhere, and particularly in bringing to the attention of the public the need for such jobs on the part of individual boys and girls, the school will be doing no more than must be done to make its educational program effective.

These various proposals as to what every secondary school should do for individual boys and girls are not based on mere idealistic theory. Neither are they based on any sentimental conception of society's "debt" to young people. They grow directly out of a consideration of the maladjustments of young people under an educational system in which schools pay little attention to individual needs, and of the harm to society as a whole which these maladjustments threaten. The school obviously cannot be a cure-all for social ills. But if it will acquaint itself with its pupils' individual needs, if it will see that each boy and girl chooses an education as much as possible in keeping with his particular abilities, and if it will help pupils who are leaving school to make the best practicable out-of-school adjustments, the school may at least make a direct and positive contribution to the betterment of a social situation which is at present none too happy.

APPRAISAL OF PUPILS' WORK

As a part of their responsibility for their pupils as individuals, the schools ought properly to assume certain new responsibilities for the appraisal of pupils' work. In particular, the schools' requirements for promotion and graduation ought to be determined more largely than at present by the individual secondary schools.

Exactly what standards any given school should use for promoting its pupils from one grade to the next can hardly be determined from outside that school. The size of the groups of pupils with which the school has to deal, the plan of teaching which the school has adopted in the light of its pupils' educational needs, special circumstances which may make it more profitable for individual pupils to be assigned to one class-group rather than to another, all need to be considered in deciding either on a general promotion scheme or on the promotions of individual boys and girls. Any one of these factors may clearly be of greater importance in a particular situation than pupils' formal "credits" in a specified list of academic subjects.

Accordingly, *each secondary school ought to assume responsibility for its own promotions.* Though the promotion plans which will result from this assumption of responsibility may not be different from the plans heretofore used, each school, as it modifies its general program, should be free to adopt whatever new plan best meets the needs of its pupils.

Each secondary school ought to be responsible likewise for the granting of diplomas. The present system of state-awarded diplomas, valuable as it has been in giving prestige to high school graduation, makes almost impossible the recognition of anything but formal scholastic achievement as a basis for graduation. It pins every pupil's fate, moreover, on his success in a series of written examinations, a measure which may be quite inappropriate for certain kinds of ability and for certain pupils. Though examinations should continue to be used in appraising each pupil's readiness to graduate from high school, they ought to be regarded as supplying only partial evidence of the pupil's accomplishment. The rest of that evidence, and the final decision as to each pupil's achievement, properly ought to be supplied by the school itself.

Eventually, individual secondary schools ought to establish a new type of high school diploma. The diplomas now in use in New York State, like most of those awarded by high schools elsewhere, consist of little more than summary reports on pupils' work in courses. Schools may properly continue to issue transcripts of credits to pupils who want such summary reports. The diploma itself ought to be a statement of what the pupil has gained from his high school education, and not just a record of the scholastic motions he has gone through. If a school has been seriously attempting to make its pupils ready for higher education or for out-of-school living, its diplomas ought to indicate that fact. They can do so most straightforwardly if, instead of certifying merely that a pupil has passed certain courses, they attest that the pupil has attained the goals which the school has been seeking for him: that in the judgment of the school faculty he is prepared either for entrance into a specified vocation or for admission to a specified type of higher educational institution, and that he can be positively recommended as likely to take an acceptable part in the out-of-school social groups to which he will perforce belong.

Serious practical difficulties clearly stand in the way of awarding any such diploma at the present time. Few schools are either well enough acquainted with the conditions which individual young people must face outside of school, or sure enough of the qualities that are likely to make for successful out-of-school accomplishment, to be able to award a diploma of this kind with confidence. Parents and high school pupils are attached to the conventional diploma; any immediate shift to a radically different measure of pupils' achievement would undoubtedly meet with strong resistance, especially from parents whose sons or daughters were entitled to the conventional diploma but could not fairly be recommended for the new one. The very strength of these obstacles, however, indicates something of the task which confronts the secondary schools if they are to achieve any fundamental reform in the nature and direction of their work. A school which is not ready to warrant the competence of its graduates is in all probability either shooting wide of the mark at which public education ought to aim, or leading its pupils through a round of activities whose value the school itself is hard put to justify. A public which conceives it to be no part of the school's duty to judge the actual competence of boys and girls is far from appreciating the part which secondary schools at their best may play in preparing young people for out-of-school living. If social competence is to be an aim of secondary school work, each school's final judgment of its individual pupils ought to be in terms wholly consistent with that aim. Each secondary school should, therefore, move as rapidly and effectively as its particular circumstances allow, against the obstacles which now keep it from a realistic appraisal of its work.

SCHOOL ORGANIZATION

Changes in the high school curriculum and in the attention which schools pay to individual pupils will be difficult to make as long as the schools hold rigidly to the conventional four-year high school organization. Provision of tryout courses on which a dependable program of educational guidance may be based will require the downward extension of secondary school work into the seventh and eighth grades. The establishment of new programs of semiprofessional training will make it necessary for certain secondary schools to add one or more grades beyond the twelfth. If it is to be effectively planned and coordinated, the work of these lower and higher grades ought to be under the same supervision as that of the four grades now included in most of the high schools. Accordingly, *the seventh grade through the twelfth grade, and in addition such higher grades as may be organized in connection with the needed upward extension of secondary school work, should be recognized in each school system as secondary grades, and instruction in all these grades should be directly supervised by the local school officer or officers primarily responsible for the program of secondary education.*

The proposal that grades above the sixth should be recognized as secondary grades does not mean that special barriers should be erected between the sixth grade and the seventh. As with promotions from one secondary grade to another, responsibility for advancing pupils from the elementary school to the secondary school should rest with the local schools. In general, *pupils should be admitted to the secondary grades whenever, in the judgment of the local school authorities, the needs of these pupils can be served better by association with older pupils or by a program emphasizing vocational preparation than by a continuance of elementary school work.*

Nor does the proposal that all the secondary grades should be under unified supervision mean that a single pattern of grade organization should be adopted by the secondary schools of the State. It is probable that an approximation of the six-year junior-senior high school plan offers the most effective scheme of organization for the majority of secondary schools at the present time, and most school systems will do well to adopt some such plan. Systematic experimentation with other forms of organization is highly desirable, however—

especially with forms of organization which make semiprofessional training above the twelfth grade a unified part of the secondary school program. The essential condition for improvement would seem to be not the adoption of any one particular scheme, but the substitution for a conventional plan which no longer fits educational needs, of whatever plans may lend themselves best to the educational programs and the educational facilities of individual school systems.

The proposal as a whole does mean, however, that *separate vocational schools (including continuation schools) for pupils who have not completed the twelfth grade should be given up as rapidly as possible*. Separate schools may appropriately be used for offering "upgrading" vocational training to young people who have had initial vocational experience, or for supplying technical courses to students who have successfully completed an appropriate high school program of twelve grades. The initial nonspecialized vocational training which needs to be given to pupils below the twelfth grade can be both economically and effectively provided in general high schools. Such training, instead of being set off by itself, ought to be an integral part of the program of secondary education which each general high school offers.

INAUGURATION OF THE PROPOSED PROGRAM

The changes in secondary education here proposed will affect the high school curriculum, the high schools' methods of guiding their pupils and providing for pupils' individual needs, the means by which the schools appraise their pupils' achievement, and the general organization of the secondary schools. In order that the proposed changes may be seen in due relation to one another, it may be well to recapitulate them briefly.

The high school curriculum should be reorganized to give first place to subjects of study and forms of pupil experience which promise fullest preparation for citizenship in a democracy. In addition, the basic curriculum should provide whatever training in fundamental skills and whatever information about opportunities for further schooling may be needed by individual pupils, to allow each pupil to go on learning in ways appropriate for him after he leaves the high school. The curriculum should also include teaching which will lead pupils to enjoy the best types of recreation open to them outside of school. Finally, the curriculum should give each boy and girl who is not going to college the minimum of practical preparation that he may need to allow him to make a successful beginning at a kind of employment appropriate to his particular interests and abilities. The high school curriculum should not furnish training in specialized craftsmanship, but it should provide such general understandings and skills, including those necessary as preparation for semiprofessional occupations in the case of young people capable of entering such occupations, as will assure each of its pupils a foothold at the bottom of a recognized field of employment.

To make its curriculum thoroughly effective, each high school should assume more responsibility than schools in general now assume for what happens to its individual pupils. It should learn as much about each of its pupils as may be necessary for a sound estimate of his abilities and needs. It should systematically adapt its teaching to its pupils' major differences in interest and ability. It should furnish its pupils with positive educational and vocational guidance. It should follow the young people who do not go on to higher institutions for at least the first few months after they leave school. It should make a systematic effort to supply wholesome recreational contacts for boys and girls just out of school, and to see that opportunities for work are provided for beginners whose need for jobs cannot be met through normal employment.

In the case of all its pupils, the high school should take independent responsibility for their promotion from grade to grade, and for the award of high school diplomas. If its appraisal of its pupils' work is to be consistent with its educational aims, the high school must eventually grant diplomas not in terms of formal credits or hours of work, but on the basis of the competence which its pupils achieve.

The organization of each high school should take whatever form best lends itself to that school's educational program and to the plant and equipment which the school has available. In most schools, the four-year high school organization should eventually be displaced by a form of organization which recognizes the grades above the sixth as secondary grades, and which places those grades under unified supervision. Separate vocational schools should not be maintained for secondary school pupils, but the high school organization may properly include grades above the twelfth, as a means of providing semi-professional training of a type not now readily available either in the secondary schools or in higher educational institutions.

Stated as they have had to be in terms of general needs, these proposals are intended not so much to furnish a set of explicit directions for individual schools as to suggest the basis for a long-term program of improvement in secondary education. It is apparent, nevertheless, that most of the changes which will be necessary to put such a program into effect will have to be made in individual high schools, by the men and women who are in immediate charge of those schools. The changes can obviously not be made quickly, nor can they be brought about by the efforts of administrative officers alone, or of teachers alone. To introduce them successfully will call for a genuinely cooperative attack on major educational problems by each school faculty as a whole. Teachers and principal, working together, will need to make of the school a laboratory in which the educational needs of individual boys and girls are given the time and thought which they rightly demand. Whether a given school becomes that sort of laboratory, rather than chiefly a smooth-running organization for providing drill on facts called for in examinations, is likely to depend most of all on the vision of its principal. There can be no escape, therefore, from the fact that the test of this program will eventually be found in the ability of the principals of the secondary schools, first of all to see what most needs to be done for high school boys and girls in local communities, and then to unite the teachers in their schools in an actively interested effort to plan, experiment, and measure the actual gain from each new undertaking.

Yet it must also be recognized that individual schools cannot independently make all the changes which have been proposed. Certain of these changes will require a relaxation of present state regulations before the schools can put them into effect. Other changes—most notably those which have to do with the curriculum—will call for a type of experimentation and research which few individual secondary schools can carry on by themselves. The whole question of financial support for the schools is also involved, a question made the more acute by the fact that the changes include the addition of various forms of educational service which are not provided for in the present system of state aid. The inauguration of the suggested program must therefore depend in part on the adoption of certain new policies and regulations by the Board of Regents and the State Education Department. The recommendations which are next to be made deal in detail with these matters.

CHAPTER XV

New Policies for the State
Education Department

IT HAS been suggested earlier that the Board of Regents and the State Education Department can contribute most effectively to the improvement of secondary education in New York State in three ways: by bringing about a better plan of school district organization, by establishing a system of examinations through which the schools may gain more information and more accurate information about their pupils' abilities and needs, and by undertaking better coordinated and more aggressive educational leadership. Recommendations for changes in the Education Law and in State Department policies and regulations may be conveniently presented in relation to these three proposals.

SCHOOL DISTRICT ORGANIZATION

The question of what ought to be done about the more than eight thousand school districts now existing in New York State is dealt with in a special report by the Inquiry.[1] In that report will be found a discussion of the present district system as it affects both elementary and secondary schools, and a detailed plan for the improvement of the system. Since the district system as a whole is considered elsewhere, the recommendations concerning school district organization which need to be made in the present report may be very briefly presented.

[1] Luther H. Gulick, *Education for American Life*, Regents' Inquiry, 1938.

They are included here for the purpose of calling attention once more to matters which will need to be taken into account in the formation of new districts, if the new districts are to provide adequately for secondary education.

Any general reorganization of the school districts ought to provide wherever possible for schools large enough to allow the offering of a comprehensive program of secondary education. Though separate school units may for a time be retained in these districts, there should eventually be a centralization of high schools within many of the districts. As part of the general plan of reorganization, some plan of support should be adopted under which each district will be able to supply for itself the minimum essentials of a basic secondary school program. Also, arrangements should be made under which the smaller districts can cooperate with one another in supplying miscellaneous services beyond the essential minimum—special health and guidance services, for example; cooperative purchasing of school supplies; forms of technical training which no one district may be able to afford independently. With these considerations in mind it is recommended:

1. That legislation be enacted to provide for the reorganization of the present school districts within a stipulated period, to the end that

a. Where geographical conditions permit, no school district shall enroll fewer than three hundred pupils in grades 7 through 12.

b. As many school districts as possible shall enroll at least 1,200 pupils in grades 7 through 12.

c. Individual secondary schools enrolling fewer than 300 pupils shall supplement, rather than duplicate, one another's programs.

2. That to encourage economy through the centralization of school services, legislation be enacted which will provide for the award of state aid in terms of total school

district enrollments (distribution of population being taken into due account), instead of in terms of individual school enrollments.

3. That state aid be so regulated as to enable each district to furnish essential educational services for itself; and that the State Department abandon the practice of providing essential services for districts unable to afford these services under present conditions. In particular, the Department should

a. Discontinue the policy of supplying traveling school libraries at direct state expense, in favor of a plan for encouraging districts to establish adequate local libraries either individually or in cooperation with neighboring districts.

b. Discontinue likewise the policy of supplying lantern slides and other visual aids for regular classroom use at direct state expense.

c. Furnish a supervisory program designed to stimulate and guide the work of local supervisors, rather than to take the place of local supervision.

4. That legal provision be made for the voluntary cooperation of two or more adjacent school districts in supplying special types of education, or special school services, which cannot be as economically furnished by any one of the districts acting independently.

The adoption of these recommendations will obviously not in itself improve the educational programs of individual high schools. Reorganization of the school districts represents no more than a way of making adequate educational programs possible. The present plan of district organization so limits a majority of the existing secondary schools, however, that reorganization must be regarded as an essential preliminary to the betterment of secondary education in most communities in New York State.

THE REGENTS' EXAMINATION SYSTEM

Changes in the Regents' Examination system will more immediately affect the educational program. Through a modification of the present plan of examinations the State Department may supply for the schools two kinds of assistance which the schools greatly need, but of which they have not thus far been able to avail themselves. The Department should be able to provide the schools, first, with comprehensive data on the outcomes of their programs, through which to evaluate those programs. Second, it should develop tests by means of which the schools themselves can appraise the work of individual pupils.

To provide the first type of assistance to the schools ought to be a major responsibility of the Department. The study of secondary education under the present Inquiry represents a kind of evaluation which the Department itself should properly undertake, not periodically, but as a continuing enterprise. Out of continued investigations of this sort should come a more definite recognition than has been possible heretofore, of local educational needs and of the strengths and weaknesses of local schools. Out of such investigations should come also a clearer formulation of educational policy for the State as a whole.

That the Department ought to withdraw from a plan under which it must officially pass on the achievements of hundreds of thousands of individual pupils is apparent for reasons which have already been discussed. The Department needs to give the schools more assistance, however, rather than less, in appraising the work of individual boys and girls. It needs especially to make available to local schools whatever testing materials may be useful in obtaining accurate information about the educational growth of pupils: general scholastic-aptitude tests, tests of achievement grade by grade in particular subjects, diagnostic tests for use with pupils who are encountering special difficulties in learning. Like the measures which the Department may employ to evaluate total educational programs, these tests should not be limited to pencil-and-paper examinations. Nor should they be restricted to tests constructed by the Department itself; excellent tests are available from other sources, and should be included among the materials which the Department encourages the schools to use. Except in connection with a general program of evaluation, the Department ought not to make the use of any of these tests mandatory, or to relieve the schools of the whole cost of any tests which they may use; but it should see to it that individual schools are able to obtain appropriate tests and know how to employ them most effectively.

As part of the assistance which it gives the schools in this connection, the Department will need to make special provision for selecting pupils for admission to higher institutions. Preliminary selection of this sort should be one of the guidance functions of the local secondary schools. Under present conditions the final selections can probably best be taken care of, as now, by a central examining authority.

This authority should not concern itself with testing all types of pupils. Its sole function should be that of selecting young people who should properly continue their education in colleges and professional schools. In exercising this function it will need to recognize that various types of higher education demand somewhat specialized abilities, and that a uniform measure of the kind of ability required by general liberal arts colleges is probably not the best measure to use in selecting candidates for other types of institutions.[2] Accordingly, it

[2] Conclusions drawn from studies recently completed at the University of Minnesota are of interest in this connection. Professor Harl R. Douglass, who was in charge of the studies, reported in a letter to the Inquiry dated April 15, 1937: "The quality of a pupil's total high school record, irrespective of the specific courses that he has taken, undoubtedly furnishes a more accurate prediction of his ability to make good college marks in general than does the nature of the courses pursued in high school, and even a better prediction than do his

may properly assume a responsibility beyond that of passing on general academic achievement. One of its most important functions should be to see that admission requirements are properly adapted to various kinds of higher education, and that each boy or girl who is to continue his education is admitted to the type of institution which will give him the further education most appropriate for him individually.

This same authority should be responsible for the award of state scholarships. Its responsibility here also should be to encourage different kinds of higher education for different kinds of young people, rather than to discriminate in terms merely of general academic attainment. In addition, it should re-examine the present plan of awarding financial stipends irrespective of the financial need of scholarship holders. A system under which honorary scholarships would be granted to all qualified students, but under which financial aid would be limited to young people of ability who could not continue their education without it, would be in many respects fairer than the present arrangement, and would make possible a more telling use of state funds. Constructive attention to this problem, as well as to the general problem of selection, should enable the selecting authority to extend notably both the opportunities and the incentives for young people of ability to make the most of their talents.

In order that the Department may furnish needed assistance to the schools in connection with all these matters, it is recommended:

1. That the Department provide for continuous appraisal of the outcomes of secondary education in New York State.

---

marks in any particular field of high school studies. There is dependable evidence, however, that school marks in special branches of college or university work—for example, dentistry, business, pharmacy, or nursing, or engineering, or the law—may be more accurately predicted if, in addition to his previous scholastic record, there be taken into consideration certain variables, particularly scores on tests of the special aptitudes which play a prominent part in the particular college."

This appraisal should be based on many other types of data than those afforded by pencil-and-paper tests. It should include systematic study of health conditions, community influences, local and state-wide employment, the adjustment of young people to their out-of-school environment, the relative social needs for various kinds of education—in short, of whatever social phenomena may provide significant clues to the effectiveness or the desirable direction of public education. Its purpose should be not to pass upon the accomplishments of individual pupils but to allow just evaluation of the educational programs of schools and school systems.

2. That the Department abandon the issuance of school diplomas or certificates, and abandon also the preparation and administration of the Regents' Preliminary Examinations.

3. That in place of the Preliminary Examinations the Department bring together or prepare standardized achievement examinations in the various branches of the school curriculum, for use by individual schools in appraising the progress of their pupils at any or all grade levels.

4. That the Board of Regents discontinue the present State Examinations Board and establish in its place a board whose sole function shall be to supervise a program for the selection of applicants for admission to the higher educational institutions of the State. Methods of selection approved by this Board should eventually be substituted for the present system of Regents' Academic Examinations. In the establishment of the proposed board it is recommended that the Regents provide

a. That the board comprise qualified representatives of the State Education Department, of the various types of institutions of undergraduate higher education chartered by the State, and of the public secondary schools of the State.

b. That responsibility for administering the plans of selection which the board may approve rest with the officers of the State Department charged with providing achievement examinations for the schools.

c. That the board appoint subcommittees to give separate attention to appropriate admission requirements for special types of higher institutions.

d. That criteria for the selection of applicants for admission to higher institutions be not restricted to the results of pencil-and-paper examinations; and that one such criterion be the judgment of local school officers as to each candidate's aptitude for the type of training to which he seeks admission.

e. That, as at present, individual institutions of higher education be not required to accept the ratings assigned by the board to candidates for admission to the institutions.

5. That, following the establishment of the board of selection, the plan of awarding state scholarships in higher institutions on the basis of pupils' ratings on uniform examinations be replaced by a plan (the details to be elaborated by the proposed board) under which

a. Each applicant for a scholarship shall be required to designate the institution or type of institution in which the scholarship is to be used.

b. No application shall be considered unless it bears the statement of the head of the school which the applicant has last attended that the applicant is prepared for the type of training to which he seeks admission, and that such training will be thoroughly appropriate in his individual case.

c. Scholarships shall be awarded in terms of (1) the public need for encouraging additional persons to seek special types of training, and (2) the applicants' possession of qualities which make particularly appropriate for them the types of training which they seek.

6. That the proposed board of selection investigate the feasibility of awarding two classes of scholarships, the awards being based on identical personal, social, and scholastic criteria, and no public announcement being made of the persons receiving the one class as contrasted with the other. The two classes should comprise

a. Scholarships carrying either no pecuniary stipend or only a nominal prize.

b. Scholarships carrying pecuniary aid in the amount of the total fixed charges for tuition and other instructional fees at the institutions which the holders are to attend. Scholarships in this class should be awarded only to applicants for whom reasonable evidence is presented that they need financial assistance in order to continue their education.

Used as a means of promoting the most effective teaching of which individual schools are capable, rather than of holding all secondary schools to a uniform program, the examination system that has been proposed may be a major factor in the influence exercised by the State Education Department. There is probably no better way to define educational goals and to encourage their achievement than to devise tests which will directly measure the realization of such goals. If the Department can give a large share of its attention to inventing or bringing together tests of this type, if it can administer such tests widely, or better, get individual schools to administer them, and if it can then help the schools to see what the test results mean as measures of each school's instruction, it can bring about marked improvement in the curricula of the great majority of high schools in the State.

LEADERSHIP THROUGH REGULATION

Though the Department's use of examinations may in itself represent an important means of leadership, the Department ought to exercise leadership in a number of other ways.

Leadership through regulation should obviously continue to be one phase of the Department's activities. Educational progress is more likely to come through showing the schools what needs to be done to bring about effective teaching, and through encouraging them to experiment with promising methods, than through requiring them to follow a set program. A minimum of regulation is nevertheless bound to be necessary if the conditions for good teaching are to be everywhere assured.

In order that they may be constructive rather than repressive, such regulations as the Department may put into effect ought to be limited to factors known to be essential to a sound educational program. They ought not to apply to practices which are legitimately debatable, or which may vary in effectiveness from school to school. The methods of instruction which make up a good school program will often differ from one school to another, and every school—subject only to the condition that it has planned its work conscientiously and with full recognition of local needs—ought to be largely free to employ the methods which it believes are most likely to be effective under local circumstances. Accordingly, regulation should be concerned much less with the details of school programs than with material provisions which will allow individual schools to do good work.

Moreover, no regulation should be adopted which the Department is unable or unwilling to enforce. The existence of large numbers of regulations enforced only occasionally, or in certain schools, may definitely weaken the Department's influence. Whether a particular regulation can be enforced is not the sole question that needs to be asked, but the answer to this question may properly furnish one criterion as to whether the regulation ought to be put into effect.

So far as the Department's general policy with respect to regulations is concerned, it is therefore recommended:

1. That the Department discontinue the plan of officially approving or disapproving the form and content of local

school offerings. As a substitute for this plan the Department may more properly set up regulations which will insure

a. That state aid is granted for new courses or fields of instruction only after local school officers have submitted *acceptable evidence of necessary preliminary planning.* This evidence should consist of detailed written reports presented in such form and containing such data as the Department may require.

b. That established courses are examined from time to time by local school officers, to determine their appropriateness. The Department should have the right to require, after due notice, a written report on a school's program in any specified field, and to withhold state aid if this report fails to give evidence of necessary planning.

2. That in order to allow local school systems necessary freedom to develop educational programs directly related to their individual needs,

a. Existing legislation or regulations requiring the devotion of specified amounts of time to the teaching of particular subjects be rescinded, and the Department oppose future tendencies to standardize the educational program by such means.

b. The award of state aid be conditioned solely on the *continuous* provision of suitable buildings, equipment, and supplies, the employment of an adequate and properly qualified staff, and the furnishing of a minimum of necessary reports to the State Department.

3. That observance of the conditions on which state aid is assigned be rigidly required before the aid is granted.

The foregoing proposals, as it has been said, have to do with the Department's general policy with respect to regulations. Certain specific regulations are needed as a means of encouraging the local adoption of desirable educational programs. In particular, it is important that the Department recognize the advantage of modifying the conventional four-year high school organization in many schools, and that it allow individual schools greater freedom than at present in devising effective plans for promoting and grouping their pupils. It is therefore further recommended:

4. That the Education Law and the Department regulations be so changed as to recognize grades 7 through 12 (and in addition, such higher grades as may be organized in connection with the needed upward extension of the secondary school program) as secondary grades.

5. That in the case of state aid assigned on a per pupil basis, the Education Law and the Department regulations provide for allotment in terms of the chronological ages of the pupils involved, rather than in terms of grade classifications. This change is necessary in order that school systems may be free to adopt whatever plans of promotion or grade classification may be locally appropriate.

A second group of specific regulations should be put into effect to insure adequate provision for pupils not suitably cared for under the existing compulsory-attendance laws. By a paradoxical requirement, pupils who reach the age of sixteen and drop out of school without obtaining jobs are at present subject to no supervision by the schools; whereas pupils who leave school at sixteen and succeed in finding work are required in the larger cities to enroll in continuation school classes. Furthermore, young people who have withdrawn from school, unless they return to school for regular class instruction, have no legal right to the advice and assistance which they often badly need and which the school might give them. Though the present laws require every pupil to remain in school for a specified amount of time, they do not insure that a pupil will be given the education or the guidance that he ought to have in order that he may speedily be able to stand on his own feet.

The present requirements as to school attendance are not merely inconsistent; they are not flexible enough to meet the varying needs of individual pupils at different times and under different conditions. Chronological age, which is the chief criterion written into the law, furnishes too crude a standard for this purpose. It does not take into account the differing abilities of pupils of the same age, and it pays no attention to variations in conditions outside the schools. Even more significant from the standpoint of an education which ought to prepare pupils for social competence, it makes school attendance a process of serving time rather than a means of acquiring important abilities.

Ideally, compulsory-attendance laws should be framed in terms of some type of direct evidence as to pupils' readiness to leave school. There would seem to be only one such type of evidence, however, which can be applied with enough impartiality at the present time to justify its being made a part of the school attendance requirements. That type of evidence consists of a pupil's ability to get and hold a full-time job.

A job requirement would have certain obvious defects. The fact that a boy or girl can get work does not mean that he has acquired all the attitudes and abilities which he ought to have acquired before he brings his full-time schooling to an end. Furthermore, to hold every boy or girl in school until a vocational opening appeared for him would prolong the school's responsibility almost indefinitely in the cases of certain pupils.

Offsetting these defects, the job requirement would possess a number of substantial merits. In conjunction with the law requiring work permits for pupils who are employed as soon as they are allowed to leave school, it would be comparatively easy to apply. It would have the virtue of determining the length of a pupil's stay in school in terms of his need for staying in order to prepare himself for at least one sort of out-of-school competence, rather than on the basis of his "putting in" a prescribed amount of time. It would tend to keep pupils under school supervision during periods when jobs are scarce, thus helping to prevent the deterioration that may result from the idleness forced on many young people during such periods.

Because of its defects, a requirement that pupils' minimum length of stay in school should be determined by their ability to get and hold a job ought not to be substituted for the present age requirements. The job requirement might advantageously be used, however, as a supplement to the age requirements. Used in this way, it would represent a step toward a much more valid definition of the least amount of schooling which any given boy or girl should have.

In addition to the desirability of more flexible attendance regulations, it is desirable that the schools be given reasonable latitude in determining the type of education appropriate for individual boys and girls. The schools are now expected to hold all their pupils to in-school work. Part-time or unpaid jobs combined with school work, out-of-school projects of various sorts, and full- or part-time apprenticeships, may all be of positive educational advantage in the cases of certain pupils, and the schools ought to be free to make use of these kinds of informal educational experience.

No change should be made, however, either in attendance requirements or in the responsibility of the schools for individual pupils, which will suddenly impose on the schools a task with which they are unprepared to cope. In the immediate future it is probable that much of what needs to be done can best be accomplished not through mandatory requirements but through permissive legislation, accompanied by special grants of state aid to schools undertaking new responsibilities.

The need for removing inconsistencies in the present law, the desirability of guidance for certain pupils who leave school early, the desirability also of determining the minimum length of each pupil's stay in school in terms of his competence rather than merely of his age, the importance of allowing the schools broad discretion in the kinds of educational experience which they prescribe for certain boys and girls, and the need for proceeding in these matters no faster than the schools can properly go, are all reflected in the following proposals. It is recommended:

6. That the Education Law be amended in such manner as to establish requirements as follows with respect to compulsory school-attendance:

a. With the exceptions which the existing laws provide in the case of subnormal pupils, all pupils shall be required to continue in full-time school attendance until they have reached the age of sixteen.

b. Pupils more than sixteen and less than eighteen years of age who obtain approved full-time employment shall be relieved of the requirement of school attendance (including continuation school attendance) for so long as they remain in full-time employment.

c. Pupils more than sixteen and less than eighteen years of age who do not obtain employment, or who obtain only part-time employment, shall be required to follow such educational programs as may be approved and supervised by the local school authorities. These programs need not be restricted to formal classroom work, in cases in which apprenticeship placement, supervised home projects, or other out-of-school activities may be of greater educational advantage to the pupils concerned than a continuance of the usual school activities.

d. Young people between the ages of sixteen and twenty-one who are no longer required to attend school shall be privileged to return to the school at any appropriate time for educational and vocational guidance, and to carry on such school work as may be of value in their individual cases.

7. That schools in cities now required to maintain continuation schools be required to provide guidance through individual interviews, for employed young people leaving

school before they reach the age of eighteen. This guidance should be provided under the following conditions:

a. Such schools shall arrange for an initial interview with each pupil concerned immediately before he begins his first full-time employment, and for a final interview at the time the school's responsibility for his guidance ends. Other interviews shall be arranged whenever the pupil is about to change either his employment or his employer, and under any circumstances, not less often than once every three months.

b. The school's obligation to furnish this guidance shall continue until the pupil has either (1) remained in full-time employment for eight consecutive months or (2) reached the age of nineteen.

c. Schools may, at their option, provide similar guidance for pupils leaving school after having reached the age of eighteen.

8. That schools required to furnish guidance to employed pupils be required also to report immediately to the State Department of Social Welfare (or to the proposed State Youth Service Council, if this council is created[3]) the name, home address, and educational, social, and vocational history of each boy or girl who has left school before reaching the age of eighteen and who reaches the age of nineteen without having made an acceptable vocational adjustment. The young people thus reported will be former pupils no longer subject to school supervision, who have not succeeded in obtaining full-time employment lasting at least eight consecutive months.

9. That all schools be required to report annually to the State Education Department the following:

[3] Bills were introduced in the New York State Senate and Assembly in March, 1938, providing for the establishment of a State Youth Service Council which should investigate and report regularly the condition of youth, coordinate and strengthen services for youth, and help communities understand and meet the problems of their young people. (Senate, Int. No. 1599; Assembly, Int. No. 1953.)

a. The total number of pupils between sixteen and eighteen years of age who have been relieved of the requirement of school attendance because of their full-time employment; the number (if any) and types of employment of the pupils in this group for whom the school has furnished individual guidance; and the number of pupils returning voluntarily to the school for special guidance or for part-time school work.

b. The total number of pupils between sixteen and eighteen years of age for whom out-of-school activities have been approved in lieu of the usual school work, and the nature of such activities.

c. The total number of pupils (if any) reported to the State Department of Social Welfare (or to the State Youth Service Council).

10. That to help school systems in meeting the requirements of the proposed legislation,

a. State aid be granted for certain pupils not recognized in the existing state aid provisions, on the same basis (the chronological ages of the pupils being taken into due account) as for pupils in full- or part-time attendance at regular day schools. Pupils for whom this allotment is recommended comprise

(1) Pupils pursuing evening or summer school work equivalent to that offered in grades 7 through 12 of full-time day schools.

(2) Pupils enrolled in advanced vocational programs.

(3) Pupils enrolled in semiprofessional programs in grades above the twelfth.

(4) Pupils being supervised in special out-of-school projects under the proposed law.

b. State aid be granted individual school systems in proportion to the numbers of young people not required to continue in school attendance, for whom the schools furnish guidance under the proposed law. Such aid should cover a part of the cost of guidance, and should be allotted only on condition that its full amount is applied to the salaries of persons devoting at least half their time to this guidance.

11. That the proposed state aid for school systems offering guidance to young people not required to continue in school attendance be made available not only to schools required by law to furnish such guidance, but to any school system undertaking the proposed program.

The exploitation to which young people outside of school are now frequently subjected suggests one further proposal in this connection. It is recommended:

12. That the State Education Department undertake strict regulation of proprietary schools in New York State, giving particular attention to their advertising practices and their sales methods. The Department should systematically provide local school officials with information about such schools, on the basis of which individual pupils may be protected against possible exploitation.

So far as concerns the basic program of secondary education, the foregoing regulations are those which most need to be put into effect. It will be noted that their intent is to give the schools greater freedom and more direct incentives for planning their programs in terms of local circumstances, to allow the schools to adopt more effective systems of grade organization and of promotion, and to focus direct attention on the out-of-school adjustment of high school pupils who are ending their full-time schooling.

LEADERSHIP IN THE SOLUTION OF MAJOR PROBLEMS

Adoption of these regulations will inevitably impose new responsibilities and new tasks on the secondary schools. If the schools are to carry these new burdens successfully, they must be able to count on leadership by the Department not through regulation alone, nor merely through regulation coupled with examinations, but through tangible help in the solution of certain major problems.

The problems with which the schools most need help are problems in connection with the improvement of the curriculum and of methods of teaching, problems of adequate guidance, and problems involved in planning each high school program in direct relation to the local situation. The State Education Department should provide for systematic advice and assistance to the schools in connection with each of these three kinds of undertakings.

The help which the Department offers on problems of the curriculum ought not to be limited to advice based on the experience of individual supervisors. Neither should this help be provided solely or chiefly in connection with the visits of supervisors to the schools. Suggestions as to appropriate methods and materials of teaching should grow out of thorough studies carried on by the Department, and should be widely and systematically disseminated through published bulletins, meetings of teachers and local supervisors, and demonstrations of particularly effective practice.

As a means of furnishing assistance of this sort, it is recommended:

1. That the Department provide for systematic, continuous, and intensive research looking toward the development of more effective methods and materials of teaching. A major share of this research should properly be concerned with recognized fields of school subject matter: English, the social studies, industrial arts, the teaching of music for pupils who will not become practiced musicians, et cetera. Certain broader problems also should receive thorough study. Among the latter are problems encountered in the

course of this Inquiry, to which the Inquiry itself has been able to provide only incomplete answers. Problems especially needing study are the following:

a. Why is the achievement of girls in New York State high schools inferior to that of boys? What specific modifications would make the present curriculum more appropriate for girls?

b. How can the secondary schools more effectively capitalize and develop the normal interests of their pupils?

c. What types of school experience beyond those now in use can be depended on to develop pupils' concern for social progress and their willingness to take an active part in advancing it?

d. By what means may the out-of-school reading of young people be extended and enriched? How can the contributions of school and public libraries be most effectively increased?

e. What curriculum materials and what methods of teaching are likely to be most effective with boys and girls who have reached the end of their rope in academic work, but who are not yet ready to leave school?

f. What curriculum materials and what methods of teaching beyond those now in use are likely to be effective in challenging exceptionally able boys and girls to the best learning of which they are capable?

2. That, in addition to course outlines of the type provided in the state syllabi, the Department prepare an extensive series of curriculum bulletins, to be furnished directly to high school teachers. Each bulletin should contain suggestions as to content and method for the teaching and testing of a single curriculum unit. Bulletins should be based on the best available teaching materials, wherever such materials may be found. The curriculum research conducted by the Department should be so planned as to result, when necessary, in definite adaptation and supple-

mentation of existing materials, as well as in the development of new materials. The Department should issue more curriculum bulletins than any one school can use, making them so varied that schools may select units adapted to local needs and pupil differences. Since the purpose of the Department should be to aid and encourage good teaching rather than to standardize the curriculum, the use of either the bulletins or the course outlines should be optional with individual schools.

3. That the Department actively stimulate more effective teaching in individual schools through

a. The establishment, in cooperation with state and regional teachers' associations, of a clearinghouse for disseminating information about superior teaching practices and for acquainting teachers with schools in which excellent teaching may be observed.

b. The development of experimental and demonstration centers in schools well equipped to provide good teaching.

c. The conduct of more frequent regional conferences of teachers and supervisors who are concerned with special phases of the curriculum.

In view of the proposed changes in the compulsory-attendance laws, assistance in the development of programs of guidance is likely to be as much needed by the secondary schools as is constructive help in the improvement of local curricula. It is therefore recommended:

4. That the State Department provide special advice and assistance in the development of local guidance programs, looking toward effective coordination, both locally and on a state-wide basis, of the present largely uncoordinated plans of pupil accounting, guidance, placement, and follow-up work.

5. That the Department take the initiative in developing plans of cooperation between the schools and nonschool agencies—particularly government placement and welfare agencies—to insure the speediest and most effective possible adjustment of out-of-school boys and girls to current vocational and social conditions.

Assistance to the schools in connection with the third major type of problem, the planning of school programs as wholes, will require a new method of attack. Though the schools' need for help in this area has already been pointed out, the fact that the Department has not previously undertaken extensive work of this sort justifies special comment on the provisions which ought to be made.

It is evident that the secondary school program ought not to consist merely of a collection of courses or of curriculum units, topped by a plan of guidance, any more than the program of the State Department itself should consist of a mere collection of specialized undertakings. If a school is to function effectively, each subject or activity which it offers ought to play a consistent and well-coordinated part in its program. To determine what that program should be, to make sure that it includes the special services that the school needs to offer, and to see that all those services function in proper relation to one another, is in most respects the task of an educational generalist rather than of a group of specialists.

The State Department ought, therefore, to provide a sufficient number of such generalists to work with the heads of individual schools. Their duties should be to acquaint themselves with the major problems which each school faces, to give as much help as each principal may need in planning the educational program most suitable for his school, to advise in matters of secondary school administration, and in the case of problems growing out of details of the school's work, to direct the principal to sources of specialized help either in the State Department or elsewhere. The State Department's general supervisors should not, under any circumstances, take over the functions of local school officers; but the advisory assistance which they can give is needed by principals quite as much as the advice which special-subject supervisors may offer is needed by local supervisors and heads of departments.

If general supervisors are to use their time effectively and are to become properly acquainted with local school conditions, they cannot be expected to work always out of Albany. Instead, they should spend much of their time in sections of the State to which they are assigned and where they may have their headquarters. Representing the State Department in outlying districts, they may eliminate much wasteful traveling by other members of the Department. They should serve, in effect, as diagnosticians as well as counselors to local schools; and the results of their diagnoses should enable specialists in the Department to direct attention to the particular schools and the particular problems where the help of specialists is most needed.

All these considerations are summed up in a final recommendation as to the type of leadership which the Department should offer:

6. That the Department provide direct advice and guidance to secondary school principals through frequent visits by supervisors especially qualified to deal with the problems which local school officers must face. The necessary advisory service cannot be rendered by supervisors chiefly interested in special fields of subject matter. Neither can it take adequate account of local needs and local conditions, if it must be offered chiefly through correspondence, conferences with visitors to the Department, or addresses before groups of administrators. Existing arrangements for field service to general school officers must be greatly extended

if the State Education Department is to exercise effective educational leadership.

ORGANIZATION OF THE STATE EDUCATION DEPARTMENT

The recommendations set forth in the preceding pages comprise all that are to be advanced in this report with respect to the general policies and regulations of the State Department. Certain supplementary recommendations need to be made, however, with respect to the plan of organization through which the Department seeks to put these policies and regulations into effect.

The reorganization of the Department approved by the Board of Regents in 1937 offers a plan of organization well calculated to further a number of the policies which have been proposed. The newly established Division of Research is in a position to assume responsibility for the continuous appraisal of the outcomes of secondary education. The Division of Examinations and Testing, having been relieved of its former duties in connection with the supervision of teaching, should be able to take full charge of the preparation of achievement examinations for the schools. The establishment of the Bureau of Curriculum Development, to work in conjunction with the Bureau of Instructional Supervision, should make possible the type of assistance to the schools which has been recommended as a means of improving methods and materials of teaching. These branches of the Department, in particular, may well undertake immediately to give new direction and significance to the Department's work with the secondary schools.

Certain further changes which ought to be made in the organization of the Department have been discussed in Chapter XII. The exact offices and lines of authority called for by those changes cannot properly be decided on without reference to other responsibilities of the Department than its responsibility for secondary education alone. Hence the final recommendations as to the organization of the Department must be left to the Inquiry's special report[4] on that subject. But a number of the further changes which need to be made are closely enough related to the development of secondary education to warrant definite proposals with respect to them in the present report. Three changes in particular deserve comment.

First, any modifications which may be made in the present organization of the Department should take account of the need for thoroughgoing coordination of the secondary school program. The present separation of vocational education from the general program of secondary education offers, it should be repeated, a serious handicap to the development of a well-balanced program. The division of responsibility between the present Bureau of Child Accounting and Attendance and the Bureau of Guidance represents an additional source of incoordination which should, by all means, be removed.

Second, there needs to be more direct provision than that made in the present organization for assistance to general school officers. The principals of secondary schools are presumably not alone in the need for such assistance; elementary school principals, directors of adult education, and superintendents of schools undoubtedly face problems in which corresponding help would be of much advantage. Whatever arrangements the Department may make for field service to school officers ought, therefore, not to be restricted to work with high school principals. Field service of this type is nevertheless clearly desirable in connection with the special problems faced by the secondary schools.

Finally, it is desirable that the Department make a clean-cut distinction between its inspectional functions and the leadership which it exercises through direct cooperation with local schools. Supervisors from the Department cannot gain

[4] Luther H. Gulick, *Education for American Life*, Regents' Inquiry, 1938.

the full confidence of school people if they are expected to use their visits to local schools as a means of enforcing Department regulations. Such further modifications as may be made in the organization of the Department ought therefore to relieve the officers whose chief duty is to work constructively with the schools, of any responsibility for enforcing formal rules. The regulations which have been recommended earlier can readily be enforced by a branch of the Department charged especially with this function; and some such branch should exercise sole responsibility in this connection.

In order that all these matters may be taken into due account, it is recommended:

1. That in the further reorganization of the Department the division responsible for development of the general program of secondary education be made responsible also for vocational education in secondary schools.

2. That, coordinate with the branch of the Department in charge of curriculum research in secondary education, there be established a branch charged with the development of programs of guidance. It should be the responsibility of this latter division to aid school officers in the observance of the compulsory-attendance law, to devise and encourage the adoption of more effective methods of directing pupils in their educational and vocational choices, and to arrange for systematic cooperation with other state agencies and with federal agencies in assisting boys and girls who have withdrawn from school. This division should unite the functions of the present Bureaus of Guidance and of Child Accounting and Attendance.

3. That there be established a branch of the Department responsible for field service to general school officers, and that this branch be represented throughout the State by regional officers. It should be the function of the field service division

a. To inform itself and the members of its regional offices of the outcomes of the educational programs in the individual school districts of the State, as these outcomes are analyzed and reported by the Division of Research.

b. To interpret to local school officers the data gathered and the conclusions reported by the Division of Research.

c. Through its regional offices, to provide advice and assistance to local school officers in improving their programs. The field service offices should bring to the attention of local schools the curriculum materials and methods developed by the Bureau of Curriculum Research. They should make arrangements for representatives of the latter Bureau and of conveniently located teacher training institutions to aid in the solution of special educational problems. Without being charged with administrative responsibilities, the field service offices should make available to schools in general the advisory assistance which the present district superintendents are expected, but are seldom in a position, to offer to schools in rural areas.

4. That the branches of the State Department concerned with research and examinations, curriculum development, and field service be granted no coercive or regulatory powers whatever with respect to the administration of local schools. Qualified members of these divisions should confer periodically with the officers of the Department in charge of the enforcement of regulations, as to the effectiveness of current requirements and as to the desirability of new or modified rules. The purpose of these divisions, however, should be to advise and assist school officers, and not to enforce Department regulations.

RELATION OF THE STATE EDUCATION DEPARTMENT TO THE SCHOOLS

In the light of the last of these recommendations in particular, a summary statement is perhaps in order as to the nature of the relations which the Department may most profitably maintain with the schools.

The Department ought first of all to insure the conditions under which good school work can be done. It should take the initiative in establishing schools and school districts large enough and well enough supported to make an adequate program of secondary education possible; it should see that local communities provide essential buildings, equipment, and staff; and it should define the duties and responsibilities of the secondary schools.

The Department ought also to make sure that local school officers recognize the problems with which their schools must deal, and that they know how well the schools are meeting these problems. It should adopt a plan for appraising the work of the schools which will bring the total strengths and weaknesses of each school, and not just its success in preparing pupils for academic examinations, into clear relief. It should then help local school officers to see exactly what the results of this appraisal mean, as a basis for planning the most effective possible educational program.

Beyond insuring the conditions for good school work and assisting school officers to analyze educational needs, the Department should make itself a source of constructive help and advice to the schools. One of its major responsibilities should be that of inventing or discovering ways of teaching, curriculum materials, methods of dealing with the varying needs of individual boys and girls, plans of organization and administration, which will offer better answers to the schools' educational problems than the schools themselves may have found. Using the new materials which the Department shall bring together, its representatives ought to work with school officers in developing local programs which will most directly meet local needs.

There is no place in this plan of work for insisting that local schools observe large numbers of formal rules. Nor is there any good reason to make a place for regulation of this sort. The great majority of school officers are quite as concerned as the Department itself that the educational opportunities which New York State offers its boys and girls shall be well planned and effective. If it is willing to rely on this concern, the Department may accomplish its best results not so much by ruling and directing as by helping the school people of the State to see clearly what needs to be done and how to do it.

CHAPTER XVI

Cost of an Improved Program

How much will a better program of secondary education cost New York State, and how can such a program be financed?

COST OF BROADER SERVICE BY THE STATE EDUCATION DEPARTMENT

The services which the State Education Department should provide for the secondary schools will demand no increase in the present budget of the Department. Both those services which represent new undertakings and certain activities which will involve a change of direction in the Department's present work can be provided for through transfers of available funds.

Among the new services must be counted an improved system of Regents' Examinations. In administering the present examination system for the school year 1936–37, the Department spent approximately $130,000.[1] Almost $100,000 of this amount was devoted to scoring the examination papers returned by the schools, and to keeping up to date the Department's records of individual pupils' marks. Under the new examination plan the greater part of the latter sum, in addition to the $30,000 now spent in preparing and distributing the examinations, should be available for devising and perfecting new measuring instruments and for carrying on fundamental research.

[1] For cost figures cited in this chapter see Alonzo G. Grace and G. A. Moe, *State Aid and School Costs*, Regents' Inquiry, 1938. For data on births and on elementary school enrollments see J. B. Maller, *School and Community*, Regents' Inquiry, 1938.

Cost of an Improved Program

The development of a field service division within the Department will represent a further new service. The field supervisors should eventually take the place of the present district superintendents. Under an improved plan of district organization the latter will presumably be elected to standard superintendencies in school districts which now have no local superintendents. The State Education Department at present contributes $594,000 a year to the salaries of the district superintendents. Out of this sum the Department should be able to provide several times the amount needed for the added supervisors recommended in the new program.

Other proposed changes within the Department will demand a redirection of work in which the Department is already engaged, rather than the setting up of entirely new divisions. These other changes will consist principally of new emphasis on curriculum research and on the development of programs of guidance—undertakings already provided for in the new plan of organization approved by the Board of Regents.

The State Department should therefore need no new funds to meet its responsibilities for secondary education. Its plan of expenditures will undoubtedly have to be readjusted from time to time as the needs for particular types of research and supervision vary. The total budget which it now devotes to the oversight of the secondary schools would nevertheless seem ample for the major services that it needs to render those schools.

SOURCES OF FUNDS FOR THE SCHOOLS

The funds which will be needed by the individual schools of the State can likewise be made available through transfer, as rapidly as the schools are in a position to use these funds effectively.

Two factors will make it possible to extend the educational program of the State and still keep within the limits of the present school budget. One of these factors is the possibility of applying millions of dollars annually, now wastefully spent, toward a more effective program. The other is the declining birth rate. The latter is already being reflected in decreasing public school enrollments, which, without any increase in the total amount of money spent on the schools, should make it practicable to devote steadily increasing sums to improving and extending the educational program. Before outlining the probable increases in cost which will be demanded by the new program recommended for the high schools, it will be appropriate to consider just how much these two items—the stopping of waste and the decline in school enrollments—may be expected to yield.

POSSIBLE ADMINISTRATIVE ECONOMIES

According to the findings of the cost studies conducted by the Inquiry, the largest single source of waste in the administration of the schools is the present school district system. The cost studies indicate that savings of from $2,000,000 to $2,600,-000 annually can be accomplished through moderate increases in the average size of classes in the small high schools—a possibility which has already been commented on in Chapter XI. The studies suggest that even greater savings are feasible in the elementary schools. Except in cases of absolute isolation, no one-room school with fewer than fifteen pupils should be permitted to operate. According to the cost study estimates, feasible consolidations among schools which now enroll fewer than fifteen pupils, or transportation of their pupils as nonresidents to near-by larger schools, should diminish annual expenses for instruction by $1,600,000 at a minimum estimate and possibly by as much as $2,600,000 at a maximum. Raising the average size of class in other elementary schools to approximately twenty-five pupils would result in further savings of some $4,500,000. The report of the general study of school costs indicates that thoroughly feasible economies of this sort in elementary schools and high schools together would release for other uses a minimum of $8,100,000 annually, and at a conservative estimate might allow an annual saving of at least $1,600,000 more.[2]

In addition to the economies which would result from a better plan of school and school district organization, the cost studies indicate further possible savings through a plan of cooperative purchasing based on scientifically established specifications for current supplies. Under such a plan school systems would agree on standard specifications developed through a study of the most economical choice and use of supplies and equipment, and would take advantage of the savings possible in large-scale buying by pooling orders in making purchases. Experience with municipal purchasing systems has demonstrated that cooperative and scientific buying of supplies and short-lived equipment may produce economies of at least 10 per cent at a very modest estimate. A saving of this amount on purchases for the New York State schools would lower the State's annual bill for the schools by approximately $1,500,000. Through the establishment of a state-wide insurance fund there could be effected a further reduction of $300,000 each year in insurance premiums. Cooperative purchasing of both types applied to current operating expenses would thus save the schools a total of some $1,800,000 annually.

Savings through increases in class size and through cooperative purchasing of current supplies would all apply against the $260,000,000 spent year by year for running the elementary and secondary schools. Cooperative buying in connection with capital outlays made from current funds would

[2] This estimate is, in fact, highly conservative, because it assumes an increase in class enrollments which would bring the average class size to no more than twenty-five pupils in schools now having class enrollments below that figure. Many states assume an average class size of thirty pupils as a desirable standard, for elementary schools especially. Were New York State schools to be reorganized to provide an average class enrollment of not less than thirty pupils, the maximum saving in current expense would rise as high as $27,500,000.

reduce annual expenses by nearly $200,000 more. If, in addition, the State adopts the pay-as-you-go policy recommended as a result of the cost studies, it might eventually eliminate all its annual bond interest on school buildings—$26,000,000 in 1935. The latter figure is obviously a maximum, only to be attained as present outstanding debts are retired. Other factors remaining equal, however, the need for new buildings will become steadily less, as the decrease in birth rate causes school enrollments to decline. Savings in interest payments therefore represent a source of economy which is by no means merely theoretical.

Adding together the minimum annual savings which the State may make as estimated in the cost studies, the total amounts to some $10,100,000. The maximum, including the eventual elimination of interest on school bonds, may reach $37,700,000. Solely through better controlled spending the State may thus avail itself of very considerable sums for improving the work of the schools.

DECREASED ENROLLMENTS

The amount of money which the State may save through better organization and administration of its schools is hardly greater, however, than the reductions in expenditure which should result from decreases in the numbers of pupils to be educated.

In 1912 there were approximately 240,000 children born in the State of New York. With minor fluctuations from year to year, births occurred in practically the same number each year through 1918. Thereafter—again with some fluctuation —the total diminished fairly steadily year by year, to 231,000 in 1923, 223,000 in 1928, 187,000 in 1933. In 1936, with 182,000 births recorded, the annual total was still decreasing, though at a somewhat slower rate.

Meanwhile the immigration into New York State of families with children of school age has almost ceased. Emigration has greatly diminished, but still remains large enough so that it has a definite effect on the school population. The net result of the shifting of population which has recently taken place has been to add slightly to the effect of the declining birth rate in decreasing the numbers of boys and girls who must be provided for each year in the public schools.

Apart from the effects of shifts in population, it is apparent that the number of births in any one year will largely determine the number of children who enter the first grade of the public schools six years later. The number of births will also determine the enrollment in each succeeding grade year by year thereafter, until pupils begin to drop out of school. At least since 1921 (the earliest year for which the Inquiry has analyzed these trends), first grade enrollments have tended to bear a fixed relation to the numbers of births six years earlier. Since 1932 the ninth grade enrollment, having reached a point of saturation because of the tendency of young people to stay longer and longer in school, has similarly corresponded with births fourteen years before. The numbers of births in recent years therefore make it possible to predict first grade enrollments as far ahead as 1942, and ninth grade enrollments as far ahead as 1950.

First grade enrollments passed their peak in 1927–28, with a total of 249,000 pupils. In 1935–36 these enrollments had dropped to fewer than 210,000 pupils. By 1942–43, as judged by the births for 1936, they will have fallen some 14 per cent below the latter figure. How much farther they may decline cannot be at all accurately predicted until further trends in the birth rate become apparent. By 1950, however, all eight of the grades now included in the elementary schools will have been affected by the births which produced the first grade enrollment for 1942–43, with the result that the enrollment in all these grades together may be expected to have fallen considerably more than 14 per cent below the elementary school enrollment for 1935–36.

Ninth grade enrollments apparently reached their maximum size in 1934–35; in that year 239,000 pupils were registered in grade 9. Enrollments in this grade in 1935–36 sank to 236,000. By 1950–51, if the number of pupils in the ninth grade is equal to the total number of children born in 1936, the enrollment will be approximately 182,000, or 22 per cent less than it was in the school year 1935–36.

It is probable that the total enrollment in all four of the upper grades will not decrease as markedly as that of the ninth grade alone. The same tendencies which have kept all pupils on into the ninth grade, even though the compulsory attendance laws would have let many of them drop out earlier, may be expected gradually to raise the average age for leaving school. Nevertheless, the period of rapid growth in the high school population, a period which brought about an increase of 400 per cent in high school attendance between 1915 and 1937, is apparently over. Except as new grades or new services are added, the high school enrollment is not likely to become much larger than it is at present, so that no new costs need to be anticipated from automatic increases in the numbers of boys and girls to be taught.

Thus, for the first time in its history, New York State faces a decreasing school population. How much of its present annual expense for schools will be freed on that account can be only crudely estimated. Within the near future, probably no reductions in expense will be possible in the operation of the secondary schools; whatever reductions are made must be looked for chiefly in the elementary grades.

The latter reductions will of course not keep exact pace with decreases in enrollment. They cannot be expected to do so for a twofold reason. In the first place, savings are likely always to lag behind theoretical chances for saving. In the second place, a decline in enrollment will to some extent lessen the possibilities for administrative economies of the kinds suggested earlier, particularly those economies depending on the organization of larger classes. Decreasing enrollment may not make it as difficult to organize larger classes as would appear at first glance, partly because the birth rate is declining more rapidly in the cities, where it is relatively easy to maintain classes of standard size, than in the rural districts; and partly because the eventual inclusion of the seventh and eighth grades in the secondary schools should allow the grouping of seventh and eighth grade pupils from several elementary schools in each high school. Nevertheless, the net reduction in expenditure that can be expected must obviously be less than the 14 per cent or more by which elementary school enrollments are likely to decline.

Balancing these various considerations as well as they can be balanced with respect to an uncertain future, it is probably not wide of the mark to assume that by 1950 decreasing enrollments will make available at least 10 per cent of the present annual cost of operating the elementary schools, in addition to the amounts which may be saved in other ways, for use wherever additional funds may be most needed, including use in the elementary schools themselves. This means that approximately $16,500,000, of the total $165,000,000 devoted to elementary education in 1935–36, may eventually be added to the $10,000,000 or more saved through administrative economies, for extending and improving public education throughout the State.

COST OF A BETTER PROGRAM

These possible savings should be kept in mind in considering the sums needed for a better program of secondary education.

A considerable part of the recommended program, namely, the revision of present elements in the curriculum, the adoption of teaching methods better suited to various degrees and kinds of ability, and the modification of the conventional plan of school organization, will demand not so much marked increases in school expenditures as a different use of the sums already being spent. The parts of the recommended program which will call for definitely new items of cost will be five in

number: (1) the offering of definite preparation for employment as a part of every comprehensive high school program;
(2) the longer retention in school of unemployed boys and
girls who now drop out before they reach the age of eighteen;
(3) the supervision of out-of-school projects in the case of
certain pupils for whom continued school attendance is no
longer appropriate; (4) the guidance of boys and girls who
have left school, until they have made a satisfactory vocational
adjustment or until they become nineteen years old; and (5)
the provision of technical and semiprofessional education in
grades above the twelfth. The Regents' Inquiry has estimated
the added annual cost of each part of this program in terms
both of present secondary school enrollments and of changes in
enrollment foreshadowed by the declining birth rate.

As a means of arriving at the cost of the recommended
program under present conditions, the Inquiry has assumed
that the group of pupils who entered the ninth grade in 1932
was fairly representative of the high school groups which will
need to be provided for in the near future.[3] To have furnished
the recommended program for these pupils during their four
years in school would have cost approximately the same as to
have supplied the program to the four classes enrolled in the
high schools in any one of these years. The difference between
that cost and the cost of the program actually offered represents the added annual expense which would be involved in
carrying out the Inquiry's recommendations. This added
expense is estimated to be as follows:

1. *Expenditure for Offering Definite Preparation for Employment as a
Part of Every Comprehensive High School Program, $1,100,000*

Two major assumptions underlie the estimate with respect
to this part of the program: first, that the added cost will re-

[3] The ninth grade in 1932–33 enrolled 234,990 pupils—a total only 1,115
smaller than that for 1935–36. As pointed out earlier, future enrollments
in the ninth grade may be expected to fall below those used as a basis for these
estimates.

sult mainly from the offering of courses requiring the use of specialized equipment—office equipment, woodworking tools, shop machinery, and the like; and second, that new courses of this type will be needed chiefly by pupils who do not now complete the high school program. The cost of such courses has been computed in terms not of the highly specialized work now offered by the separate vocational schools, but of the general industrial arts courses in schools in which such courses have been approved by the State Department. Assuming classes of normal size, this cost will be approximately 30 per cent greater than the cost of the classroom subjects which the pupils enrolled in these subjects would otherwise be taking. To allow an estimate of the total enrollments to be expected in such courses, it has been assumed (*a*) that for secondary school pupils who stay through to graduation each year's program should be composed, on the average, of 90 per cent classroom work and 10 per cent work requiring specialized equipment; (*b*) that in the case of pupils who do not graduate, the program up to the beginning of the final year should consist of these same proportions of classroom work and special work; and (*c*) that for pupils who do not graduate the program of the final year should consist (apart from extracurricular activities and study assignments) of approximately 75 per cent classroom work and 25 per cent work requiring special equipment. Since the program involving 10 per cent of special work is essentially that now provided, no additional expense need be expected from this source. As judged by the pupils who entered school in 1932, approximately 410,000 boys and girls each year may well be engaged in this type of program. One hundred twenty-six thousand may be expected to have programs in which 25 per cent of their regular class time, on the average, will be spent in work requiring special equipment. For each of the latter pupils this will mean the substitution of one shop or laboratory course for an academic course, in a program normally consisting of four "credit" courses. The cost of the academic program in 1935–36 averaged $175 a year for each pupil. The 75-25 program should cost approximately $183.75 for each pupil. The added cost of $8.75 for each of 126,000 pupils thus makes up the total of increased expense.[4]

2. *Expenditure for Keeping in School Unemployed Boys and Girls Who Now Drop Out Before They Reach the Age of Eighteen, $5,250,000*

The proposed changes in the compulsory-attendance laws will require either continued school attendance or work on projects supervised by the school, on the part of the majority of pupils who now leave school before graduation without obtaining employment. For half the pupils who are unsuccessful in finding jobs it is assumed that continued school attendance for an average of one year more will be desirable. The additional year in school may properly give these pupils a chance to spend half their regular class time in subjects demanding specialized equipment. The cost of the latter subjects has been estimated in the same way (allowing for the greater amount of time spent on these subjects) as for pupils enrolled in the 75-25 program. Assuming that the employment situation discovered among pupils who left school in 1936 is reasonably typical, it is estimated that the half-classroom-half-shopwork program may need to be provided for some 28,000 pupils each year. The fact that the full year's work for each of these pupils will represent an addition to current costs of approximately $187.50 explains the much greater expense of providing this work than of changing the programs of the larger numbers of pupils still in school.

[4] Because the amounts of federal aid for vocational education, and the conditions under which this aid may be supplied, are largely unpredictable, no deduction of federal aid is made in these estimates. For a discussion of the policy which New York State may wisely adopt with respect to grants for educational purposes from the federal government, see Alonzo G. Grace and G. A. Moe, *State Aid and School Costs*, Regents' Inquiry, 1938.

Cost of an Improved Program

3. *Expenditure for Supervising Out-of-School Projects Carried on by Pupils Who Have Not Obtained Full-Time Employment, $5,450,000*

The other half of the pupils who now fail to find any kind of work after leaving school will presumably be subject to supervision by the school in connection with approved out-of-school projects. In addition, the pupils employed only part-time will be subject to similar supervision; and it is assumed that the schools will need to supervise for an additional year about half the pupils who were in school during the preceding year under the half-classroom-half-shopwork program. The annual cost per pupil for supervision of this type, allowing for the equivalent of one half-day visit by a supervisor to each pupil each month, is estimated at $75. Judging again by the employment situation among the pupils who left school in 1936, and by the numbers of pupils dropping out of the group which entered the ninth grade in 1932, the number of pupils for whom such supervision will have to be provided in any one year may total approximately 73,000.

4. *Expenditure for the Guidance of Boys and Girls Who Have Left School, Until They Have Made a Satisfactory Vocational Adjustment or Until They Become Nineteen Years Old, $950,000*

This estimate is based on the assumption that every school will eventually provide the counseling required of certain schools under the proposed law, and that such counseling will be made available not merely to pupils who leave school before they are eighteen, but to all who leave the high school to go to work. Three groups of pupils are likely to be eligible for such counseling: (*a*) about half the pupils engaged during the preceding year on the half-classroom-half-shopwork program; (*b*) practically all the pupils whom the school has supervised for a year on out-of-school projects; and (*c*) about one-fourth

· 329 ·

the high school graduates (the rest of the graduates either going on into higher institutions, continuing under the supervision of the secondary school until they obtain employment, or taking advantage of their right to leave school without further supervision). The counseling of each pupil will presumably need to be continued for an average of about a year. Its cost, assuming that a counselor interviews four pupils a day and sees each pupil five times a year, should be approximately $15 per pupil. Estimated in terms of the pupils who entered the high schools in 1932, the total number of pupils who may be eligible for this counseling in any one year will be approximately 161,000. The cost of interviews for these pupils will be slightly under $2,450,000. Against this cost, however, must be balanced the saving which will come from the proposed closing of the continuation schools. These schools accounted in 1935–36 for a total current expense of approximately $1,500,000. The net added cost of the counseling service will therefore amount to less than $1,000,000.

5. *Expenditure for the Provision of Technical and Semiprofessional Education in Grades above the Twelfth, $6,700,000*

In the absence of any experience in New York State with technical and semiprofessional training as part of a secondary school program extending beyond the twelfth grade, an estimate of the cost of such training for all pupils who may reasonably take advantage of it may be wide of the mark. It is assumed, however, that further education of this sort may be appropriate for as many as half the high school graduates who do not go on to college. In terms of the group entering grade 9 in 1932, this would mean a total of slightly less than 23,000 pupils to be provided for. The annual cost of such training would probably approximate $200 for each pupil, and its average length would presumably be about a year and a half. In any one year the total cost would therefore amount to some

Cost of an Improved Program

$6,860,000. From this cost should be deducted savings of over $160,000 in the counseling service, resulting from the fact that approximately 11,000 of the pupils who may be enrolled in the extended training have been counted among those to whom the schools should offer guidance after they graduate. The net added cost of the technical and semi-professional training will thus be in the neighborhood of $6,750,000 each year.

These five major items together represent an added cost of $19,450,000. Obviously, no estimate of this sort can be more than an approximation. The present estimate is based, however, on what would seem to be the maximum rather than the minimum needs of a representative group of pupils. The prediction can therefore fairly safely be made that to adopt the program of secondary education which has been recommended will require, under present conditions, a new expense of less than $20,000,000 annually.

Present conditions may, of course, not persist. On the one hand, it is conceivable that the tendency of boys and girls to remain in school may overbalance the declining birth rate to such an extent that there will continue to be marked increases in the total secondary school enrollment. All boys and girls entering the ninth grade may eventually, for example, stay through the twelfth grade. Were this to happen in the case of the 182,000 pupils who will presumably enroll in the ninth grade in 1950, the added cost of the proposed program over the present secondary school budget would rise to approximately $41,500,000.[5]

On the other hand, pupils may continue in the future to drop out of school at about the same points and in about the same proportions as now—subject only to the increased retention

[5] This estimate, and the estimate which follows, are based on the assumption that per pupil costs due to salaries and expenses for school supplies and equipment will be approximately the same in 1950 as at present. Any such assumption is clearly open to debate. It would seem quite impossible, however, to take the changes that may occur in these factors into account.

which the proposed changes in the compulsory attendance laws may bring about. If this should come to pass, the budget of current expense for schooling from the ninth grade on of the pupils entering that grade in 1950 would be some $6,250,000 *less*, under the proposed program, than the present high school budget. The cost of technical and semiprofessional training beyond the twelfth grade would represent an addition of more than $5,000,000 over present expenses, but the smaller enrollments in the other grades would require, despite the added services in these grades, an expenditure nearly $12,000,-000 below the total of $95,000,000 allotted to the secondary schools for the school year 1935–36.

The new amounts which will actually need to be spent almost certainly lie well away from either the conceivable maximum or the conceivable minimum. This being the case, the exact total which they may reach is of less significance than is the fact that any such total will be smaller than the total of the savings which may be made in other directions.

The estimates which have been presented have been based on total eventual costs and total possible savings. Briefly summarized, the estimates indicate that against annual savings and reductions in expense which should amount to not less than $26,000,000 and which in the long run may exceed $50,000,000, New York State must plan for additional expenditures of approximately $20,000,000 each year, in order to make the changes that most need to be made in the state-wide program of secondary education.

IMMEDIATE STEPS IN THE IMPROVEMENT OF SECONDARY EDUCATION

Not all the added $20,000,000 which should eventually go to the secondary schools each year can be wisely spent in the immediate future. Before the recommended changes which call for this expenditure can be put into substantial effect, the specific needs of local communities must be canvassed, definite local plans must be formulated for the addition of new school services, and persons competent to undertake these new services must be added to many local school staffs. The improvement of the educational program ought properly to be undertaken as a gradual process, with new responsibilities being placed on local schools only as rapidly as the schools can become prepared to assume new duties.

The expenditure of added sums for secondary education, moreover, will require a revision of the basis on which the cost of the schools is now divided between the State and the local communities. Certain of the changes which have been recommended involve new grants of state aid; other changes are likely to demand new methods of apportionment in order that the total cost of the schools may be properly distributed. To take account of general problems involved in the sharing of educational costs, the whole question of state aid has been examined in a separate study under the Inquiry.[6] Before new sums are allotted to the secondary schools, the plan of state aid which that study recommends should be made a part of the general educational program.

For all these reasons, the expenditures for secondary education in New York State probably ought to be increased only as rapidly as new funds for the secondary schools become available through the economies which the State can make in its school program as a whole. Planning for new services should not wait on these economies; the State Department and local schools together should systematically prepare for an extension of the educational program in advance of actual commitments to new undertakings. Nor should desirable changes which can be made within the present secondary school budget be postponed. Improvements in the examination system, in the established curriculum, and in methods of teaching, in particular, need to be put into immediate

[6] See Alonzo G. Grace and G. A. Moe, *State Aid and School Costs*, Regents' Inquiry, 1938.

effect in order that local schools may begin to render the service that they ought to render to the boys and girls in their communities. But if New York State moves promptly to take advantage of the economies which the Inquiry has recommended, extensions of the secondary school program calling for greatly increased expense can safely be postponed until financial support for these extensions is thoroughly assured.

New York State thus has the opportunity, without increasing the expenditures for its schools, to add greatly to the preparation which it gives its boys and girls for citizenship, for further learning, for leisure, and for jobs. If it is to preserve and enhance the reputation which its schools have justly earned in the past, it will take full advantage of that opportunity.

Appendix

Special Investigations in the Study
of Secondary Education

CHAPTER I of this report outlines the major steps in the study of secondary education under the Regents' Inquiry. The study as a whole included a considerable number of subordinate investigations. The latter were designed to contribute either to the second step in the general plan—the appraisal of educational outcomes—or to the third—the analysis of school practices in relation to those outcomes. For the benefit of readers interested in the techniques of the study, there is presented in the following pages a brief account of each of the special investigations, indicating its purpose, its method, and its part in the general plan. More detailed explanations of procedures in certain of these investigations will be found in the monographs supporting this general report. There is also presented, in the final section of this Appendix, a brief statement of the relation of the study of secondary education to other divisions of the Inquiry.

1. THE APPRAISAL OF EDUCATIONAL OUTCOMES

The appraisal of educational outcomes involved the use of three chief instruments: a battery of tests given to large numbers of pupils who were on the point of leaving school; reports from the schools themselves on individual leaving pupils; and interviews of pupils who had left school, and of their employers or adult acquaintances.

The Survey Testing Program

One of the first projects undertaken in the general study of secondary education was to draw up a working definition of social competence in relation to which an appropriate plan of evaluation might be formulated. A thorough canvass of the literature on curriculum making revealed that the most comprehensive and most carefully elaborated definition of this sort is that which was presented by Professor Franklin Bobbitt, of the University of Chicago, in 1924.[1] Professor Bobbitt's definition appears in the form of a list of the desirable outcomes of secondary education. Members of the Inquiry staff made certain revisions in this list to render it more readily usable for the purposes of the present investigation. They then examined all the tests which they could discover, selecting from these tests the ones which offered reasonably direct measures of any of the various qualities included in the revised list of desirable outcomes. Certain tests had obviously to be excluded because they could not be satisfactorily used under survey conditions, or because their reliability or validity was doubtful. The eventual battery included only tests which had already been widely enough tried out, by their authors or others, to give reasonable assurance of their value.[2]

The search for pertinent tests led to the somewhat discouraging conclusion that social competence, as such, has apparently been thus far a matter of subordinate concern to makers of tests. Tests of achievement in school history or mathematics or Latin are numerous and comprehensive; tests of the kinds of ability which boys and girls may normally be expected to use day by day outside of school tend to be scarce and fragmentary. In spite of this fact, the eventual battery in-

[1] In *How to Make a Curriculum*. Boston: Houghton Mifflin Company, 1924. Members of the staff were aided in revising this definition for use by the Regents' Inquiry, by suggestions made by Professor Bobbitt through correspondence.

[2] Professor Ralph W. Tyler, formerly of the Ohio State University, now of the University of Chicago, served as adviser to the staff on all major matters connected with the selection and administration of the test battery. In the preliminary canvass of available test materials Mr. Oscar K. Buros, of Rutgers University, assisted Dr. Herbert G. Espy, of the Inquiry staff, in examining published tests.

cluded twenty-seven separate test-units embracing a wide variety of measures of the types of ability with which the study was chiefly concerned—tests of pupils' knowledge of certain fundamental rules of physical health, of their acquaintance with public affairs, of their attitudes on social questions, of their ability to understand straightforward prose and to express themselves intelligibly and forcefully, of their current reading and their acquaintance with contemporary music and art, of the nature and direction of their chief interests, of their knowledge of practical arts as applied to problems round their homes, of their command of commonly useful skills in arithmetic, of their attitudes toward school and toward their associates, of the definiteness and sensibleness of their plans for further education or for a vocation.[3]

To these tests of social competence was added a group test of mental ability. The results from such a test may have important predictive value with respect to out-of-school achievement. It was included in the battery both because of its value in this connection and in order to make possible some estimate of the success of individual schools in adapting their programs to the varied capacities of their pupils.

Also included in the battery were certain tests of the usual academic type. They comprised one test each in American history and civics, a test in general science, a test in elementary algebra, and a test in "classical" English and American literature. These tests were chosen to conform reasonably closely to the requirements of the New York State syllabi. Their results provided certain significant clues to the connection, or lack of connection, between achievement in conventional school subject matter and ability to deal with out-of-school problems.

The total group of tests eventually selected was specially printed for the Inquiry in a series of seven test booklets, of

[3] The titles, authors, and publishers of the tests used are listed in Ruth E. Eckert and T. O. Marshall, *When Youth Leave School*, Regents' Inquiry, 1938.

which six were so arranged as to demand approximately one forty-five-minute period of class time each. The seventh booklet contained a comprehensive interest inventory, which was given to pupils to be checked outside of school.[4]

While the test battery was being prepared, members of the staff called on the superintendents and principals of each of the sixty-two general high schools in the sampling list to make arrangements for the testing. The conferences with the principals provided data from which it was possible to determine the school grades containing large numbers of pupils likely to leave school in the near future. Arrangements were made to test twelfth grade pupils and postgraduates in all schools, and to test the pupils in any other grades from which extensive elimination was expected. The conferences also made possible the planning of a definite testing schedule for each school, approved by the principal well in advance of the actual testing. The testing was in all instances distributed over two or more days in the week of June 1, 1936, that week having been selected, as a result of conferences with the Commissioner of Education and other members of the State Education Department, as the latest period at which the tests could be given without undue interference with the official Regents' Examinations.

A number of the school principals generously offered to assign members of their staffs to take charge of the administration of the tests. Assistance was gladly accepted—it was, in fact, requested from schools where it was not volunteered—in proctoring the examinations and in providing for the prompt and orderly admittance and dismissal of the pupils to be tested. It seemed best, however, not to allow local teachers or school officers to give the tests, partly because a general request for assistance of this sort would quite naturally

[4] The editing and printing of the test booklets, and the preparation of a manual for the test administrators, was under the charge of Dr. J. W. Wrightstone of the Inquiry staff.

have been regarded as an imposition by many schools, and partly because of the difficulty of securing uniform administration of the tests if some schools were to be tested by local teachers and others by outside examiners. Instead, a special staff of examiners was recruited from graduate students of education recommended by faculty members of their institutions as having had training and experience in group testing.[5] These students were brought together at various centers for preliminary study of the tests and of the accompanying manual, and for instructions as to the special arrangements for testing in the schools to which they were assigned. In their subsequent work in the schools each of the examiners was responsible to one of six area supervisors who had made the initial arrangements for the testing.

The original plans for the testing called for the administration of the tests in the twelve specialized vocational schools at the same time that they were given in the sample general high schools. Visits to a number of the vocational schools made it apparent, however, that arrangements for testing in these schools would need to be more complex than in the general schools, and that satisfactory schedules could not be drawn up in the limited amount of time available for this purpose. Testing in the specialized schools was therefore postponed to the latter part of May, 1937. The battery used in these schools in 1937 was of the same nature as that devised for the general schools, and the tests were given under the same conditions.

The total number of pupils tested in the spring of 1936 was 22,584, of whom 3,626 were enrolled in the ninth grade, 4,676 in the tenth grade, 3,143 in the eleventh grade, and 10,486 in the twelfth grade; 653 were postgraduates. In 1937, 2,426

5 The examiners were drawn from Columbia University, New York University, the College of the City of New York, Brooklyn College, Cornell University, Syracuse University, the University of Buffalo, the University of Rochester, and the New York State College for Teachers at Albany.

vocational school pupils were similarly tested; 219 of these were enrolled in the ninth grade, 470 in the tenth grade, 645 in the eleventh grade, 1,023 in the twelfth grade, and 69 were postgraduates.

Except for the analysis of the interest inventories and of pupils' reports on their plans for the future, the scoring of the general high school tests and a preliminary tabulation of the resulting data were completed during the summer of 1936.[6] Separate scores for each of the tested schools, showing grade medians in each test, were transferred to charts which indicated graphically the standing of the individual schools as compared with the medians for the total group of pupils tested. Charts for each school, with accompanying explanations, were sent to the principal and the superintendent of the school in question. Between November 12, 1936, and May 27, 1937, each of the tested schools was visited by the director of the study of secondary education. Charts were sent to the vocational schools, and similar visits were made, in the fall of 1937. The visits afforded opportunity to discuss the test results in detail with the school officers immediately concerned, to check the dependability of the test scores, and to gain a measure of insight into local conditions or special school practices which might explain scores deviating markedly from expectancy, as indicated by the general ability of the pupils tested.

An important outcome of these visits was to make possible the elimination from the test data of results which were questionable because of local circumstances connected with

[6] Through the courtesy of Dr. Ben D. Wood of Columbia University, working space and a certain amount of equipment were provided by the Educational Records Bureau for a special staff engaged in the scoring of the secondary school tests. The scoring of the tests was under the charge of Dr. J. W. Wrightstone, of the Inquiry staff. The scoring was greatly expedited by the cooperation of the International Business Machines Corporation in making available for the use of the Inquiry the laboratory model of their recently developed electrical scoring machine. Four of the test booklets had been arranged by Dr. Wrightstone to permit scoring on this machine.

the testing. Directions were found to have been misunderstood in a few instances, arrangements for the testing had occasionally not been carried out by the test administrators according to the approved plans, and in certain schools unavoidable distractions had interfered with pupils' performance. Wherever local conditions seemed to have affected the reliability of group scores from specific test units, these scores were discarded in the cases of the schools concerned. One test unit, that covering practical arts knowledge, yielded median scores which varied from school to school in such a way as to throw serious doubt on their general value for the purposes of the Inquiry. Since the fluctuation in scores could not be accounted for without a greater amount of special study than seemed justifiable, all the scores for this test were eventually rejected, and the test was omitted from the vocational school battery. Except in this single instance the results which had to be discarded were so few as not to affect the representativeness of the final data.

The visits to the schools had the added and unexpected advantage of furnishing somewhat unusual evidence of the dependability of the test data in general. A number of schools reported that they had followed the Inquiry tests with similar tests locally administered. Every instance of such retesting yielded a corroboration of the group scores obtained from the survey tests. Moreover, one school, whose officers and faculty had been hesitant to accept the test results, submitted the scores on separate test units for individual pupils (the individual scores having been furnished for this purpose by the Inquiry staff) to examination by those teachers who were well acquainted with the pupils concerned. The consequence of this detailed appraisal was the thoroughgoing acceptance by the school of the group scores on all sections of the battery except one which had already been marked for discard because of a local misunderstanding as to the conditions under which the test was to have been administered.

The reliability of the test results made their use in selecting schools for special study highly fruitful. The initial purpose of the testing, it will be recalled, was to identify those schools meriting study by the Inquiry's subject-specialists. The test results, arranged in such form as to show the relative standings of individual schools on separate sections of the battery, were submitted to the specialists, together with notes on other available data concerning the schools and the local communities. Subsequent investigations by the specialists were based in considerable part on the general information thus presented.

The testing program had a further purpose—that of contributing to a description of the educational equipment with which boys and girls leave New York State high schools. The test scores for pupils who were found to have withdrawn from school within four months after being tested were accordingly grouped together for special analysis. At the same time a tabulation was made of the data from the interest inventories and from the questionnaires on pupils' plans for the future, which the staff had not been able to prepare for use in selecting the individual schools visited by the specialists.[7] Test results for pupils enrolled in specialized vocational schools were included in these further studies.[8] The supplementary studies in general were so planned as to add to the information gained from school reports and interviews with pupils, thus making possible a reasonably comprehensive inventory of the social competence of boys and girls who had finished their full-time work in the secondary school.

[7] The scoring of the interest inventories and of the questionnaires on pupils' plans for the future was under the charge of Dr. Ruth E. Eckert, who supervised a special statistical staff occupying quarters at the University of Buffalo. Dr. Eckert was also responsible for the retabulation of a considerable part of the test data for pupils who had left school. The remainder of this retabulation was performed by Dr. Wrightstone's staff in New York City.

[8] The survey tests were given in the vocational schools too late to allow the use of the test data in selecting individual schools for intensive study. All the specialized vocational schools, however, were visited by one or more specialists from the Inquiry staff.

Investigations in the Study of Secondary Education

Reports by School Officers on Individual Leaving Pupils

The survey tests given in the sample New York State high schools were administered to practically all the pupils in certain grades in each school. To permit an appraisal of the attainments of the leaving pupils, as distinguished from tested pupils who continued in school, some means had to be found for identifying the pupils who had actually withdrawn from school, and for obtaining necessary information as to the school histories and the home backgrounds of these pupils. Even in the cases of pupils who had left school, however, the test results alone could be expected to yield only a partial measure of the products of secondary education. The tests used in the present study failed to cover numerous educational outcomes which deserved analysis. Still more important, they offered no comprehensive answer to the question with which every school ought sooner or later to tax itself in the case of each of its pupils: Is this boy or this girl ready to leave school?

These various considerations suggested the desirability of securing from the schools themselves somewhat extensive reports on individual leaving pupils. In the spring and summer of 1936 a number of conferences were accordingly arranged with members of the State Education Department, with the Committee on Secondary Education of the New York State Council of School Superintendents, with officers of the Associated Academic Principals of the State of New York, and with individual school officials. The conferences resulted in a plan which had a twofold purpose: to supply pertinent information not obtained through the survey tests, and to give the schools themselves an opportunity to undertake a direct appraisal of the results of their own educational programs.

In accordance with this plan, members of the Inquiry staff prepared a special report form for use by individual schools. The form called for a brief summary by the school of the school history of each leaving pupil; for general information as to the pupil's home background, including the vocational and economic status of his parents, their attitude toward the school, the presence of exceptional factors in the home environment; for a statement as to whether the pupil himself was exceptional in any important respect; and for such information as the school could readily supply concerning the pupil's educational and vocational activities after leaving school. In addition, the report form asked the school to answer two questions of vital importance. The first of these questions had to do with the pupil's vocational preparation: "At the time this pupil left school, could the school have recommended him for any type of full-time employment which would have permitted self-support, with confidence that he would be reasonably successful at this employment?" The second question concerned the pupil's preparation for social living: "At the time this pupil left school, could the school have recommended him as ready to participate responsibly, sensibly, and honestly both in the informal non-vocational phases of adult community life and in the more formal duties of citizenship?" In answering each question the school was requested to indicate the strengths or weaknesses in personal characteristics which dictated the answer with respect to a given pupil.

Report forms were separately prepared for pupils withdrawing from school before graduation, for graduates, and for postgraduates. Detailed folders of instructions for responding to the individual items on the forms were drawn up, and a schedule was arranged by which reports were to be submitted at three four-month intervals, covering withdrawals during the calendar year from June 1, 1936 (the date of the first survey tests) to May 31, 1937.

Though the report forms were prepared for use primarily by the tested schools, cooperation from other schools was sought in order to secure more widespread appraisal by individual schools of the competence of their leaving pupils. An explanation of the purposes of the reports and requests for the cooperation of school officials were presented at meetings of the Associated Academic Principals, the Council of Superintendents, and the District Superintendents' Association. The project was separately discussed with the New York City principals at a special meeting called for the purpose, following a conference with members of the school headquarters staff. In addition, a full explanation of the undertaking, accompanied by a letter from the Commissioner of Education urging cooperation, was mailed to each of the public high school principals and school superintendents in the State.

The result of these efforts was the receipt of reports covering at least one, and in most instances all, of the three four-month periods, from 61 of the 62 tested general high schools, and from 4 of the 12 vocational schools. Of the 947 untested secondary schools in the State, 338 (36 per cent) supplied reports for at least the first period. The total group of reports provided supplementary information concerning 10,321 of the 22,584 pupils tested in general high schools. Similar information was available for 42,770 untested pupils, of whom 2,977 had been enrolled in specialized vocational schools.

The data thus obtained were tabulated[9] separately for the tested and the untested pupils. Comparison of the results for the two groups indicated that the pupils in the tested schools were fairly representative of the total school population. In certain detailed analyses, therefore, the smaller group of reports only was used.

The reports provided important indications of pupils' strengths and weaknesses as the local schools conceived them. In the case of the tested pupils, objective data on some of the matters concerning which the schools were asked to report were available in the test results. Thus, the testing

[9] By the staff supervised by Dr. Ruth E. Eckert at the University of Buffalo.

program yielded evidence as to the pupils' general scholastic ability, their vocational plans, and their acquaintance with current political affairs. For a considerable sampling of the tested group still further information was obtained through personal interviews with the pupils after they had left school, and with adults who knew them. The latter information also bore on questions raised in the report forms, particularly questions relating to the pupils' out-of-school environment and their activities after leaving school. A comparison was undertaken of what the schools reported concerning individual pupils, with what the facts about the pupils actually were, as determined through these other sources of information. The results made it possible to define important areas of misunderstanding or ignorance which commonly exist in the schools' acquaintance with their pupils.

The schools which supplied the reports were in numerous instances seriously concerned because of their lack of information about individual pupils. An offer to furnish duplicate copies of the report forms for the schools' own use met with widespread acceptance, and a number of schools volunteered the information that they were making these forms the basis for more adequate systems of pupil records and guidance. That the forms were put to this local use is evidence of the strong interest of school officers in the difficult problems of individual pupil adjustment.

Interviews with Former Pupils

More dependable evidence concerning leaving pupils than that supplied by the schools themselves was forthcoming from the third means of appraisal, namely, interviews with a large number of these pupils, and with their employers or other adults acquainted with them.

The majority of the pupils selected for interviewing comprised a random sampling of those tested in the spring of 1936 who were reported by school officials as having withdrawn from school prior to September 30, 1936. Pupils who had entered college were not interviewed, since the needs of these pupils were being considered in the Inquiry's study of higher education; nor were interviews arranged with pupils who had merely transferred to other full-time educational institutions. Because of their inaccessibility certain pupils whose names appeared in the initial sampling had to be omitted from the list; these pupils comprised chiefly boys who had enlisted in the Army or Navy, and those who had enrolled in the Civilian Conservation Corps and had been sent to camps outside New York State.[10] With these exceptions the group interviewed comprised a representative selection of leaving pupils from the sixty-two general high schools included in the 1936 testing program. The total number of pupils from these schools with whom interviews were obtained was 1,626— 19 per cent of the tested pupils reported by the schools as having left school between June 1 and September 30.

[10] The original plans for the study of secondary education included provisions for a special investigation of boys enrolled in CCC camps. Mr. Kenneth Holland, director of a special study of the CCC for the American Youth Commission, was to have supervised this investigation. Preliminary work carried out by Dr. Wrightstone, in part under Mr. Holland's direction, made it apparent that boys enrolled in the CCC whose educational histories were known through their having been previously enrolled in schools studied under the Inquiry were so few and so widely scattered that the expense of locating them and analyzing their activities would have been out of proportion to the value of the information gained. Furthermore, the study planned by the Youth Commission promised to secure on a broad scale data which the staff of the Inquiry had intended to gather for New York State alone. A decision was eventually reached, therefore, to limit the Inquiry study to interviews of those CCC enrollees whose names appeared in the random sampling used as the basis for all the interviews, and to leave to the Youth Commission the more comprehensive study of the effects of the CCC program.

Special acknowledgement should be made of the willingness of Dr. Homer P. Rainey, Director of the American Youth Commission, to make part of Mr. Holland's time available to the Inquiry, and of the assistance which Mr. Holland himself rendered. Mr. Holland cooperated with the Inquiry both in the preliminary canvass of possibilities for a study of the CCC and in making it possible for staff members from the Inquiry to locate and interview CCC enrollees.

Since tests had not been given in the specialized vocational schools at the time the interviews were arranged, the selection of pupils from these schools was made on the basis of special lists of leaving pupils submitted by the schools. The total number of vocational school interviews was 341, making a grand total of 1,967 interviews of pupils from the sample schools.

The pupils interviewed from both the general high schools and the specialized vocational schools had been out of school for periods ranging from six to eleven months. Information concerning the activities of young people whose full-time schooling was further behind them would obviously have supplied an additional, and perhaps a more dependable, check on the effectiveness of the school curriculum. Tentative plans were therefore made to interview a group of young people who had been out of school for at least five years. Shortly after the reports on leaving pupils began to be received from the schools, however, it became apparent that almost none of the schools reporting to the Inquiry possessed sufficiently detailed and accurate records to allow reliable connections to be established between the activities of a representative group five years out of school and the school experiences of those pupils. Accordingly, the study had to be restricted to boys and girls newly finished with their full-time schooling, due care being used to guard against interpretations which might be faulty in view of the youth and inexperience of these pupils and the recency of their schooling.

The purpose of the interviews was to explore the activities of out-of-school boys and girls in three principal fields— vocational, educational, and recreational. Detailed interview forms were drawn up, listing questions to be asked both of the pupils and of the adults who were approached for supplementary information. In general, the questions paralleled, with added detail, those on which the schools had already been asked to report concerning individual leaving pupils. The interview questions focused chief attention on what the pupils had done or were then doing, rather than on matters of judgment or opinion. As a means of perfecting both the questions themselves and the techniques to be used in interviewing, trial interviews with 152 pupils and with at least one adult acquainted with each pupil were conducted in a city not included in the testing program. The experience thus gained led to certain modifications in the original interview forms, and provided the basis for a detailed manual of instructions for interviewers.[11]

Interviewers were selected in part from graduate students who had assisted in the administration of the testing program, in part from other qualified persons recommended to the Inquiry by the departments of education of various New York universities. A primary criterion for the selection of interviewers was their possession of personal qualities which would make it easy for them to gain the confidence of young people and their parents. Once selected, the interviewers were given preliminary instructions in the purposes of the study and in the methods of interviewing which had been found successful, and were carefully supervised in their first few interviews.

To get young people and their employers to talk freely about vocational, social, and educational problems proved not at all difficult. Both groups cooperated willingly in supplying information, often expressing satisfaction at the official interest which the interviews suggested. Only in the case of adults other than employers who were approached concerning unemployed boys and girls, were serious obstacles encountered. The adults interviewed in such cases were those named by the pupils as the persons outside their families who were best acquainted with their activities. Difficulties in securing information from these adults resulted not from their unwillingness to tell what they knew, but from the meagerness of their

[11] Preparation of the interview forms and of the manual, selection and supervision of the interviewers, and preparation of a report on the results of the interviews were under the charge of Mr. Thomas O. Marshall, Jr., of the Inquiry staff. The tabulation of the interview data (except the data from the trial interviews, which were tabulated by Mr. Marshall) was undertaken by Dr. Ruth E. Eckert, working in close cooperation with Mr. Marshall.

knowledge. In hundreds of instances, indeed—and this circumstance seemed of much significance in interpreting the results of the interviews in general—no adult could be discovered aside from someone in the pupil's immediate family who knew a given pupil well enough to provide any reliable information whatever.

The use of the data provided through the interviews in checking the accuracy of the reports by the schools has already been mentioned. In addition, these data were so organized as to furnish an independent measure of the effectiveness of the school curricula. The activities in which pupils engage or in which they fail to engage more or less immediately after leaving school obviously reflect in considerable degree the extent to which the school program is functioning in preparing pupils to meet normal out-of-school problems. Examination of these activities in relation to the school courses which the boys and girls concerned have elected may bring to light both major strengths and major weaknesses or omissions in the work of the schools, at least in so far as that work is designed to provide for the needs of pupils who do not continue into college. Examined in this way, the information provided by some two thousand boys and girls who were no longer in school afforded an especially revealing insight into the adequacy of the present high school curriculum.

2. ACCOUNTING FOR EDUCATIONAL OUTCOMES

In connection with the third major step in the general study—the determination of cause-and-effect relationships between the programs of the schools and their educational outcomes—the most extensive separate studies were those carried on by specialists in various fields of teaching.

Special Studies of Selected Fields of Teaching

From the beginning, a strong effort was made to avoid narrow attention to separate secondary school "subjects," merely as such. The intent was to investigate, instead, whatever in-school or out-of-school experiences might contribute to pupils' competence in significant fields of activity.

Eight such fields were originally selected as deserving special attention. These comprised the fields of general health activities and physical recreation; social relationships, including civic activities; the use and interpretation of the English language; computation, and the appreciation of quantitative relationships; the application of science both in practical-use situations and in interpreting the normal environment; reading for pleasure or profit; the enjoyment of music, art, and the drama; and direct vocational adjustment. Before the studies by specialists were well under way, it became apparent that financial restrictions would prevent separate attention to all these fields. The fields in which special studies promised to yield results of greatest immediate significance were therefore chosen for intensive investigation, the analysis of instruction related to the other fields being carried out in connection with a general survey of trends in the development of the secondary school program of studies. The fields in which studies by specialists were ultimately conducted were those of health activities, social activities, the use and interpretation of English, general reading, and vocational adjustment.

Except in the field of vocational adjustment, which first becomes the concern of the schools at the secondary level, the specialists who analyzed high school instruction also studied the programs of representative elementary schools. The conclusions of the secondary school studies were therefore not confined to the influences which affect boys and girls merely while they are high school pupils, but took into account the whole vertical range of the average pupil's school life.[12]

---

[12] Detailed conclusions and recommendations with respect to the elementary school program were, of course, presented in the reports submitted by the specialists as a basis for the general report on elementary education. The secondary school reports contained direct references to the elementary school program

Moreover, each specialist was made definitely responsible for the investigation of out-of-school influences related to his special field. In addition to the test data which were available for the sampling schools, a summary of the outstanding social and economic characteristics of each of the sample communities, abstracted from the information used in selecting these communities, was prepared for the specialists at the beginning of their work. As rapidly as significant information was secured from individual schools through the visits by the director of the general study, this information also was made available to the specialists. Data from the interviews and from the school reports on leaving pupils were received too late to be of direct use in certain of the special investigations, but tentative generalizations from these data played an important part in shaping the specialists' conclusions with respect to the social studies, the encouragement of pupils' reading, and vocational education. Furthermore, the plans for the special studies included a number of investigations directly concerned with pupils' out-of-school influences and activities—studies of home reading, motion picture attendance and habits of listening to the radio, local attitudes toward various types of vocational education, and the like. Horizontally as well as vertically the attention of the specialists was thus addressed to many factors outside the high school program as such.

The existence of varied problems within the several special fields made necessary the organizing of the studies according to varied patterns. Variations in procedure consisted for the most part, however, in minor departures from one fundamental plan. The latter included, first, visits to selected schools by each of the specialists, for the purpose of obtaining first-hand knowledge of local curricula and teaching materials, classroom methods, the quality and interests of the teaching staff, and the out-of-school factors likely to have chief bearing on educa-

only where such references were necessary to support or clarify recommendations with respect to the work of the high schools.

tional results in the specialist's particular field. In obtaining information on these matters, the specialists were ordinarily guided by detailed check lists, prepared in advance of the visits to individual schools and modified as successive visits revealed new items which deserved attention. Each specialist visited those schools which ranked either unusually high or unusually low in the competence of leaving pupils in his field, as measured by the general survey tests. Specialists visited also schools not included in the testing program, which were known to be employing unusually promising methods not found among the sampling schools.[13] The schools whose work was intensively studied varied from approximately 20 to 40 for each of the several fields. Nearly all the sampling schools were visited by one or more of the specialists, the exceptions consisting of a handful of schools (for the most part very small) whose test results were either so near the median for schools in their types of community, or so similar to those of schools already included in the specialists' schedules, as not to make separate studies profitable.

A second part of the basic plan provided for supplementary testing in the field of each specialist's particular interest. In some fields the additional testing was designed to furnish a more exact picture than that afforded by the survey tests, of pupils' grade-by-grade growth in achievement. Thus, special tests in reading-comprehension were given in grades 2, 4, 6, 8, 10, and 12 of selected schools, to supplement the survey tests in grade 6 and in the four high school grades.

[13] Possibly because of the care with which the sampling list was prepared, only a few such schools were discovered. An effort was made to draw up a list of all the secondary schools in the State which were doing especially promising work in specified fields, on the basis of replies to a letter addressed in May, 1936, to all high school principals, asking for the names of such schools. In terms of numbers of replies the response to this letter was excellent (64 per cent of the principals addressed responded), but the replies failed to yield data of much value, largely because, as many of the principals frankly wrote, opportunities for school officers to become acquainted at first hand with the work of other schools than their own are exceedingly limited.

In other fields the further tests were intended to measure knowledge, abilities, or attitudes not touched on in the general battery. Specially formulated tests were used in the field of the social studies, for example, to provide data on pupils' appreciation of social problems in their local communities, and to explore pupils' attitudes toward certain fundamental principles of American democracy.

Third, the specialists were asked to analyze the state syllabi in their fields, to take definite account of relevant policies of the State Education Department, and to investigate the effects of the Regents' Examination system. For this purpose copies of the pertinent syllabi were provided for each specialist, and numerous conferences were arranged with members of the State Department.

Fourth, copies or detailed descriptions of local course outlines were requested from every secondary school which had developed instructional methods or materials notably different from those presented in the New York State syllabi. Few such outlines were actually received, chiefly because the official syllabi furnish the basis for the overwhelming majority of secondary school courses. Analysis by the specialists of the materials which were submitted resulted in visits to certain schools not included in the sampling list. The materials in general, studied in relation to the state syllabi, provided a basis for descriptions of the total range of practice within the various fields, and for more detailed attention to the practices likely to be of greatest value.

Finally, each specialist was asked to prepare a report embodying the results of his investigation. Particular attention was directed to the need for an interpretation of educational outcomes; the specialists were asked to suggest the minimum of achievement in their fields which ought to be sought for pupils on the point of leaving school, and to indicate the extent to which New York State schools are now attaining this minimum. Detailed analysis of those factors chiefly accounting for present results was also requested, with particular consideration of out-of-school influences, the characteristics of the various groups of pupils with whom the schools must deal, the instructional methods and materials commonly in use, and the qualities of the present teaching staff. The individual reports, like the report for the study of secondary education as a whole, were planned to culminate in proposals for an improved secondary school program, together with recommendations for definite action on the part of the Board of Regents and the State Education Department.

The studies in the field of health education and physical recreation followed essentially this basic plan. The complexity of this particular field, and the somewhat indeterminate nature of its relationship to the general field of public health, resulted in the assignment of detailed problems to a number of different investigators. Separate studies were carried on by individual specialists in health education, physical training, mental hygiene, and public health, the whole group of investigations being supervised and coordinated by the specialist in public health.[14] The studies were so planned as not merely to lead to recommendations for improvement in the school health program, but to clarify the relative responsibilities of the schools and the state or local nonschool health agencies.

The special investigation in the field of social activities likewise adhered closely to the basic plan. Despite the breadth of this field, the problems which it presented seemed so closely interwoven as to make undesirable any division of responsibility in their analysis. The investigation as a whole was therefore entrusted to a single specialist.[15]

[14] Dr. C.-E. A. Winslow of Yale University assumed general charge of the health studies. Except in their initial stages, these studies were planned and conducted somewhat independently of the general study of secondary education. Since their scope and method are described in a separate report by Dr. Winslow, they are not here dealt with in detail. See page ii of this report.

[15] Dr. Howard E. Wilson of Harvard University. In the construction of special tests in this field Dr. Wilson was assisted by Mr. Roy A. Price, of the School of

Studies in the field of the use and interpretation of English, and in the field of general reading, were divided among a number of specialists. To one person[16] was assigned a special investigation of pupils' ability in the mechanics of reading at the high school level. Because of the slight attention paid in New York State high schools to the systematic development of reading ability, fewer schools were studied intensively in this connection than in most of the special studies; the general plan of investigation otherwise paralleled that for the studies already mentioned. A second specialist[17] assumed responsibility for analyzing pupils' abilities in oral and written expression, for studying the range and quality of pupils' reading, and for investigating the reading opportunities presented by a number of representative school and public libraries. In addition, this specialist undertook a brief analysis of pupils' habits with respect to movies and the radio, two influences not inherently associated with the use of English or with general reading, but conveniently studied in this connection.[18] A third specialist[19] conducted an intensive appraisal of the reading habits of pupils, parents, and teachers in two of the communities included in the general testing program, as a means of providing an illustrative analysis of the influence of school and public libraries. This third study involved also a necessarily brief assessment of the adequacy of existing library provisions in New York State. The three studies devoted to the

Citizenship of Syracuse University, Mr. Alfred M. Church, formerly of the Punahou School of Honolulu, and Dr. Ruth E. Eckert of the Inquiry staff.

[16] Dr. William S. Gray of the University of Chicago. Much of the detailed work in connection with this investigation was performed by Dr. Bernice E. Leary, under Dr. Gray's supervision.

[17] Dr. Dora V. Smith of the University of Minnesota.

[18] A special study of the motion picture and the radio, with particular reference to the possibility of putting these devices to systematic school use, was conducted independently of the general study of secondary education by Dr. Elizabeth Laine.

[19] Dr. Douglas Waples, of the University of Chicago, with the assistance of Dr. Leon Carnovsky.

fields of reading and the use of English were coordinated not by any one of the specialists concerned, but through close co-operation in the planning of work and the sharing of data on the part of all three of the persons directly responsible.

The special study of the influence of libraries referred to above deserves separate comment. Both the general educational importance of school and public libraries, and the fact that in New York State such libraries are under the direct supervision of a branch of the State Education Department, suggested the desirability of a thoroughgoing analysis of current library problems as a part of the Regents' Inquiry. A preliminary review of the broad range of problems which would need to be dealt with, however, made it apparent that no adequate analysis could be financed with the resources at the Inquiry's disposal. The staff was therefore faced with a choice between making a large-scale study of the superficial survey type, or of planning a more intensive study which did not pretend to deal in thoroughgoing fashion with the library program as a whole. Of these alternatives the latter seemed preferable. The study finally undertaken was intended to illustrate needs rather than to lay the basis for a comprehensive program. Out of it may eventually come, it is hoped, provision by the Board of Regents for the type of comprehensive study which constitutes one of the pressing needs in this educational area.

The final major field in which special studies were carried out was that of vocational adjustment. In the analysis of this field certain important departures from the basic plan used in the other special studies were necessary. The chief departure was occasioned by the radical changes which have recently taken place outside the schools in the need for vocational education, coupled with adherence by the schools themselves to a program largely standardized as a result of the Federal Smith-Hughes Act twenty years ago. Present needs seemed to call for the definition of fundamental policies rather than for the evaluation of instructional details. The investigation was therefore planned in such a way as to emphasize the social and economic factors which must be taken into account in developing a sound program of vocational education.

To insure adequate attention to these factors, an economist[20] was invited to take charge of the investigation as a whole. Working with him were specialists in each of the major subordinate fields of vocational education: industrial and technical education, agriculture, homemaking, and commercial education.[21] In addition to the separate studies for which each person was responsible, this group of specialists undertook to frame a statement of fundamental policies with respect to vocational education in New York State, to which the members of the group could unanimously subscribe.

Besides this major variation in the basic plan, certain other departures were necessary in the study of vocational adjustment, largely because of the present lack of reliable tests of vocational skills. The absence of such tests in the survey battery required the selection of specialized vocational schools for intensive study chiefly on the basis of preliminary information as to their programs, rather than in terms of test results. Moreover, the problem of devising adequate and readily usable tests proved to be so complex that no attempt was made to supplement the survey testing program through vocational tests given to pupils in school; data from the interviews of leaving pupils were used instead, wherever these data allowed direct appraisal of pupils' vocational competence. The study of vocational adjustment thus differed from the other special investigations in its somewhat greater reliance on the observation and judgment of specialists, and in its extensive use of general social and economic data as con-

[20] Dr. Thomas L. Norton, of the University of Buffalo.

[21] These specialists were, respectively, Dr. Walter B. Jones, of the Pennsylvania Department of Public Instruction; Dr. Z. M. Smith, of Purdue University; Miss Alice L. Edwards, of the President's Advisory Committee on Education; and Dr. H. G. Shields, of Simmons College, Boston.

trasted with information about definitely identified individual pupils.

Studies of Course-Outlines Not Analyzed by Specialists

In major fields not studied intensively by specialists, a general view of instructional methods and materials was obtained through the analysis of course-outlines. As in the case of the fields dealt with intensively, the available outlines were of two types: the official state syllabi and local syllabi prepared by individual schools and school systems. Study of the outlines was supplemented by conferences with members of the State Education Department concerning general policies in the instructional fields represented, and by an analysis of Regents' Examination procedure in these fields. The resultant data made possible certain important conclusions with respect to instruction in all the major secondary school subjects.[22]

Analysis of Recent Trends in Secondary Education

Studies of separate fields of instruction, however revealing these studies may be with respect to important educational outcomes, necessarily fail to take into account the effects of the secondary school program as a whole. For this reason it seemed desirable to undertake an analysis of the total secondary school program in New York State, as this program is reflected in the range of offerings within individual schools, in the extracurricular activities sponsored by the schools, and in the extent to which schools have adopted forms of grade organization other than that of the conventional four-year high school.[23]

[22] Dr. Herbert G. Espy, of the Inquiry staff, was responsible for the analysis of course-outlines in the fields not covered by specialists. Study of the Regents' Examinations in these fields was conducted by Dr. D. A. Worcester, of the University of Nebraska.

[23] This analysis was carried out by Dr. Espy, with the aid of an extensive clerical staff. Miss Evelyn G. Cummings, of the Inquiry staff, assisted in the interpretation of many of the data, particularly those secured from the files of the State Department.

Information as to the range of offerings within individual schools was sought from two different sources. For strictly factual information concerning the subjects included in secondary school programs of studies and the numbers of pupils enrolled in these subjects within recent years, the reports submitted periodically by individual schools to the State Education Department were consulted. The reports used covered a period of sixteen years, and included one report especially obtained by the Department at the request of the Inquiry, for the purpose of making current figures available for this study.

A different type of information, consisting of principals' judgments as to relative values and effectiveness of separate elements in the program of studies, was secured through questionnaires addressed directly to the high school principals. The effectiveness of the programs in individual schools must inevitably depend largely on the criteria used by school officers for estimating the results of instruction in their own schools, on the views of these officers as to the parts of the program which should be emphasized and those which should be minimized or abandoned, and on their attitudes toward special provisions for various types of pupils. Questions on all these matters were therefore included in a questionnaire addressed to each of the public secondary school principals in the State.[24] Replies were received from 720 principals, 71 per cent of those to whom the questionnaire was addressed. The replies contributed notably to an understanding of current tendencies in the schools.

The study of trends with respect to extracurricular offerings was originally planned to parallel the study of the general curricular program. A search for factual information on extra-curricular activities in the New York State schools revealed,

[24] Questionnaires were not sent to private school principals because of a staff decision to restrict studies of private elementary and secondary school programs to the analysis of such data as might be included in records of the State Department.

however, that no comprehensive information of this type was available. It was consequently necessary to obtain descriptive information directly from the schools, and in doing so to reduce to a minimum the number of questions calling for evaluative judgments, in order not to burden school officials unduly. Data were furnished by 727, or again approximately 71 per cent, of the school principals to whom special questionnaires on the subject were sent. The resultant information, though more limited in scope than that obtained with respect to curricular offerings, bore on similar questions of practice and policy.

Data on trends in grade organization, like the data on subject offerings and on enrollments, were obtained from State Department records.

Supplementary Studies

In addition to the studies of special fields of instruction and of the secondary school program as a whole, a number of briefer investigations were carried on to throw light on certain detailed problems.

The first of these investigations was undertaken at an early stage in the general study of secondary education. A letter was addressed to each of the public secondary school principals in the State, asking for a description of the two or three educational problems which had caused each principal most concern in the administration of his school during the preceding year or two years.[25] The 628 replies which were received, many of them strikingly trenchant in their descriptions of specific problems, provided a valuable supplement to the returns from the questionnaires in which principals were asked to express their judgments as to the values of various parts of the secondary school program.

[25] This letter also requested the names of schools which were known to be doing especially promising work in certain specified fields. The replies to the latter request have been commented on elsewhere.

A further study dealt with examinations, plans of guidance, and provisions for individual differences in each of the schools included in the survey testing program. Specific inquiries with respect to these matters were made by the director of the general study in connection with visits to individual schools. As in the case of the replies to the letters to principals, the resultant data served to corroborate the generalizations suggested by other studies.

The desirability of knowing why pupils leave school, as well as what their characteristics are when they leave, led to a third study in which the Inquiry received exceedingly valuable cooperation from the officers and members of the Associated Academic Principals.[26] Pupils who have withdrawn from school have frequently been asked why they withdrew, but the conclusions based on their replies have been of questionable validity because of rationalization, failure to remember actual circumstances, or the desire to impress the questioner which is likely to color pupils' answers to a question of this sort. In the present instance the procedure adopted was that of asking pupils still in school whether or not they would leave under specified circumstances. To lessen rationalization and to minimize responses designed to create a favorable impression, the pupils were given a careful explanation of the purpose of the questions and of the entirely impersonal use to which their answers would be put. The circumstances described to the pupils covered a wide range of specific situations which might conceivably influence young people either to continue in school or to withdraw. Pupils' replies accordingly reflected their attitudes toward such diverse matters as the scope of the school program, the value of what they were learning, their opportunities to elect subjects of interest to them, their relationships with their teachers, the local systems of promotion

[26] This study was officially sponsored by the Associated Academic Principals. Dr. Everett B. Sackett, of the Inquiry staff, made all initial arrangements for the study and was responsible both for its general planning and for the interpretation of its results.

and graduation, state and local examinations, the advice of parents and friends, opportunities for employment, and individual financial circumstances.

In both the preparation of a list of statements to which pupils were asked to respond and the eventual use of the resulting check list, members of the Associated Academic Principals contributed extensive advice and assistance. A group of principals selected by the President of the Association examined a tentative list of statements and submitted detailed suggestions for revisions. Four principals tried out the revised list in their own schools, securing from both teachers and pupils further suggestions for specific improvements. The ultimate returns from the questionnaire were secured through the cooperation of the principals of sixty-nine individual secondary schools, in which the questionnaire was administered either by the principals or by teachers under their immediate supervision to a total of 10,965 pupils.

Replies to a questionnaire of this type obviously do not answer completely or with finality the question of why pupils leave school. The fact that pupils had to be asked to imagine themselves in particular situations meant that at best the results provided only an indication of what boys and girls thought they would do—which might have been different from what they would actually do—in the face of situations of the sort described. The replies unquestionably reflected, however, the pupils' valuations of important phases of school work and out-of-school experience. Interpreted from this standpoint, they played an important part in accounting for the outcomes of the school programs in the types of communities from which these pupils came.

The final supplementary study consisted of a special investigation of the operation of the Regents' Examination system.[27] Specialists in the various fields of teaching had been

[27] A study of the Regents' Preliminary Examinations and of the district superintendents' examinations was carried out by Dr. Sackett in connection

asked to consider the influence of the Regents' Examinations in accounting for the outcomes of instruction in their fields. Both because the major secondary school fields were not completely represented in these studies, and because the specialists had only incidental opportunities to familiarize themselves with the machinery for preparing and administering the examinations, a separate study of the examination system as a whole was undertaken. Through the courtesy of the State Department, members of the Inquiry staff were able to attend as observers a majority of the committee meetings at which the papers for June, 1937, were prepared. The Examinations and Inspections Division provided access to its files for data on examination results, and brought together for the use of the Inquiry a number of summary statements covering various phases of the examination procedure. Since extensive and well-conducted studies of the merits and defects of the system had already been made, both by members of the Department and by outside investigators, no detailed studies of this type were undertaken by the Inquiry staff, but the reports of all previous studies were carefully examined and their major conclusions noted. The insight gained through these various means into the purposes, the scope, and the effectiveness of the examination system provided a basis for important recommendations.

3. RELATION OF THE STUDY OF SECONDARY EDUCATION TO OTHER DIVISIONS OF THE INQUIRY

It will be apparent that the investigations described in the preceding sections stopped short of a complete examination of certain important problems. This was intentional where these

---

with the general study of elementary education. Dr. Sackett's report was made available to Dr. D. A. Worcester, of the University of Nebraska, who was asked to study the Academic Examinations and the operation of the examination system as a whole.

investigations touched on matters being dealt with by other divisions of the Inquiry. A brief statement concerning problems which inevitably bear on the development of secondary education in New York State, but which were not directly dealt with in the study of secondary education, may serve to indicate the relation of this study to the ⌊Inquiry as a whole.

The study of secondary education was planned on the assumption that responsibility for the outcomes of school work must be jointly shared by the elementary school and the secondary school. A definite effort was therefore made to coordinate the study of secondary education with that of elementary education, both in methods of investigation and in fundamental point of view. Noticeable differences in emphasis between the two studies resulted from the fact that the problems of the secondary school are in many respects those of a terminal institution, whereas certain major elementary school problems grow out of the school's concern with pupils whose full-time schooling is just beginning or is at least far from complete.

The study of secondary education has led to suggestions as to needed educational provisions for certain types of pupils not ordinarily admitted to post-secondary institutions and not adequately served by the usual postgraduate high school offerings. This study has not, however, given direct attention to the entrance requirements of established higher institutions, nor has it attempted to discover how many or what types of students should be admitted to such institutions. Recommendations with respect to these matters grow out of the separate studies of higher education and of teachers colleges.

In the case of young people who have left the secondary school to go to work, the present study has been limited to considering ways in which secondary schools may help inexperienced boys and girls to make a successful beginning in their out-of-school activities. The provision of continued education for these young people represents a problem which has been dealt with in the study of adult education.[28]

Except incidentally, the study of secondary education has not considered means for improving the quality of the teaching and administrative personnel in the schools. Recommendations for the more effective recruiting of teachers and the better education of teachers-in-training are to be found in the report of the separate study of school personnel.[29]

The question of possible changes in school district organization and in the system of state aid is one of much consequence to the future of secondary education in New York State. The present study has not attempted, however, to define a general pattern of improved district organization or to suggest comprehensive modifications in the plan of state aid. It has sought only to identify specific factors which need to be taken into account if new plans are to be substituted for those now in effect. Definite proposals for the improvement of the present plans are to be found in the reports of the separate studies of school districts and of state aid.[30]

[28] Floyd W. Reeves, T. Fansler, and C. O. Houle, *Adult Education*, Regents, Inquiry, 1938.

[29] Charles H. Judd, *Preparation of School Personnel*, Regents' Inquiry, 1938.

[30] Alonzo G. Grace and G. A. Moe, *State Aid and School Costs*, Regents' Inquiry, 1938.

INDEX

A

Academic curricula, compared with vocational curricula, 83–92
"Adult Education," 248n, 271n, 368n
Adults, contacts with young people, 30–32, 82
influence of, 256, 257
Agriculture, courses in, 124–125, 142–144, 211
graduates of, 84, 85
American Youth Commission, 349
Arithmetic, courses, 180
teaching of, 265–266
tests, 41, 42, 95–96
Associated Academic Principals, cooperation with Inquiry, 364–365
Athletics, as leisure-time activity, 49–50, 144–145, 148, 278
participation in, of graduates and nongraduates, 81
Attendance, compulsory, cost to school of proposed change in, 328
recommendations on, 300–305

B

Bobbitt, Franklin, 338, 338n
Books (see Reading)
Boy Scouts, 29, 146
Boys, competence of compared with girls, 100–106
Buros, Oscar K., 338n
Business courses, 124–125, 129–134, 212
enrollment in, 168
Business curriculum, graduates of, 85, 87–88
Business schools, 111

C

Carnovsky, Leon, 358n
Centralized schools, as remedy for present defects, 218–223
Character-building organizations, 146
Church, Alfred M., 358n
Church groups, value of in citizenship training, 29, 87–88
Citizens, rights of, pupils' attitudes toward, 23–24
Citizenship, attitude toward responsibilities of, 24–26, 32
deficiencies in recognized by schools, 17–18
in improved curriculum, 263–265, 285–286
meaning of in a democratic state, 16–17
out-of-school activities of leaving pupils, 27–29
preparation for, 15–32, 98, 244
as problem of nongraduate, 80–81
readiness of leaving pupils for, 26–27
relation of to curricula, 86–88
Civic competence, as responsibility of educational program, 149
of girls compared with boys, 101–103
Civic interests, of rural and urban youth, 96
Civics tests, 95, 339
Civilian Conservation Corps, 279, 349
Clubs, church, 29, 87
extracurricular, 182
farm, 29, 146
out-of-school, 48–49, 278–279
school, 144–148
among unemployed, 71, 124–129

· 369 ·

Index

Educational program, effectiveness of
summarized, 116–120
inequalities of outcomes, 118
positive outcomes of, 117–118
and social competence, 118–119,
148–149
Educational Research Division, reports of, 233–234
Educational Screen, 47
Edwards, Alice L., 360n
Elementary school tests, 7–8
Employment, chances for advancement, 66–68
factors influencing success in getting,
61–62, 71
of girls compared with boys, 104
preparation for cost of in proposed
plan, 326–328
of vocational school graduates, 89–
91
(*See also* Jobs, Vocational guidance)
English, clubs, 145
courses, 124–127, 153, 167, 180,
212–213
enrollment, 168
special studies on, 353–359
teaching of, 265–266, 268
tests, 40–42, 96, 339
Enrollment, effect of size on achievement, 209–225
effect of decreases in on cost of proposed plan, 322–325
Equipment, school, lack of, 183, 241–
243
Espy, Herbert G., 338n, 361n
Examinations, study of, 364
(*See also* Regents' Examinations)
Exceptional pupils, educational outcomes of, 106–114, 182
higher education of, 110–111
Extracurricular activities, program of,
144–148
effective practice, 151–152
study of by Regents' Inquiry, 361–
363

F

Fansler, T., 248n, 271n, 368n
Finances, as factors in college enrollment, 111–113
Foreign affairs, pupil information on,
20
Foreign language, clubs, 145
courses, 124–125, 127, 168, 212–213
enrollment, 168

G

Girl Scouts, 29, 146
Girls, competence of, compared with
boys, 100–106
Grace, Alonzo G., 9n, 223n, 224n,
318n, 328n, 333n, 368n
Graduates of different curricula, competence of, 83–91
Gray, William S., 358n
Guidance, cost of in proposed plan,
329–330
programs in junior high schools,
171–172
recommendations on, 275–281, 309–
310, 314
study of, 364
(*See also* Educational guidance,
Vocational guidance)
Gulick, Luther H., 219n, 246n, 272n,
289n, 313n

H

Health activities, special studies on,
353–357
High school group, composition of in
New York State, 3
High school subjects, general, 124–129
Higher education, of rural and city
graduates, 113–114
Higher institutions, factors influencing
choice of, 111–114
History tests, 19, 95, 338, 339